Critical Thinking in Psychology

Developmental Psychology

Critical Thinking in Psychology – titles in the series

Critical Thinking in Psychology

Developmental Psychology

Penney Upton

Series Editor: Dominic Upton

Los Angeles | London | New Delhi
Singapore | Washington DC

First published in 2011 by Learning Matters Ltd
Reprinted 2013

British Library Cataloguing in Publication Data
A CIP record for this book is available from the British Library

ISBN 978 0 85725 276 0

This book is also available in the following ebook formats:

Adobe ebook   ISBN 978 0 85725 278 4
ePUB ebook   ISBN 978 0 85725 277 7
Kindle   ISBN 978 0 85725 279 1

Cover and text design by Toucan Design
Project management by Diana Chambers
Typeset by Kelly Winter
Printed and bound in Great Britain by Henry Ling Limited, at the Dorset Press, DT1 1HD

Learning Matters
An imprint of SAGE Publications Ltd
1 Oliver's Yard
55 City Road
London EC1Y 1SP

SAGE Publications Inc.
2455 Teller Road
Thousand Oaks, California 91320

SAGE Publications India Pvt Ltd
B 1/I 1 Mohan Cooperative Industrial Area
Mathura Road
New Delhi 110 044

SAGE Publications Asia-Pacific Pte Ltd
3 Church Street
#10-04 Samsung Hub
Singapore 049483

Contents

Acknowledgements

Many thanks to Lee Badham, Tracey Price and Emma Jackson for their technical assistance.

A big thank you must also go to my husband for his advice and encouragement while writing this textbook, and to my three favourite children – Francesca, Rosie and Gabriel – who have taught me a lot about the practical aspects of child development!

Series editor's introduction

Studying psychology at degree level

Being a student of psychology is an exciting experience – the study of mind and behaviour is a fascinating and sprawling journey of discovery. Yet, studying psychology at degree level brings with it new experiences, new skills and knowledge. This book, one in a comprehensive new series, brings you this psychological knowledge, but importantly brings with it directions and guidance on the skills and experiences you should also be developing during your studies.

Psychology is a growing discipline – in scope, in breadth and in numbers. It is one of the fastest-growing subjects to study at GCSE and A-Level, and the number of students studying the subject at university has grown considerably over the past decade. Indeed, psychology is now one of the most popular subjects in UK higher education, with the most recent data suggesting that there are some 45,000 full-time students currently enrolled on such programmes (compiled from Higher Education Statistics Agency (HESA) statistics available at www.HESA.ac.uk) and it is likely that this number has not yet peaked.

The popularity of psychology is related to a number of reasons, not the least of which is its scope and its breadth – psychology is a sprawling discipline that seeks to analyse the human mind and behaviour, which is fascinating in its own right. Furthermore, psychology aims to develop other skills – numeracy, communication and critical analysis to name but a few. For these reasons, many employers seek out psychology graduates – they bring a whole host of skills to the workplace and any activities they may be involved in. This book brings together the knowledge base associated with psychology along with these critical skills. By reading this book, and engaging with the exercises, you will develop these skills and, in this way, will do two things: excel in your studies and your assessments; and put yourself at the front of the queue of psychology graduates when it comes to demonstrating these skills to potential employers.

Developing higher level skills

Only about 15–20 per cent of psychology graduates end up working as professional psychologists. The subject is a useful platform for many other careers because of the skills it helps you to develop. It is useful to employers because of its subject-specific skills – knowing how people act is pertinent in almost any job and is particularly relevant to those that involve working directly with people. Psychology also develops a number of generic and transferable skills that are both essential to effective undergraduate study and valuable to employers. These include higher-level intellectual skills, such as critical and creative thinking, reflection, evaluation and analysis, and other skills such as communication, problem solving, understanding and using data, decision making, organisational skills, teamworking and IT skills.

The Quality Assurance Agency in Higher Education (QAA) subject benchmarks for psychology (www.qaa.ac.uk/academicinfrastructure/benchmark/honours/psychology.asp), which set out the expectations of a psychology degree programme, highlight the sorts of skills that your degree should equip you with. The British Psychological Society (BPS), which accredits your degree course, acknowledges that graduate employability is an important area of focus for universities and expects that opportunities for skills development should be well embedded within your programme of study. Indeed, this is a major focus of your study – interesting as psychology is, you will need and want employment at the end of your degree.

The activities in this book have been designed to help you build the underpinning skills that you need in order to become independent and lifelong learners, and to meet the relevant requirements of your programme of study, the QAA benchmarks and the needs of you and your potential employer.

Many students find it a challenge to develop these skills, often learning them out of context of their study of the core knowledge domains of psychology. The activities in this book aim to help you to learn these skills *at the same time* as developing your core psychology knowledge, giving you opportunities continuously to practise skills so that they become second nature to you. The tasks provide guidance on what the skill is, how to develop basic competence in it and how to progress to further expertise.

At the same time, development of these skills will enable you to better understand and retain the core content of your course – being able to evaluate, analyse and interpret content is the key to deepening understanding.

The skills that the activities in this book will help you to develop are as presented in Table 0.1.

Table 0.1: *Skills developed in this book*

Generic skills	Transferable skills
• critical and creative thinking	• communication: oral, visual and written
• reflection	• problem solving
• analysing and evaluating	• understanding and using data
	• decision making
	• organisational skills
	• teamwork
	• information technology
	• independent learning

In addition to review and essay questions, each chapter in this book will contain novel learning activities. Your responses will be guided through these activities and you will then be able to apply these skills within the context of developmental psychology.

Features in this book

At the start of each chapter there will be **learning outcomes**. These are a set of bullet points that highlight the outcomes you should achieve – both skills and knowledge – if you read and engage with the chapter. This will mean at the outset of the chapter that we try to orientate you, the reader, and demonstrate the relevance of the topic.

We have also included learning features throughout the individual chapters in order to demonstrate key points and promote your learning.

- **Bulleted lists** are used within the chapter to convey key content messages.

- **Case studies** are included as part of a critical thinking activity.

- **Tasks** are a series of short review questions on the topic that will help you assess yourself and your current level of knowledge – use these to see if you can move on or whether you need to reread and review the material.

- **Critical thinking activities** allow for the review of the text by encouraging key critical and creative thinking of the psychology material presented, and provide development of the generic skills. Each of these activities is followed by a **Critical thinking review** which unpicks the activity for you, showing how it should have been tackled, the main skill it develops and other skills you may have used in completing the activity.

- **Skill builder activities** use the psychology material presented in the text but will be focused on one particular transferable skill as outlined in Table 0.1. Each of these activities is followed by a **Skill builder review** which may provide further hints and which makes explicit the skills it helps to develop and the benefits of completing the activity.

At the end of the chapter there will also be some pedagogic features that you will find useful in developing your abilities.

- **Assignments** In order to assess your awareness and understanding of the topic, we have also produced a series of questions for you to discuss and debate with your colleagues. You can also use these questions as revision materials.

- **Summary: what you have learned** at the end of each chapter we present a summary of the chapter as a series of bullet points. We hope that these will match the learning outcomes presented at the outset of the chapter.

- **Further reading** we have included items that will provide additional information – some of these are in journals and some are full texts. For each we have provided the rationale for suggesting the additional reading and we hope that these will direct you accordingly.

- **Glossary** entries are highlighted in bold in the text on their first appearance in a chapter.

Finally, there is a full set of **references** to support all of the material presented in this text.

We hope you enjoy this text, which is part of a series of textbooks covering the complete knowledge base of psychology.

Professor Dominic Upton
June 2011

Chapter 1

Themes and theories in developmental psychology

Learning outcomes

By the end of this chapter you should:

- *understand how developmental psychology has evolved as a discipline;*

- *be able to critically evaluate the main themes and theories in developmental psychology;*

- *know who the key historical and contemporary figures are in developmental psychology;*

- *have a critical understanding of the research methods commonly applied in developmental psychology;*

- *have developed your written communication and independent learning skills;*

- *be able to engage in reflection on contemporary and traditional approaches in psychology.*

Introduction

Developmental psychology is the scientific study of age-related changes in mind and behaviour. Originally it was believed that the development of all our skills and abilities was completed in childhood. We now understand that development is a lifelong process; change does not stop because we have reached adulthood. The purpose of this chapter is to introduce the **lifespan approach** to the study of development and to show you the importance of examining changes that occur in adulthood, as well as those that occur in childhood. In Chapter 7, for example, we see the way in which cognitive skills can continue to increase in adulthood or decline depending on personal experiences. Developmental psychology informs several applied fields, including educational psychology, child clinical psychology and child forensic psychology, and also complements the other main fields in psychology, including social, cognitive and individual differences.

Themes in developmental psychology

There are a number of themes that run right through developmental psychology. These are:

- the influence of nature verses nurture;

- continuity versus discontinuity in change;

- critical versus sensitive periods of development;

- stability versus change;

- the role of the individual in development.

Nature versus nurture

As a student of psychology you will come across the nature–nurture debate throughout your studies. It is one of the most fundamental and oldest issues in psychology and philosophy, and one that we will return to in later chapters. The debate concerns the relative contributions of inheritance and the environment in determining our knowledge and behaviour. Philosophers such as Plato and Descartes supported the idea that we are born with knowledge and **innate** skills. Other thinkers such as John Locke argued for the concept of **tabula rasa** – the idea that the mind is a blank slate at birth, with experience determining what we know. These philosophical viewpoints have influenced some of the great thinkers in developmental psychology as you will see later on in the chapter.

In developmental psychology the debate centres around two main questions.

- Are children born with innate knowledge or skills or are these acquired from interaction with the environment?

- Is development driven by external factors or by something inside each individual?

In this context, nature refers to traits, abilities and capacities that are inherited. It includes anything produced by the predetermined unfolding of genetic information. Development that relies on nature alone is known as **maturation**. In contrast, nurture refers to the environmental influences that shape development. These can be biological; for example, substance misuse in pregnancy may result in changes in growth and development of the unborn child. More often than not, nurture refers to the social and cultural factors that shape our environment and way that the behaviours of those around us influence our development. This includes the way we are raised as children, the attitudes and behaviours of our peer group, our experiences and even the choices we make as we get older. Societal factors, such as the socio-economic circumstances in which we find ourselves, may also be important.

One area where this debate has been quite prominent is that of language acquisition, a topic we will return to in more detail in Chapter 3. A major question here is whether or not certain properties of human language are specified genetically or simply acquired through learning. The **nativist** position argues that the environmental input from language is insufficient for infants and children to acquire the structure of language. A well-known proponent of this view is linguist Noam Chomsky, who asserted that there is a 'universal grammar' that applies to all human languages and is pre-specified (Chomsky, 1979). He calls this the **language acquisition device (LAD)**. This view is supported by some contemporary psychologists, including Steven Pinker, who argues convincingly that language is a human instinct, wired into our brains by evolution (Pinker, 2007).

In contrast, the **empiricist** position on the question of language acquisition suggests that language input is sufficient to provide the information we require to learn the structure of language. This perspective proposes that infants acquire language through a process of statistical learning. Language is acquired by the general learning methods that apply to all aspects of human development.

There is evidence to support components of both the nativist and the empiricist position, both for language and for other aspects of development. In contemporary psychology the consensus view is that development results from an interaction between genes and environment. However, that does not mean that this issue has been put aside. The debate now concerns the relative role of nature and nurture for different aspects of development. In language development, for example, theorists such as Jerome Bruner (1983) agree with Chomsky's notion of an LAD. However, Bruner asserts that Chomsky gives too big a role to this aspect of language acquisition, noting that social context, and the behaviour of parents in particular, have a significant impact on language development. This aspect of the environment he calls the **language acquisition support system (LASS)**. According to Bruner, the LAD cannot function alone and every LAD therefore needs a LASS.

Continuity versus discontinuity

This issue concerns whether development follows a smooth continuous path, or whether it is a discontinuous stage-based process. In continuous change, development is gradual and cumulative. Changes are quantitative in nature and the underlying processes that drive change are the same over the course of the lifespan. In this view, one behaviour or skill builds upon another, such that later development can be predicted from what occurred early in life. Physical growth and changes in height provide one example of continuous change in childhood. In discontinuous change, development occurs in distinct, usually abrupt stages. Each stage is qualitatively different from the last. Examples sometimes cited from nature include the caterpillar that turns into a butterfly, or the tadpole that becomes a frog.

The question for developmental psychology concerns whether psychological skills and abilities in childhood are qualitatively different from those of adults. Or are children merely mini adults, who simply lack the knowledge that comes with experience? One area in which this debate has been of primary concern is cognitive development. Jean Piaget, for example, proposed a four-stage **theory** to describe how children reason and interact with their surroundings (1952, 1962, 1983). According to Piaget, children's thinking is characterised at each stage by different forms of mental organisation. This gives rise to qualitative differences in thinking and reasoning at each stage. This, in turn, means that a child's view of the world is different from that of an adult. In contrast to this, information-processing models of cognitive development have proposed that this idea is flawed and that cognitive change occurs because of an increase in quantitative advances, not qualitative differences. A child's ability to engage in more sophisticated reasoning processes is believed to stem from a change in their capacity to handle information. This increased capacity, along with improved processing speeds, makes processing more efficient.

Once again, psychologists generally agree that neither approach is complete. It is more likely that some processes may be better described as continuous and others as occurring through stages. There is also some suggestion that continuous and discontinuous processes may interact. *Neo-Piagetian theory* (e.g. Case, 1999) suggests that the changes in information-processing mechanisms, such as speed and memory capacity, are responsible for the progression from stage to stage.

Critical versus sensitive periods for change

A critical period is a specific time during development when a particular event has its greatest impact. As you will see in Chapter 2, maternal diseases, such as **rubella**, have greater consequences for foetal development in the eleventh week of pregnancy than in the thirtieth week. Rubella contracted in the eleventh week may lead to blindness, deafness and heart problems. Rubella in the thirtieth week may have no significant impact on **prenatal** development. In this case, specific events during the critical period lead to **atypical development**. In developmental psychology, a critical period for development usually implies that certain environmental stimuli are necessary for typical development to occur. John Bowlby (1951), for example, suggested that, if children did not receive the right kind of care in the first two years of life, their emotional development would be adversely affected. According to Bowlby, between six months and two years of age is a critical period for relationship formation. If children are not able to form a strong attachment with a carer during this period, their ability to form relationships later in life will be permanently damaged.

Better understanding of the **plasticity** and **resilience** of human nature has led to a reassessment of this idea. Most developmentalists now agree that, rather than suffering permanent damage from a lack of stimuli during early periods of development, it is more likely that people can use later experiences to help them overcome deficits. It is now more common to talk about 'sensitive' rather than 'critical' periods. In a sensitive period we may be more susceptible to particular stimuli; however, the absence of those stimuli does not always result in irreversible damage.

Stability versus change

This issue concerns the extent to which early traits and characteristics persist throughout life or are able to change. Does the shy child become a shy adult? Can a shy child become a gregarious adult? The stability–change issue involves the degree to which we merely become older versions of our younger selves. Theorists who believe in stability in development often argue from a nativist stance, emphasising the role of heredity for the development of psychological characteristics. We inherit aspects of our personality, for example, in much the same way that we inherit eye colour. From this perspective we cannot change our psychological self, only learn to control it. Thus, the shy child remains shy as an adult even if he or she learns to act in an outgoing manner in social situations.

From an empiricist viewpoint, stability in psychological characteristics stems from the impact of early experiences that cannot be overcome. An individual is shy not because of a genetic predisposition, but because during early experiences of interacting with others they encountered considerable stress, leading them to avoid social interaction. This has much in common with the idea described in the preceding section, that there are critical periods of development during which specific experiences permanently influence later behaviour.

The alternative viewpoint is that there is potential for change throughout the life span. Later experiences are believed to be able to influence development just as early ones do. The majority of contemporary theorists accept this perspective. However, there is still some debate as to how much change is possible. On the one hand, Baltes (2003) argues that, while adults are able to change, their capacity to do so is less than that of a child and diminishes over time. On the other hand, Kagan (2003) argues that personality traits such as shyness have a genetic basis; yet he also provides evidence that even these inherited traits can be subject to change over time.

The role of the individual in development

This concerns the extent to which development is driven by external factors or by something inside each individual. Are children active agents who influence their own development or passive agents who merely respond to forces in the developmental progression? Traditional views of development see the individual as passive in their development. Empiricists see the child as a passive recipient of stimuli, while nativists see the child as passively following a biological programme. Most contemporary theories of development recognise an active role for children in their own development. This thinking has its roots in the philosophy of Immanuel Kant, who argued for a synthesis of nativism and empiricism. He proposed that we are born with certain mental structures that help us to interpret input from our senses in particular ways. By themselves, they cannot give us knowledge. It is only through interaction with the environment that these structures order and organise experience. He also proposed an active role for individuals as organisers of this experience.

Modern theories of development recognise children as central to their own development. The individual is able to influence development directly through the choices they make and increasingly, as they get older, by selecting their environment. They are also able to affect development indirectly through their behaviour, which can affect how others respond to them and, to some extent, the experiences they encounter.

Theories of development

Miller (2002) defines a *theory* as a set of interconnected statements including definitions, axioms, postulates, hypothetical constructs, laws and testable hypotheses, which describe unobservable structures, mechanisms or processes and relate them to observable events. Complete theories of development are rare in contemporary psychology, according to Miller. Rather, developmental theories serve as frames of reference for examining change in specific aspects of mind or behaviour, such as cognition or emotional functioning. In this way, they are perhaps better viewed as *models* of development – that is, informal theories of more limited scope.

However, developmental psychologists usually have a particular theoretical perspective. Their view of development is usually based on a general set of assumptions about how change occurs and the factors they believe to be most significant in producing developmental change. You may well have come across some of these theoretical perspectives in other areas of psychology. While there are many approaches in psychology, the most significant from a developmental standpoint include the psychodynamic, learning, constructivist and social constructivist perspectives, which are described briefly here. We will return to these theories later in the chapter when we look at some key figures in development on pages 10–19.

Psychodynamic theories

Proponents of the psychodynamic perspective believe that behaviour is motivated by inner forces, memories and conflicts, of which a person has little awareness or control. These inner forces usually result from childhood experiences and continue to influence behaviour across the lifespan. The best-known theorists in this perspective are Sigmund Freud (1856–1939) and Erik Erikson (1902–94).

Learning theories

This perspective suggests that the key to understanding development lies in observable behaviour and an individual's response to environmental stimuli. The assumption here is that behaviour is a learned response to **reinforcement** provided by the environment. The learning and conditioning principles described in the **behavioural** theories of BF Skinner (1936) and John B Watson (1913, 1924) account for human development.

One area that behaviourist theories do not explain is the type of learning that takes place when someone learns by observing a **model**. Called **social learning** by Albert Bandura (1963), this is the process by which someone imitates the behaviour observed in another person when it appears to have reinforcing consequences, and inhibits such behaviour when the observed consequence is punishment.

Constructivist and social constructivist theories

Constructivism argues that learning and development occur when an individual interacts with the environment around them. Individuals are seen as active learners who construct their own under-standing and knowledge of the world from their actions upon the environment. Development is suggested to take place in sequential stages and children's thinking is proposed to be different from that of adults. The most well-known theorist in this perspective is Jean Piaget (1896–1980), who developed an important theory of cognitive development.

Social constructivist theories are a variant of this perspective and emphasise the influence of the social and cultural environment on development. The social context of development and an individual's interactions with other people are seen as playing an important role in development. The most significant theorists to take account of social and cultural factors in development are Lev Vygotsky (1930/1978) and Urie Bronfenbrenner (1977).

How has developmental psychology evolved as a discipline?

There are two key areas to be aware of with regard to the progress of developmental psychology as a discipline. First, there has been a change in the focus of interest from development in childhood, to development across the lifespan. Second, there has been a gradual change in the way that this development has been studied.

From child development to lifespan development

The scientific study of children began in the second half of the nineteenth century, when Charles Darwin (1809–82) first put forward his theory of evolution. In his book *On the Origin of Species* (1859), Darwin focused attention on the significance of the immaturity of human infants. In particular, he proposed that **ontogeny** recapitulates **phylogeny**. According to this recapitulation theory, individual development replicates the evolution of the species. For example, in the very early stages of development the human **embryo** looks like a fish, even having gill slits. This fits well with the evolutionary idea that humans evolved from other vertebrates. Darwin also kept a detailed record of his infant son's development, which he later reported in the journal *Mind* (1877). Baby biographies such as this one were popular during the late nineteenth century and are often credited with being some of the first studies in human development. While not scientifically sound, these single **case studies** made human development a legitimate topic for study.

A number of other scientists of the time were influenced by these baby biographies and Darwin's theories, most notably Granville Stanley Hall (1846–1924), the founder of the American Psychological Association. Well aware of the shortcomings of the baby biographies, Hall became a strong advocate of the need to base child-rearing on scientific principles. His own studies used questionnaires in an attempt to collect more objective data and to explore *the contents of children's minds* (Hall, 1891). At around the same time in England, James Sully (1842–1923) established a new subject at London University called 'Child Psychology'.

Initially, developmental psychology focused on the changes that take place in childhood. It was only in the early twentieth century that adolescence began to be studied as a distinct life stage. One of the first psychologists to study and write about adolescence was Hall (1904), who suggested that this was an important period of change, typified by intense emotional turmoil, which he called 'storm and stress'. The importance of psychological development as a process that continues throughout adulthood as well as childhood and adolescence was not fully recognised until much later in the twentieth century. Hall himself wrote about changes in adulthood in 1922; however, one of the most important theories to suggest that psychological development continues across the lifespan was that of Erik Erikson (1950).

Although some early theorists such as Hall saw all phases of the lifespan as worthy of investigation, for much of the twentieth century the study of human development was divided into age-related specialities. Some researchers focused on infancy and childhood, others specialised in adolescence and some focused on gerontology, the study of ageing and old age. So while many areas of the lifespan were being studied, this was being done in quite separate, self-contained disciplines. In this traditional approach to studying development the emphasis is on the idea that most developmental change occurs in childhood and adolescence. This is followed by adulthood, a period of relative stability. Finally, old age is believed to be characterised by decline. This is quite different from the lifespan perspective, which began to emerge as a distinct discipline in the 1960s and 1970s. According to this perspective, developmental change occurs throughout the lifespan and changes in adulthood are as important as those in childhood. No age period dominates development. Changes that occur as we age may also be positive; ageing is not defined by decline. Development is therefore **multidirectional**. This means that, as some capacities or behaviours decrease, others expand. Furthermore, development includes both gain and loss throughout the lifespan and these may even occur together. Development is also believed to be **multidimensional**; that is, it consists of biological, social, emotional and cognitive changes, all of which are interrelated. The study of development should therefore be seen as **multidisciplinary**;

neuroscientists, psychologists, sociologists and medical researchers have different but comple-mentary perspectives on age-related change, making multidisciplinary research an important goal. It is also recognised that development can be influenced by the environment in which an individual lives. Thus, the **socio-cultural context** of development is seen as highly relevant to developmental change. Finally, the *plasticity* of human development – the idea that we retain capacity for change in response to environmental factors right across the lifespan – is emphasised.

This lifespan approach to development has become increasingly popular in recent years, perhaps in response to increases in life expectancy. This is undoubtedly because of the optimistic view it gives of ageing. Rather than being seen as the endpoint of development as it is in the traditional view, adulthood is seen as an important time of growth and change. Furthermore, adulthood and ageing are no longer portrayed as a period of decline; positive change is seen to take place even for older adults. As we shall see in Chapter 7, there is a lot of evidence that supports this positive view of ageing.

From the traditional to a new research paradigm

In the late nineteenth century, the new study of child development used a systematic approach to investigating age-related changes. The methods used were based on those used in the natural sciences and involved evaluating theories of development by generating and testing hypotheses. This is known as the *hypothetico-deductive* method. When following this scientific **experimental** method, the aim is to collect objective data and carry out a **quantitative** analysis in order to provide accurate descriptions and explanations of how and why change occurs. It is also common to carry out data collection under controlled conditions in a laboratory.

An underlying assumption in this traditional scientific approach is that there is an objective reality in the world that can be observed, measured and categorised. This is sometimes referred to as a **positivist approach** and has been used widely in developmental psychology since the study of human development began. This approach has produced much of the theoretical work and research described in this book. However, in the last 20 to 30 years, there has been increasing debate about whether the approach taken in traditional science is appropriate for the study of human development. One important objection that we will encounter throughout this book is that, in traditional lab-based research, development is being studied outside a meaningful social context. The findings may therefore lack **ecological validity**, which means that they may no longer hold true when people are behaving naturally in their everyday settings. It is also argued that people's behaviour during a research study may also be changed because of other factors, such as the uneven power relationship between the researcher and the participant. It has also been suggested that researchers may impose on participants their own ideas of what is being measured, by the research tools that they use and the way they design the study. Thus a parti-cipant's behaviour during the study may not be completely natural but may, in part, be an artefact of participating in the research. The problem of the uneven power relationship has been sug-gested as a particular issue when working with children and is something we will return to in later chapters.

These objections to the positivist approach have resulted in a different emphasis in the way that some developmental psychologists conduct their research. They may do this while still following the core principles of the traditional scientific approach. For example, studies have been carried out to investigate the influence of context on people's behaviour, but using traditional experimental methods. A good example of this is the work of Margaret Donaldson (1978), which looked at how children's cognitive performance changed according to the language used and the meaningfulness of the situation. More studies have been carried out to research people's behaviour in everyday situations using *observations* and **quasi-experimental** methods. The collection of more **qualitative** data, using open-ended questions in questionnaires and **interviews** that allow participants to raise ideas that the researcher had not included, has also become more common.

Other psychologists have shown a more radical reaction to the debate about the traditional scientific approach. They reject the idea that human thought and behaviour can ever be studied objectively. This is because they argue that there is no single objective reality; rather, each one of us constructs our own understandings and interpretations of 'reality', which are embedded in the context of our interactions with others. 'Reality' is therefore highly individualised and subjective. These psychologists argue that it is the interactions between people that should be the focus for psychological research. The aim is to describe the subjective experience of participants and understand individuality in order to build 'local theories' that apply to the specific social context of an event. Unlike 'scientific' theories, they are not concerned with generating predictions as much as making sense of phenomena. These are some of the key features of what is referred to as a qualitative approach, and sometimes called 'new paradigm' research. The difference between this and the traditional approach is illustrated by Grieg and Taylor's (1999) suggestion that, in the positivist approach, children are determined, knowable, objective and measurable, whereas in the qualitative approach they are subjective, contextual, self-determining and dynamic. It is important to recognise that there is some overlap between these differing approaches. Many researchers use a variety of methods and seek to gain both quantitative and qualitative data.

Key figures in developmental psychology

There are a number of key figures in developmental psychology. These are the theorists whose ideas and research have changed the way we think about human development. The afore-mentioned Granville Stanley Hall (1904, 1912, 1922), for example, is often called the 'father' of developmental psychology, as he carried out some of the first systematic studies of children. He also taught one of the first courses in child development and established scientific journals for the publication of child development research. His belief that children's development recapitulates the evolution of the species has long since been discredited. However, he retains importance as a historical figure as he inspired a great deal of the work on human development upon which this book is based. The theories of those who followed in Hall's footsteps have also not always stood up to close scrutiny. However, there are some theorists whose work remains critical to our understanding of human development.

John B Watson (1878–1958)

Watson created the behaviourist approach to psychology at the beginning of the twentieth century (Watson, 1913). He believed that human behaviour can be understood in terms of experiences and learning. He rejected the introspective approach of late nineteenth-century theorists, which attempted to understand internal mental experiences based on self-reports. He called instead for the objective study of observable, measurable behaviours. In 1928, in his book *Psychological Care of the Infant and Child*, he presented his view that all behaviour is the product of environment and experience. Biological factors had no role, according to Watson. His theory was that all learning takes place through a process of association.

Watson believed that learning occurs through **operant conditioning**, when an association is made between a behaviour and the consequence of that behaviour. Consequences will either reinforce a behaviour, thus making it more likely to reoccur, or will be aversive, thus decreasing the likelihood of the behaviour reoccurring. A reinforcer is therefore any event that strengthens or increases the behaviour that it follows. There are two kinds of reinforcers.

- Positive reinforcers are favourable outcomes presented after the behaviour. In positive reinforcement, a response or behaviour is strengthened by the addition of something such as praise or a direct reward.

- Negative reinforcers involve the removal of an unfavourable outcome after the display of a behaviour. In negative reinforcement a response is strengthened by the removal of something considered unpleasant.

Conversely, punishment occurs when an adverse outcome causes a decrease in the behaviour it follows. There are two kinds of punishment.

- Positive punishment involves the presentation of an unfavourable outcome in order to weaken the response it follows.

- Negative punishment occurs when a favourable outcome is removed after a behaviour occurs.

Although we now believe development to be far more complex than behaviourism allows, modern application of many of the ideas presented in Watson's learning theory can still be found, most especially in **Applied Behavioural Analysis (ABA)** – an intervention programme often used with children with behavioural or learning difficulties.

Albert Bandura (1925–)

Bandura believes that behavioural learning theories are inadequate as a framework for under-standing human development. He suggests that many human behaviours are learned from observing others. According to Bandura's social learning theory (1963), people learn through observing others' behaviour and attitudes, using this as a model for their own behaviour. However, there are certain conditions that are necessary if modelling is to be effective.

- Attention: in order for the behaviour to be learned, the observer must see the modelled behaviour.

- Retention: the observer must be able to remember the modelled behaviour.

- Reproduction: the observer must have the skills to reproduce the action.

- Motivation: the observer must be motivated to carry out the action they have observed and remembered, and must have the opportunity to do so. Motivation may include seeing the model's behaviour reinforced, while punishment may discourage repetition of the behaviour.

According to Bandura, the observer will imitate the model's behaviour only if the model possesses characteristics that the observer finds attractive or desirable. Therefore, we do not always imitate others' actions. We choose who to imitate – learning is not an automatic response but depends on internal processes as well as environmental ones. This is very different from Watson's view of learning, and social learning theory has sometimes been called a bridge between behaviourist and cognitive learning theories because it encompasses attention, memory and motivation.

Sigmund Freud (1856–1939)

Sigmund Freud is best known in developmental psychology for his model of psychosexual development (1905). This theory is in sharp contrast to the objective approach advocated by Watson. His is one of the best known, but also one of the most controversial theories of develop-ment. It was based on his own and his patients' recollections of their childhood. According to Freud, personality develops through a series of stages, during which the psychosexual energies of the *id* become focused on different areas of the body as the child grows to adulthood. This psychosexual energy, or **libido**, was described as the driving force behind behaviour. Freud proposed five stages of development (see Table 1.1). If each psychosexual stage is completed successfully, the result is a healthy personality. However, if certain issues are not resolved at the appropriate stage, fixation occurs. Until this issue or conflict is resolved, the individual remains stuck in this stage. For example, a person who is fixated at the oral stage may be overdependent on others and may seek oral stimulation through smoking, drinking or eating.

Table 1.1: *Freud's five stages of psychosexual development.*

Stage	Age	Characteristics
Oral	Birth to 1 year	An infant's primary interaction with the world is through the mouth. The mouth is vital for eating, and the infant derives pleasure from oral stimulation through gratifying activities such as tasting and sucking. If this need is not met, the child may develop an oral fixation later in life, examples of which include thumb-sucking, smoking, fingernail biting and overeating.
Anal	1 to 3 years	Freud believed that the primary focus of the libido was on controlling bladder and bowel movements. Toilet training is a primary issue with children and parents. Too much pressure can result in an excessive need for order or cleanliness later in life, while too little pressure from parents can lead to messy or destructive behaviour later in life.
Phallic	3 to 6 years	Freud suggested that the primary focus of the **id**'s energy is on the genitals. According to Freud, boys experience an **Oedipal complex** and girls experience and **Electra complex**, both of which are an attraction to the opposite sex parent. To cope with this conflict, children adopt the values and characteristics of the same-sex parent, thus forming the superego.
Latent	6 to 11 years	During this stage, the superego continues to develop, while the id's energies are suppressed. Children develop social skills, values and relationships with peers and adults outside the family.
Genital	11 to 18 years	The onset of **puberty** causes the libido to become active once again. During this stage, people develop a strong interest in the opposite sex. If development has been successful to this point, the individual will continue to develop into a well-balanced person.

Freud's model is an interactionist one, in which development is determined by both biology and the environment. Thus, the sequence and timing of the stages are biologically determined; however, successful personality development depends on the environmental experiences of the child at each stage. The details of Freud's developmental theory have been widely criticised, and few psychologists today accept his theory of development as accurate. One problem with his theory is that concepts such as the libido are impossible to measure, and therefore cannot be tested scientifically. Furthermore, Freud's theory is based on case studies and not empirical research. Freud based his theory on the recollections of his adult patients, not on actual **observation** and the study of children.

Erik Erikson (1902–94)

Erikson, like Freud, was a psychoanalyst and he accepted a lot of Freud's ideas. However, he put much more emphasis on the social and cultural aspects of development than Freud. He also believed that development continued across the lifespan, rather than our childhood experiences determining our adult psychological health. His theory outlines eight stages of development from infancy to late adulthood, which he called 'The Eight Ages of Man' (Erikson, 1963). These stages are described in Table 1.2. In each stage the person confronts, and hopefully masters, new challenges. Each stage builds on the successful completion of earlier stages. As with Freud's theory, the challenges of stages not successfully completed are likely to reappear as problems in the future. Erikson's theory is an important one and we will explore some of his ideas in later chapters.

Jean Piaget (1896–1980)

Jean Piaget is considered one of the most influential developmental psychologists of the twentieth century, and his stage theory of cognitive development revolutionised our view of children's thinking and learning. His work has also inspired more research than any other developmental psychologist. Initially, he was not interested in child development, but in the nature of knowledge and how it could be seen as a form of adaptation to the environment. He described his work as **genetic epistemology**. Piaget (1952, 1962) argued that children develop progressively more elaborate and sophisticated mental representations of the world. These mental representations, or schemas, are based on their own actions on the environment and the consequences of these actions. He therefore saw the child as taking an active role in his or her own development. According to Piaget, children construct their knowledge through the processes of **assimilation**, in which they evaluate and try to understand new information based on their existing knowledge of the world, and **accommodation**, in which they expand and modify their mental representations of the world based on new experiences. He described four sequential stages of cognitive development (see Table 1.3). Some of the details of these stage theories have been criticised and the evidence now suggests that he underestimated children's abilities. However, many of his concepts are still accepted. In addition, his work has provided the foundations for our understanding of cognitive development and his ideas continue to influence educators across the world. We will explore Piaget's ideas in greater detail in Chapters 3–6.

Lev Vygotsky (1896–1934)

Vygotsky developed his theory at the same time as Piaget. However, because he was working in Marxist Russia, although he was aware of Piaget's theories, his work was not known in the West until long after his death in the 1970s. Some of his conclusions about the constructive and active nature of development are similar to those of Piaget. However, he differed in the role he attributed

Table 1.2: Erikson's eight stages of psychosocial development

Stage	Basic conflict	Important events	Outcome
Infancy (birth to 18 months)	Trust vs. mistrust	Feeding	Children develop a sense of trust when caregivers provide reliability, care and affection. A lack of this will lead to mistrust.
Early childhood (2 to 3 years)	Autonomy vs. shame and doubt	Toilet training	Children need to develop a sense of personal control over physical skills and a sense of independence. Success leads to feelings of autonomy, while failure results in feelings of shame and doubt.
Preschool (3 to 5 years)	Initiative vs. guilt	Exploration	Children need to begin asserting control and power over the environment. Success in this stage leads to a sense of purpose. Children who try to exert too much power experience disapproval, resulting in a sense of guilt.
School age (6 to 11 years)	Industry vs. inferiority	School	Children need to cope with new social and academic demands. Success leads to a sense of competence, while failure results in feelings of inferiority.
Adolescence (12 to 18 years)	Identity vs. role confusion	Social relationships	Teens need to develop a sense of self and personal identity. Success leads to an ability to stay true to oneself, while failure leads to role confusion and a weak sense of self.
Young adulthood (19 to 40 years)	Intimacy vs. isolation	Relationships	Young adults need to form intimate, loving relationships with other people. Success leads to strong relationships, while failure results in loneliness and isolation.
Middle adulthood (40 to 65 years)	Generativity vs. stagnation	Work and parenthood	Adults need to create or nurture things that will outlast them, often by having children or creating a positive change that benefits other people. Success leads to feelings of usefulness and accomplishment, while failure results in shallow involvement in the world.
Maturity (65 to death)	Ego integrity vs. despair	Reflection on life	Older adults need to look back on life and feel a sense of fulfilment. Success at this stage leads to feelings of wisdom, while failure results in regret, bitterness and despair.

Table 1.3: Piaget's stages of cognitive development

Stage	Approximate age	Characteristics
Sensorimotor	0 to 2 years	Begins to make use of imitation, memory and thought. Begins to recognise that objects do not cease to exist when they are not in view. Moves from reflex actions to goal-directed activity.
Preoperational	2 to 7 years	Gradually develops use of symbols, including language. Able to think operations through logically in one direction. Has difficulties seeing another person's point of view.
Concrete operational	7 to 11 years	Able to solve concrete problems. Understands some mathematical operations such as classification and seriation.
Formal operational	11 years to adult	Able to solve abstract problems in a logical fashion. Becomes more scientific in thinking. Develops concerns about social issues and identity.

to the social and cultural environment of the child. According to Vygotsky (1930/1978), human history is created through the construction and use of cultural tools. It is this inventive use of tools that makes humans unique. A hammer is a physical example of a cultural tool. It is a means of knocking sharp objects such as nails into surfaces, in order to create a new structure. The form and function of the hammer are the result of generations of cultural evolution and adaptation. The meaning and use of a hammer are not immediately obvious to someone who has never come across one before, or who has never needed to knock nails in. The information about how to use tools is also culturally transmitted. Each generation may adapt the hammer for its own needs or use it in new ways. Vygotsky calls this 'appropriation'. Thus, the hammer that we buy from a hardware store in the twenty-first century is very different from the one first constructed by our ancestors.

Not all cultural tools, however, are physical objects. According to Vygotsky, they include ways of thinking as well as ways of doing. One of the most important cultural tools people use is language. Like the hammer, the language we use today is the result of long-term cultural development, adaptation, transmission and appropriation. Vygotsky proposed that ways of thinking are transmitted to children through social interaction and are then appropriated by children. Our knowledge and understanding of the world is therefore constructed in a social context, not, as Piaget thought, by children acting on the environment alone. Vygotsky also argued that the child follows the adult's example at first, gradually developing the ability to do tasks without help. He called the difference between what a child can do with help and what he or she can do alone the

zone of proximal development (ZPD). To be effective, learning must take place within the child's ZPD. New tasks should neither be too difficult for the child to master with help, nor so easy that they can be completed alone. The ZPD is an important concept and one we shall return to in later chapters.

Urie Bronfenbrenner (1917–2005)

Bronfenbrenner is best known for his bioecological systems theory (1977). This model provides us with a framework for looking at the different factors that influence human development. Bronfenbrenner acknowledges the importance of biological factors for development, but also points to the fact that, more than any other species, humans create the environments that help shape their own development. Development always occurs in a particular social context and this context can change development. Bronfenbrenner maintained that human beings can therefore develop those environments to optimise their genetic potential.

Bronfenbrenner labelled the different aspects of the environment that influence development as the microsystem, the mesosystem, the exosystem, the macrosystem and chronosystem (see Figure 1.1).

- *Microsystem*: this includes the immediate environment we live in and any immediate relationships or organisations we interact with, such as the family, school, workplace, peer group and neighbourhood. How an individual acts or reacts to the other people in the microsystem will affect how they are treated in return. Each individual's unique genetic and biological traits will also affect how others treat them.

- *Mesosystem*: this level describes the connections between immediate environments. According to Bronfenbrenner, the way in which the different groups or organisations in the microsystem work together will have an effect on how we develop as individuals. For example, if parents take an active role in their child's schooling, and school and home agree on what is best for the child, development will be well supported and optimal. If, however, the school and home have different goals and attitudes, the child will be given conflicting information from the two environments, which may impact on the child's development.

- *Exosystem*: this refers to the external environmental settings that only indirectly affect development, such as a parent's workplace. Workplace structure can influence the choices a parent makes regarding childcare, for example. Changes in these settings can have both positive and negative effects on microsystem relationships. A promotion at work, for example, may mean more money for treats and activities, but may also mean less time at home for the parent.

- *Macrosystem*: this is the larger cultural context and includes cultural and social norms and attitudes, national economy, political culture and so on. Although this layer is the most remote from the individual, it still influences development, for example by shaping how the micro- and

Figure 1.1: *Bronfenbrenner's ecological model of development*

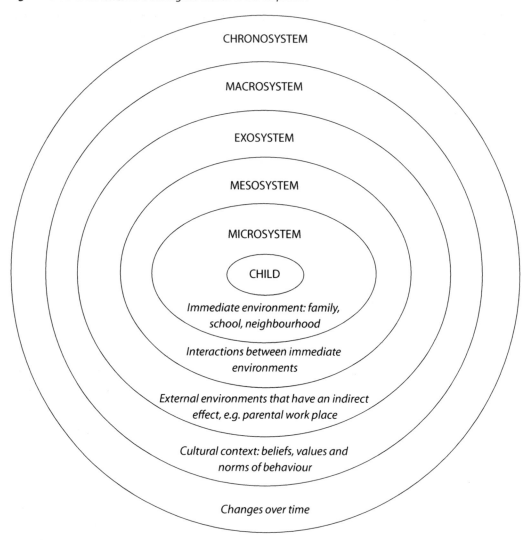

CHRONOSYSTEM

MACROSYSTEM

EXOSYSTEM

MESOSYSTEM

MICROSYSTEM

CHILD

Immediate environment: family,
school, neighbourhood

Interactions between immediate
environments

External environments that have an indirect
effect, e.g. parental work place

Cultural context: beliefs, values and
norms of behaviour

Changes over time

exosystems are organised. For example, if it is the belief of the culture that parents alone should be responsible for raising their children, that culture is less likely to provide financial or other resources to help parents. This will then affect the structures in which the parents function – will both parents need to work to support the family, for instance? The parents' ability or inability to carry out that responsibility towards their child within the context of the child's microsystem is therefore affected.

- *Chronosystem*: this system refers to the dimension of time as it relates to an individual's environments. Elements within this system can be either external, such as the timing of a loved one's death, or internal, such as the physiological changes that occur with ageing. As individuals get older, they may react differently to environmental changes and may be more able to determine more how those changes will influence them. It also includes socio-historical circumstances, for example how the opportunities for women to pursue a career have increased during the last 30 years and the impact that this might have on family structures.

The framework Bronfenbrenner provides is an important one and we will return to his ideas throughout the book.

Research methods in developmental psychology

The research methods used in developmental psychology are similar to those used in other areas of psychology and include both experimental and non-experimental designs. As research tends to be concerned with age-related changes, one of the first decisions a researcher must make is whether to use a cross-sectional or a longitudinal approach. **Cross-sectional research** involves looking at groups of people of differing ages. For example, if you are interested in how the self-concept differs in childhood and adolescence, you could compare a group of 10 year olds to a group of 14 year olds. This approach is commonly used because it is easy to complete and takes little time. The main limitation is that, even if you find that **self-concept** is different for your two groups of children, it is difficult to be sure of the extent to which this is due to age or some other **cohort** factor such as experiences at school. The only way to determine whether or not changes are age-related is to carry out a **longitudinal study**. This involves looking at the same group of people over a long period of time. The data are collected at the beginning of the study and then throughout, giving researchers the ability to look at changes over time. The main limitation with this type of research is that it is expensive and requires a large amount of time and dedication from both researchers and participants.

Researchers must also decide whether or not to use an experimental design. In an experiment, the researcher sets up two or more situations in which the variable of interest (known as the dependent variable or DV) can be measured and compared. The conditions vary only in terms of the variable whose effect is being tested (the independent variable or IV). The researcher attempts to control all other factors that may affect the DV so that there is a valid test of the predicted **causal relationship**. For example, if you wanted to see if aerobic exercise during pregnancy (IV) changes the sleeping patterns of newborn babies (DV), you might compare two groups of pregnant women. This is known as a **between-group design**. One group you would ask to attend regular aerobic classes and the other would do no exercise. Women would then be allocated to one of the two study groups using either **random sampling** or a **matched design**. With random sampling it is assumed that there is no systematic difference between the two groups. However, if the groups are small this assumption may not be correct. In a matched design the researcher tries to ensure the groups are similar by matching individuals across the groups according to characteristics that are thought to be relevant to the study; for example, here you might use the mothers' age, length of pregnancy and number of children.

A different technique is to have all the participants experience both conditions. This is known as a **within-group design**. This method avoids the need to assume that the different groups are equivalent because everyone experiences everything. However, there are limitations. The researcher has to ensure that the results are not due to participant fatigue or practice when they experience the second condition. One way to control for this is to have half of the group experience the conditions in one order and the other half experience them in the reverse order. This is known as **counterbalancing**. Using a within-group comparison is not always possible. For example, how would we know if it was the aerobics that had influenced the babies' sleeping patterns if all mothers experienced both conditions?

Experimental designs are helpful when the aim of a study is to test a prediction that there is a *causal relationship* between two variables. However, there are limitations to this approach. One possibility is that the researcher's choice of factors to control was wrong. There may be other variables that had an influence on the results but were overlooked. If one of these systematically biases the results it is called a **confounding variable**. This could prevent the researcher from obtaining valid results. In the example above, it was suggested that women could be matched on a number of factors including age, length of pregnancy and number of children. If a difference is found in babies' sleeping patterns where the mum has attended aerobics, it would be tempting to assume that the hypothesis has been supported and the aerobics has changed the infants' sleep patterns. But what if there was another factor that only became evident after the study was completed? Perhaps those mothers who attended aerobics were also more likely to use lullabies to get their newborns to sleep and it is this that has changed the sleep patterns. A second issue is that of ecological validity (refer back to page 9).

However, in developmental psychology the main problem with experimental designs is that there are many situations where it is not possible or ethical for the researcher to manipulate a variable that is thought to have a causal effect on behaviour. For example, if you were interested in the effect of smoking during pregnancy on the child's development at six months of age, it would not be ethical to manipulate the amount that a group of mothers smoked during pregnancy, as we know smoking is potentially toxic to both mother and child. However, it might be possible to use what are called natural or *quasi-experiments*. This is where the independent variable has been created already and so presents the opportunity for a comparison. In this case, we could compare a group of known smokers to a group of non-smokers. Alternatively, you might conduct a **correlational study**, looking for evidence of whether the number of cigarettes smoked by a sample of mothers was related to a measure of their children's development at six months of age. It is important to remember that correlational studies look for a relationship between variables rather than seeking to establish cause and effect. Other non-experimental designs aim to describe and explain behaviour without looking for causes. Case studies, for example, may be used to explore extreme or unique behaviours.

There are also different ways of collecting data in psychological research. *Observation* is one of the most common forms of data collection in developmental psychology. Systematic observations can be carried out either in a laboratory or in a naturalistic setting. The advantage of the former is that it allows the researcher to control the situation and focus on the variables of interest. The disadvantage is that the artificial nature of the setting makes it less ecologically valid. Observations in a natural setting have the advantage of being highly ecologically valid. However, the lack of control of extraneous factors is a limitation of this type of study.

Another way of collecting data is to use self-report survey methods, such as interviews or questionnaires. **Questionnaire surveys** can be conducted in person, over the phone or via the internet. The advantage of this method is that it allows you to collect a lot of data very easily and often in a short period of time. However, the use of fixed-response categories may mean that you miss an important issue you had not thought of. *Interviews* allow for a much richer data set and are often preferred in qualitative studies. However, they are time-consuming and usually result in a lot of data from fewer individuals, meaning that it is harder to generalise from the study findings.

Sometimes **standardised tests** are used to measure someone's performance. Examples of standardised tests include the Stanford-Binet Intelligence Scale, the Wechsler Intelligence Scale for Children (WISC) and the Wechsler Adult Intelligence Scale (WAIS). Scores on these tests can be compared to established *norms* to determine skills and abilities at different ages.

It is important to understand about research methods and how they are applied to the study of human development. This chapter has only given a brief overview of the methods used and some of the advantages and disadvantages. As noted earlier, there is some debate about the relative merits of different approaches for explaining development and this is something that is discussed further in later chapters.

Critical thinking activity

Research methods

Critical thinking focus: reflection (on contemporary and traditional approaches in psychology)

Key question: *What is the value of the traditional positivist approach versus a more contemporary qualitative research model for studying development?*

Consider the following research question.

What is the relationship between the number of friends a teenager has and their academic success?

To answer this question consider the following.

- How could you carry out a study using experimental research design?

- What variables would you need to control and why?

- How could you answer this question using an alternative (non-experimental) approach?

- Which approach best answers the research question?

Critical thinking review

This activity helps develop your ability to reflect upon the material you are learning and consider a range of options. It is important to recognise that, in research and other areas of life, there is often more than one solution to a problem. If you are able to reflect critically, you will be able to consider the options open to you with a view to analysing and evaluating them. Reflection is an important skill that will help you to solve real-world problems, as well as developing you as an autonomous learner.

Skill builder activity

Key figures in developmental psychology

Transferable skill focus: written communication and independent learning

Key question: Use the information in the chapter to complete the following table, which compares the theories of Piaget, Vygotsky and Bronfenbrenner. Consider the extent to which the statements in the left-hand column apply to each of these theories. Write a few sentences in each box to explain your thinking.

In order to complete this task you will need to consider the differences and similarities between these theorists in terms of their position concerning the key themes in development, such as the role of the environment and whether or not development is stage-based.

	Constructivism (Piaget)	Social constructivism (Vygotsky)	Bioecological systems theory (Bronfenbrenner)
The environment plays an important role in development.			
Innate factors drive development.			
Development follows a smooth continuous path.			
Providing the right experiences in early childhood is critical for optimal development.			
Even as adults we can develop higher critical thinking skills.			
Interacting with others can promote our development.			
Children are active in their own development.			

Skill builder review

This task requires you to extract information from within the text and reorganise it. Because you need to find information from different areas of the chapter, the task encourages you to learn independently. You are also able to develop your written communication as you have to summarise in your own words how the key themes in developmental psychology are dealt with by these three key theories.

Assignments

1. How have experimental design and methodology evolved to allow us to observe and model developmental change?

2. Critically evaluate Bronfenbrenner's ecological model of development. Illustrate your answer with evidence from across the lifespan.

3. 'Development is a function of gene-environment interactions.' Critically evaluate this statement, providing evidence from at least two areas of development to support your argument.

Summary: what you have learned

Now you have finished studying this chapter you should:

- understand how developmental psychology has evolved as a discipline and the changes in methods and thinking that this has engendered;

- be able to evaluate critically the main themes in developmental psychology and recognise how these themes are addressed in different theories;

- know who the key historical and contemporary figures are in developmental psychology and recognise their contribution to our understanding of human development;

- have a critical understanding of the research methods commonly applied in developmental psychology and be aware of the different approaches that can be used;

- have developed your written communication and independent learning skills by completing a comparison of Piaget, Vygotsky and Bronfenbrenner.

- be able to engage in reflection on contemporary and traditional approaches in psychology by evaluating possible research approaches.

Further reading

Bronfenbrenner, U (1977) Toward an experimental ecology of human development. *American Psychologist*, 32: 513–31.

Provides a useful background to Bronfenbrenner's theory.

Bronfenbrenner, U and Crouter, AC (1983) The evolution of environmental models in developmental research, in Mussen, PH and Kessen, W (eds) *Handbook of Child Psychology, Vol. 1: History, theories, and methods.* New York: Wiley.

Update to Bronfenbrenner's original model.

Harris, P (2002) *Designing and Reporting Experiments in Psychology* (2nd edn). Maidenhead: Open University Press.

Useful further information on positivist approaches to research.

Newcombe, NS (2003) Some controls control too much. *Child Development,* 74(4): 1050–2.

Discusses the disadvantages using a positivist approach to study real life issues.

Sameroff, AJ (1987) The social context of development, in Eisenberg, N (ed.) *Contemporary Topics in Developmental Psychology.* New York: Wiley.

Describes transactional models of development which, like Bronfenbrenner's and Vygotsky's, place great emphasis on the bidirectional influences on development.

Spelke, ES (1998) Nativism, empiricism and the origins of knowledge. *Infant Behaviour and Development,* 21(2): 181–200.

Discusses the main approaches to studying development.

Chapter 2

Prenatal development, birth and the neonate

Learning outcomes

By the end of this chapter you should:

- *be able to describe the main stages of prenatal development;*

- *understand the factors influencing prenatal development;*

- *be able to evaluate how the environment and genetics interact to influence development;*

- *be aware of the main threats to typical prenatal development;*

- *be able to evaluate critically the evidence concerning prenatal learning and later cognitive development;*

- *understand critically the importance of social and cultural factors surrounding the birth process;*

- *have developed your ability to analyse and evaluate written text;*

- *have developed your organisational skills and visual communication.*

Introduction

During the *prenatal* period, many of the foundations for later development are established. It is therefore important to know what happens during the main stages of prenatal development and this is the starting point for this chapter. Physical maturation of the unborn child is described and the genetic factors that influence this early development are presented.

However, it is also important to remember that you are studying psychology, not biology. Consideration must be given to the long-term impact of prenatal experiences on later social, emotional and psychological development. For this reason, the focus of prenatal development in psychology tends to be on how development may be negatively affected by environmental factors such as **teratogens**, and on the short- and long-term consequences for child development. Of course, the flip side of this is the way in which avoidance of teratogens can be beneficial for future infant well-being. The sort of advice that could be given to expectant parents in order to give their child the best developmental opportunities should therefore be considered. Other important environmental factors that are discussed include the social and cultural context in which development occurs and, especially, how this might impact on the **perinatal** experiences of the *neonate* and the birthing choices made by parents.

It is also important to consider the interaction between these genetic and environmental factors, especially with regard to future skills and behaviour. What is the nature of the influence on the unborn child: are certain features clearly a result of genetic inheritance; or can the environment be seen to provide the basis for some developmental outcomes; or do genetic and environmental factors interact to impact on development?

It is also important to recognise that developmental psychology is just one element of an extensive discipline. Making links between the different areas of psychology is an important part of the learning process – demonstrating such a synthesis of knowledge is therefore encouraged throughout this chapter.

Stages of prenatal development

Prenatal development lasts approximately 266 days, beginning with fertilisation and ending with birth. It can be divided into three periods.

The germinal period

- This describes the first two weeks after conception.

- The newly fertilised egg is known as a zygote.

- Rapid cell division takes place within the zygote by **mitosis**.

- The zygote comprises the **blastocyst**, which becomes the embryo, and the **trophoblast** – an outer layer of cells that will provide nutrition for the *embryo* in the next stage of development.

- The zygote implants in the uterus wall 10–14 days after conception.

The embryonic period

- This describes the period lasting from two to eight weeks after conception.

- The embryonic period begins once the blastocyst (now known as an embryo) has implanted in the uterus wall.

- Cell differentiation now intensifies and organs appear.

- The embryo comprises three layers:

    ○ **endoderm** – inner layer, which develops into the digestive and respiratory systems;

Figure 2.1: *Main processes of the germinal period of development*

Single egg from ovary is drawn into fallopian tube at 9–15 days of 28-day menstrual cycle

Fertilisation occurs in upper third of fallopian tube within 24 hours of ovulation

24–30 hours after fertilisation: male and female chromosone material unite and rapid cell division begins as zygote travels down fallopian tube to the uterus

36 hours: structure comprises 2 cells

48 hours: structure comprises 4 cells

3 days: zygote is now a small compact ball of 16–32 cells

4 days: zygote becomes a hollow ball of 64–128 cells

4–5 days: inner cell mass is formed. Zygote is within uterus, but not yet attached

6–7 days: attaches to wall of uterus

11–15 days: zygote implants in uterus wall

- ○ **ectoderm** – outer layer, which develops into the nervous system, sensory receptors (eyes, ears) and skin, hair and nails;

- ○ **mesoderm** – middle layer, which develops into the circulatory system, bones, muscles, excretory system and reproductive system.

- The embryo is protected by the amnion, a bag containing the amniotic fluid in which the embryo floats. Together the amnion and the amniotic fluid provide a temperature-controlled, shock-proof environment.

- The **umbilical cord** contains two arteries and one vein, and connects the baby to the **placenta**.

- The placenta contains tissues in which blood vessels from the mother and offspring entwine but do not join. Oxygen, water, food and salt pass from the mother's bloodstream to the embryo and waste products (carbon dioxide, digestive waste) pass from embryo to the mother. Only small molecules can cross the placental barrier – many harmful substances such as bacteria are too large to pass into the child's bloodstream.

- Major organs are formed during this period and so are most vulnerable at this stage. More details about what develops when can be found in Table 2.1.

Table 2.1: *Critical periods of development for the major organ systems*

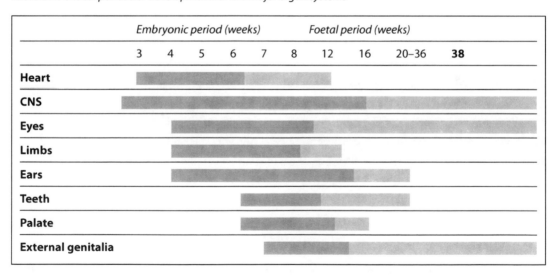

	Embryonic period (weeks)					Foetal period (weeks)				
	3	4	5	6	7	8	12	16	20–36	**38**
Heart										
CNS										
Eyes										
Limbs										
Ears										
Teeth										
Palate										
External genitalia										

Note: Darker areas of shading indicate the most sensitive period for teratogenic effects: exposure during these sensitive periods is more likely to result in more serious structural abnormalities.

The foetal period

- This period begins two months after conception and lasts on average for seven months.

- The organism is now known as a **foetus**.

- The foetus is active, moving arms and legs, and opening and closing the mouth.

- Facial features can be distinguished and genitals can be identified as male or female.

- By the end of the fourth month, a growth spurt occurs in the lower body and the mother begins to feel movement of her unborn child.

- Activity increases over the fifth month and preferences are shown for particular positions.

- The **grasp reflex** develops by the end of the sixth month and irregular breathing movements occur.

- At seven months the foetus is viable, but will need help breathing if born now.

- During the last two months of prenatal development, fatty tissues develop and organ functioning improves ready for birth.

Influences on development

Genes and heredity

The importance of genetics and inheritance for physical traits such as eye colour, height etc. is well established. Likewise, it is known that chromosomal abnormalities can result in atypical development as seen in **Down's syndrome** or **Fragile X** (McGuffin et al., 2001). Such syndromes are often associated with specific cognitive or behavioural deficits. However, the extent to which other cognitive or behavioural problems have a genetic basis is not known. Likewise, the importance of inheritance for psychological traits such as intelligence and personality remains highly controversial.

Focus on: biological bases of behaviour

In the paper 'Reactivity in infants: a cross-national comparison' Kagan et al. (1994) argue that behavioural traits, such as the amount of motor activity seen in infants, are innate. In this study, Kagan provides evidence for very different patterns of motor arousal in four-month-old infants in three different cultures – China, Ireland and the USA. The data suggest that Chinese infants are much calmer, quieter and less fretful than the American and Irish infants, which Kagan cites as evidence for *biological* differences in temperament between Caucasian and Asian infants.

Task — Read the paper described above (Kagan et al. (1994) Reactivity in infants: a cross-national comparison. *Developmental Psychology*, 30: 342–5) and answer the following review questions.

– What methods did the study employ?

– What evidence is provided to support the hypothesis presented by Kagan and colleagues that temperament has a biological basis?

– Is it possible to interpret this evidence in a different way?

Comment

The study used a well-controlled experimental design to test infant reactivity to a range of auditory, visual and olefactory stimuli. Infant behaviour was then coded on a number of features, including motor activity, smiling, fretting, crying and vocalisation. Coding was standardised and carried out by experienced, independent researchers. However, despite the good research design and implementation, it is important to think very carefully about the evidence Kagan provides. Can we be certain that these differences are biological? He cites evidence of earlier studies showing this difference in younger infants. Does this therefore negate the experiential factor? At what point in development is experience relevant? For example, how might prenatal experiences have influenced the behaviours shown by these infants? How might this idea be tested further? For instance, would it be useful for studies to test Asian infants born in the USA?

An important issue highlighted by this paper is the role of culture in development, which is one of the environmental factors also discussed in this section. The social context of development is clearly important as it helps define beliefs and social practices. Remember, though, that culture is not defined by geography: culture refers to the attitudes and behaviours that are characteristic of a particular social group or organisation. These attitudes and behaviours may therefore be influenced by social and economic factors as well as ethnicity. Can you think of different cultural groups in the UK, for example? This paper therefore also highlights one of the many links between social and developmental psychology.

Environmental factors

A range of environmental factors has been suggested to impact on development, including culture, socio-economic status and family context (Nebot et al., 1997). Such factors are relevant from before birth as they will impact on issues such as access to and uptake of prenatal care, maternal and paternal lifestyle choices, exposure to potential teratogens and so on. They may also confound some of the other factors thought to influence prenatal development (Nebot et al., 1997).

Gene–environment interactions

There is evidence to support a role for both inheritance and environment in the development of a range of psychological functions, including intelligence and personality, as well as psychological disorders such as **schizophrenia**. In terms of intelligence and personality, it is suggested that, while the **genotype** (a given combination of genes) is inherited, the **phenotype** (that which is observed) develops over time in response to environmental factors. Likewise, it may be that an individual inherits a particular genotype that predisposes them to developing schizophrenia, but whether the disorder is actually manifest in an individual will depend on the presence of environmental triggers (**diathesis-stress model**). While the relevance of genetics prenatally may be evident, the role of the prenatal environment should also be considered; factors such as maternal health and well-being should not be dismissed lightly. Indeed, there is increasing evidence that prenatal stress combined with a genetic predisposition affects changes in brain development associated with schizophrenia (Koenig et al., 2002).

Threats to development

A teratogen is any agent that has the potential to cause a birth defect, or have a negative affect on cognitive and behavioural outcomes. The effects of teratogens may not always be evident at birth. Severity of damage is linked to a range of factors, including dose, developmental period during which exposure takes place (see Table 2.2) and genetic susceptibility. The most common teratogens are as follows.

Maternal health

Illness in pregnancy can have devastating effects, depending on the timing. *Rubella* in the eleventh week of pregnancy can cause blindness, deafness, heart defects and brain damage due to the critical developmental stage of organ development. Rubella at later stages of pregnancy may, however, have no long-term impact on the unborn child (Dontigny et al., 2008). Other infections with the potential to harm include **chicken pox**, some sexually transmitted diseases (e.g. **syphilis**) and **Aids** (Avril and Ornoy, 2006). Table 2.2 lists other common diseases and their effects. An important issue here for psychologists is how these risks can be reduced. Strategies to reduce risk may be employed at either a social or an individual level, but in either case the emphasis is usually on increasing knowledge in order to change people's attitudes and behaviour. For example, the risk of HIV infection to infants born to mothers who are HIV positive can be reduced by a number of simple measures, including birth by **Caesarean delivery** and not breastfeeding (RCOG, 2004).

Maternal diet is also important as the developing embryo or foetus relies solely on the mother for its own nutrition (Derbyshire, 2007). Maternal malnourishment increases the risk of deformity,

Table 2.2: *Threats to prenatal development due to maternal health problems*

Disease or health condition	Common effects for the unborn child	Impact of timing on teratogenic effect
Rubella	Blindness Deafness Cognitive deficits Heart defects Cerebral palsy Microencephaly	Infection in weeks 1–8 most likely to lead to deficits (60–85 per cent of cases), reducing to 50 per cent in weeks 9–12 and 16 per cent in weeks 13–24.
Chicken pox	Premature birth Slowed growth Limb, facial or skeletal malformation	Infection in weeks 1–12 most likely to lead to deficits. Infection up to 4 days before birth can also have implications for perinatal health resulting in neonatal death in 30 per cent of cases.
Aids	HIV infection	Infection is more likely during the birth process or perinatally than prenatally.
Chlamydia	Premature birth Low birth weight Neonatal conjunctivitis Pneumonia in newborn infant	25 per cent of infants born to infected mothers contract pneumonia and 50 per cent contract conjunctivitis. In both cases infection is transmitted during the birth process.
Syphilis	Blindness Deafness Cognitive deficits Heart defects	Syphilitic organisms cannot cross the placental barrier until week 18. Thus, if treatment can be given before this time, teratogenic effects are rarely seen.
Herpes	Microencephaly Hydrocephalus Cognitive deficits Eye defects	Prenatal infection occurs in only 8 per cent of cases. Infection is more likely to occur during the birth process.
Toxoplasmosis	Blindness Deafness Cognitive deficit	Infection in weeks 1–8 most likely to lead to deficits.

while maternal obesity has been linked to foetal death, stillbirth and central nervous system (CNS) defects. **Folic acid** deficiency has been linked to **neural tube** defects such as **spina bifida**.

Maternal age

Delayed childbirth is increasingly common in Western societies; however, this can increase risks to the health of both mother and child (Jacobsson et al., 2004). Risks to the infant include prematurity, low birth weight and certain chromosomal abnormalities such as Down's syndrome. Risks are thought to be greatest for mothers over 30 years of age and have been linked to the declining condition of a woman's eggs; however, there is some evidence that in women with no pre-existing maternal health difficulties the risk of problems in pregnancy is lower. There are also risks for the offspring of younger mothers; adolescent pregnancies are more likely to result in premature birth and infant mortality rates for this age group are higher than for any other (Frazer et al., 1995). However, there are possible confounding factors here related to social circumstances and social support; teenage mothers are more likely to be from lower-income families and live in areas of greater deprivation.

Maternal stress

Intense emotional states during pregnancy can affect the unborn child as the physiological changes experienced by the mother may have consequences for uterine blood flow and available oxygen levels. High levels of corticotrophin-releasing hormone (CRH) have been linked to maternal stress and subsequent premature birth and infant distress. Maternal stress may also have an indirect effect on the health of the unborn child by increasing the likelihood of maladaptive behaviours, such as drug taking, smoking and alcohol use (Talge et al., 2007).

Prescription and non-prescription drugs

Potentially harmful prescription drugs include certain antibiotics (e.g. streptomycin), anticonvulsants, antidepressants and synthetic hormones (e.g. **DES**). **Thalidomide**, prescribed for morning sickness in the 1960s, is a commonly cited example of the disastrous effects of drugs on the unborn child. Non-prescription drugs with potential to harm include diet pills and aspirin. Further examples of the known effects of prescription and non-prescription drugs on the foetus are shown in Table 2.3.

Illegal drugs

Cocaine use in pregnancy has been linked to low weight, body length and head circumference at birth, as well as more long-term neurological and cognitive deficits, including impaired motor development at two years of age, lower arousal, poorer self-regulation, higher excitability and poorer reflexes at one month of age (Lester et al., 2002). However, confounding variables linked to the environment and lifestyles of drug users should also be considered (e.g. poverty, malnutrition). Children born to heroin users have been found to show withdrawal symptoms immediately after birth, including tremors, irritability, abnormal crying, disturbed sleep and impaired motor control. Heroin use in pregnancy has also been linked to behavioural problems and **attention deficits** in later childhood.

Table 2.3: Drugs and their effect on prenatal development

Drug	Drug type and use	Effects
Carbemazepine and phenytoin	Prescription drugs used to control seizures (anticonvulsants)	Cleft lip and palate Neural tube defects Kidney disease Restricted growth
Aspirin, ibuprofen, and other non-steroidal anti-inflammatory drugs (NSAIDs)	Non-prescription pain relief; occasional use is not problematic	Neo-natal bleeding Raise the risk of delayed labour
Sotretinoin and etretinate	Prescription drugs used to treat chronic acne and psoriasis	May cause chronic malformations during the stage of organ development
Ergotamine and methysergide	Prescribed for migraine attacks	Raise the risk of premature labour
Coumarin	Anticoagulant drugs used in the treatment of heart disease and stroke, to slow blood clotting	Taken during early pregnancy, they are associated with facial malformations and mental retardation; later on they raise the risk of uncontrolled bleeding
Tetracycline	Antibiotic; safe to use in the first four months of pregnancy	Discolouration of teeth Reduced bone growth

Alcohol

Consistent heavy drinking in pregnancy can result in foetal alcohol syndrome (FAS) – a cluster of abnormalities that include facial deformity, defective limbs, heart problems and cognitive impairment (Caley et al., 2008). Binge drinking has also been found to lead to cognitive impairment and behavioural problems in offspring. Some studies have suggested that even moderate drinking in pregnancy can result in reduced attention and alertness, which lasts at least through early childhood (four years of age).

Tobacco

Smoking cigarettes during pregnancy reduces the oxygen content while increasing the carbon monoxide content of the mother's blood and this in turn reduces the amount of oxygen available to the unborn child (Shea and Streiner, 2008). This has been shown to increase the chance of premature birth, low birth weight, foetal and neonatal death, **sudden infant death syndrome (SIDS)** and respiratory problems. Nicotine withdrawal has also been noted in neonates of smoking mothers. Links have also been made to **attention deficit hyperactivity disorder (ADHD)** in childhood. Second-hand smoke may also affect the mother's health and thus the health of her unborn child; a father's smoking may therefore have negative consequences for his child's health.

Environmental hazards

Radiation can cause **gene mutations**; chromosomal abnormalities are higher in the offspring of fathers exposed to high levels of radiation through their occupation. X-rays in the first few weeks of pregnancy (when expectant mothers often do not know they are pregnant) increase the risk of **microencephaly**, cognitive problems and **leukaemia** (Hertz et al., 2008).

Other hazards include pollutants such as carbon monoxide, mercury (sometimes found in fish such as tuna), certain fertilisers and pesticides.

Paternal health

As noted earlier, fathers who smoke risk affecting the health of their unborn child through effects on the mother's health. However, a father's health before conception is also important and can directly influence the development of the child. Thus, exposure to environmental pollutants, poor diet, and drug and alcohol use have all been suggested to cause abnormalities in fathers' sperm, resulting in miscarriages, childhood diseases such as cancer, and infant deformity (Cordier, 2008). More recently, fathers' age has also been suggested to increase the risk of birth defects (Yang et al., 2007).

Prenatal learning

In addition to the physical development described so far, there is some suggestion that cognitive development also begins before birth. The evidence to support such early cognitive ability comes from evidence of prenatal learning, which is linked to infant auditory perception. Hearing develops at around the sixth month prenatally and it has been well established that the foetus can perceive and respond to sounds, such as speech and music. The recognition of, and preference for, their mothers' voices shown by neonates is thought to be a learned response based on prenatal experience. Research studies have also shown that neonates can recognise either music or prose they have been exposed to prenatally, suggesting the development of cognitive skills such as memory before birth. A burgeoning industry has also built up around the idea that prenatal sonic stimulation with classical music (by, for example, Mozart and Bach) can have a positive effect on prenatal development, even though the evidence for this is equivocal.

Hormonal levels have been found to influence later cognitive skills, including sex differences. Increased levels of testosterone are thought to result in more rapid growth of **neurons** in the foetal brain and have been linked to enhanced spatial skills.

Focus on: 'The cat in the hat'

In this study by DeCasper and Spence (1986), mothers were asked to read a three-minute passage from the Dr Seuss story 'The cat in the hat' to their foetuses twice a day during the last six weeks of pregnancy. After these infants were born, 16 of them participated in a **non-nutritive sucking preference procedure**, in which they were given dummies linked to recordings of this or another previously unheard story being read aloud by their mothers. By sucking on the dummy, the infants were able to trigger the recording. The number of times the infants triggered the familiar, versus the previously unheard, recording was compared to a group of control infants who had never been exposed to either story. Infants in the study group triggered the tape recording of the prenatal story more frequently than the novel recording. For the control infants, however, there was no systematic preference. Infants tested using recordings in which the familiar story was read by an adult other than their mother also showed preference for this story. This shows that newborns could recognise the story read aloud by their mothers prenatally and has therefore been cited as evidence for prenatal learning.

Task — Read the paper described above (DeCasper, A and Spence, M (1986) Prenatal maternal speech influences on newborns' perception of speech sounds. *Infant Behavior and Development*, 9: 133–50) and answer the following review questions.

– What sort of evidence does the study provide concerning prenatal learning?

– What was the dummy sucking used to measure?

– What feature of language have infants learned in order to recognise the Dr Seuss story?

Comment

This is one experiment in which post-natal experience does not explain infant response to prenatal events. Because the researchers used both mothers and unfamiliar adults to read out the test story, they concluded that the infants were responding to the story itself, not simply the sound of their own mother's voice reading the story. The study therefore provides good evidence for prenatal learning. The dummy sucking was used to measure infant recognition of the story. Increased sucking in order to hear the familiar story is suggestive of prenatal learning since, in order to show recognition, a representation of the story must be held in the memory, which suggests learning has occurred. However, it is important not to over-interpret when evaluating the results from such experiments. Remember that, just because infants show a response to something, or demonstrate that they can discriminate between two things, this does not mean that they perceive them in the same way that adults or older children do. Infants may be able to differentiate between two words, but this does not mean that they know anything about what each word means. The recognition of the prenatal story demonstrated here does not suggest that the infants have learned the meanings of words, but that they have learned about patterns of speech and language – what linguists call 'acoustic cues'. This skill is the precursor to developing an understanding of what words mean, and the ability to recognise and remember speech sounds, and to segment words from the speech stream – in other words, to identify where words begin and end from the flow of sounds people make when they speak.

When taken together, this and other studies suggest that:

- foetal sensory experience shapes the developing brain;

- prenatal experience with the maternal voice provides a sensory and perceptual bridge into post-natal life (Moon and Fifer, 2000).

There is evidence, for example, that newborn infants have already learned to identify their native language. They can also recognise different speech patterns within that language; for example, they can differentiate 'happy talk' from other patterns of speech (Mastropieri and Turkewitz, 1999). This prenatal learning is thought to influence infants' responsiveness to speech and voices, which in turn provides a foundation for later language acquisition.

Task ─┐ The findings from this study have also been used as evidence to support the burgeoning industry that has developed around prenatal learning programmes. See www.babyplus.com/WhatIsIt.php for one example of such a programme. Once you have explored this website and have some understanding of the aim of prenatal learning programmes, reread the paper and consider the following question.

─ Does the study provide *any* evidence to support the idea that education should begin prenatally?

Comment

The research carried out by DeCasper and Spence (1986) provides exceptional evidence of prenatal learning. It shows that infants not only recognise their mothers' voices from before birth (which in itself suggests learning has taken place), but that the recognition of language and speech patterns is established through prenatal experience. It therefore supports the idea of prenatal learning and suggests how this may link to later learning. However, it is important to note that the study does not demonstrate any developmental benefit to providing 'extra' learning experiences during gestation. While most psychologists would agree that a healthy and enriched prenatal environment is of vital importance to an individual's long-term development and learning ability, this does not necessarily mean that there is a need to provide stimuli over and above those that are available to the foetus naturally.

Birth and neonatal development

In a normal full-term foetus, birth is triggered by the release of a hormone in the foetal brain, which stimulates the contractions that will deliver the baby. On average, this process takes 12–14 hours, although this varies and many births take longer, especially for first-born children. Most babies are delivered head first; in only 4 per cent of births does the baby present with another part of the anatomy (**breech birth**), which can make birth harder and more dangerous for both mother and child. There are three stages involved in the birth process: stage one begins when the mother experiences regular contractions of the uterus and ends when her cervix is fully dilated so that the baby's head can pass through. The second stage of labour is delivery, which begins as the baby's head passes through the cervix into the vagina and ends when the baby emerges from the mother's body. The final stage is the delivery of the placenta, which normally takes only a few minutes.

In the majority of cases, the birth process goes smoothly; however, there may be circumstances in which difficulties arise either for the mother or for the unborn baby (**foetal distress**). In extreme cases, such problems may lead to **anoxia**. Anoxia at birth can have a negative impact on neurological development, as brain cells die if starved of oxygen for more than a few minutes. Extreme cases of anoxia can lead to **cerebral palsy**. Milder anoxia, however, leads to irritability in the perinatal period but has no long-lasting effects.

Medical intervention is sometimes necessary to ensure the well-being of mother and child. A Caesarean section may be indicated if the baby is very big or the mother too small. Medical advances mean that this is as safe as a normal vaginal birth for both mother and baby. Perinatal and later development also appears to be normal, suggesting no lasting impact on the child. Recent research (Swain et al., 2008) suggests, however, that mothers who have experienced a Caesarean birth are less sensitive to their own baby's cry in the early perinatal period. What, if any, implications this may have for later development is not as yet known.

Other medical interventions include the use of pain control medication such as an **epidural** or **analgesics** such as pethadine. Pethadine and other sedatives may cross the placental barrier, resulting in the **neonate** being sleepy and more difficult to feed in the first few days. Epidural anaesthetics are also able to cross the placental barrier, although the research in this area is somewhat ambiguous. Despite this, most studies suggest that some babies will have trouble **latching on**, which can lead to breastfeeding difficulties. Another disadvantage is that they may result in longer labour and so increase the likelihood of an assisted delivery.

Assisted delivery refers to the use of instruments such as **forceps** or **ventouse** to help pull the baby out of the birth canal. They are needed in difficult deliveries where the labour has proceeded for too long and the mother is too tired to push, the infant appears distressed or there are concerns about the health of the mother. While these procedures can be potentially life-saving, their use can mark or even injure the soft tissue of the infant **cranium** and can be very uncomfortable for the mother.

Socio-cultural influences on birthing choices

Although childbirth is a universal biological event that occurs in all cultures, it is not independent of cultural influences. Culturally based beliefs and values influence women's experiences of childbirth and determine the practices a society believes are appropriate for providing care for pregnant and post-partum women. Birth is almost never simply a biological act (Davis-Floyd and Sargent, 1997). Cultural views about women and reproduction lead to a wide variation in the kinds of care women receive during both pregnancy and birth. Polynesian culture, for example, values the female body and bestows a high status on pregnant women, who are treated with great consideration and benefit from the attention of respected midwives. In comparison, in Bangladesh and rural north India, menstruation and birth are regarded as 'intensely polluting' and women are reluctant to assist others in childbirth for fear of being tainted by the pollution of birth.

The extent to which a culture embraces technology also affects the dominant views on childbirth (Fiedler, 1997). A culture that values technology highly, such as the United Kingdom, tends to view the process of childbirth as requiring a high level of medical intervention. Recent figures (DH, 2004) suggest that 20 per cent of deliveries are **artificially induced** or accelerated. Thirteen per cent of women have an **episiotomy** and one third have an epidural, general or spinal anaesthetic during labour. These same figures also suggest that 11 per cent of women have instrumental deliveries.

The number of babies born by *Caesarean section* has also increased in the last 15 years. The World Health Organization (WHO) recommends that the Caesarean rate should be no more than 10–15 per cent. The average rate across the UK is, however, 22 per cent, with many hospitals having rates that exceed 25 per cent. It has been suggested that this increased medicalisation of childbirth can be attributed to the kinds of choices that women themselves are making. While it is true that women themselves are increasingly choosing a Caesarean birth, it should be noted that only 7 per cent of Caesareans are performed at the mother's request. As noted earlier, we do not yet know whether or not the use of such interventions impacts on later development.

Neonatal development

Human infants are born before they have fully developed and they are vulnerable, needing to be cared for by others. For example, infants enter the world with virtually no muscle control; they can't hold their heads up on their own and they can't even roll over. However, they are born with some, albeit limited, survival skills.

Neonatal reflexes

The neonate can turn its head, suckle, grasp your finger and cry out when startled. These are all examples of neonatal reflexes. These unconditioned reflexes are not learned or developed through experience, but are innate. Normally, developing neonates are expected to respond to specific stimuli with a specific, predictable behaviour or action. The absence of such a response may be a sign of atypical development and indicate further assessment. Some neonatal reflexes disappear with maturation; others persist into adulthood. Some of the most important reflexes for survival are described in Table 2.4.

Table 2.4: *Neonatal reflexes and their survival value*

Reflex	Stimulus	Behavioural response
Rooting	Stroking the cheek, mouth, or lips (e.g. with the teat of a bottle or the nipple)	Head turns towards the stimulation, mouth opens and tongue moves forward. Infant searches for the object by moving the head in steadily decreasing arcs until it is found. This reflex helps the neonate find a source of nourishment.
Sucking	Stimulating the roof of the mouth	Neonate automatically sucks and swallows in a coordinated fashion. This reflex is common to all mammals and enables feeding.
Palmar grasp	Placing an object in the neonate's palm	Neonate's fingers curl tightly around the object. This automatic grasp reflex fades over the first few months to enable the infant to grasp objects voluntarily.
Babinski	Stroking the side of the sole	Toes spread and the big toe extends upward. This Babinski reflex is the opposite of the normal adult response, in which the big toe turns downward. Fades over the first year of life.
Stepping	Holding infant upright, so that the soles of the feet are touching a firm surface	Neonate alternately bends each leg as though walking. This reflex fades rapidly but reappears months later as learned voluntary behaviour in preparation for true walking.
Moro or startle	A loud noise or rough handling	The legs and head extend while the arms jerk up and out with the palms up and thumbs flexed. Shortly afterwards, the arms are brought together and the hands clench into fists, and the infant cries loudly. This reflex normally disappears by three to four months of age.

Sensory capacity

The neonate has the capability to see, hear, taste, touch and smell. However, some of these senses are more developed than others. Touch is an important method of communication during the first months of an infant's life. Rhythmic motion or rocking can be comforting to a fretful infant, for example. Neonates also experience pain and there is evidence that children who experience repeated pain exposure as neonates, such as frequent heel-pricks or intramuscular injections, may be more fearful of pain than their peers during later childhood.

Neonates are also able to respond to different tastes, including sweet, sour, bitter and salty substances, and show a preference towards sweet tastes. It has also been demonstrated that neonates show a preference for the smell of foods that their mother ate regularly during pregnancy. The neonate also has a developed sense of smell at birth, and within the first week of life can already distinguish the differences between their mother's breast milk and the breast milk of another female.

Vision is less well developed in the newborn infant. Acuity is limited and they are only able to focus on objects approximately 12 inches directly in front of their face. This is because both the anatomical and neurological structures that support vision are not yet fully formed. The optic nerves are all formed by birth, but are not fully **myelinated**. Likewise, the *neurons* of the **visual cortex** are formed, but **interconnectivity** is limited and **axons** are poorly myelinated. This process is not complete until the infant is approximately six months of age. The muscles that move the eyes to help them both focus on an object to produce a single image are also immature at birth. This visual coordination improves over the first six–eight weeks post-natally. Neonates cannot perceive depth and this skill does not develop fully until the infant is mobile. Colour perception is also immature at birth. However, infants can perceive contrast and, when not sleeping, feeding or crying, may spend a lot of time staring at random objects. Preference is shown for anything that has sharp contrasting colours or complex patterns, and there is some evidence that the greatest preference is for looking at human faces (Bushnell, 2003).

As discussed earlier, hearing develops prenatally and at birth the anatomical structures are remarkably mature in contrast to the visual system. The fibres throughout the auditory nerve are also fully myelinated at birth, although the neurons in the auditory projection areas of the cortex (**Heschl's gyrus**) do not complete their interconnectivity until adolescence. Neonates usually respond to a female voice over a male voice, which may relate to prenatal experience. As discussed in 'Prenatal learning' (page 36), preferences are shown for sounds that were a regular feature of their prenatal environment.

Post-natal brain development

The majority of neurons form before birth but continue to develop during the first six years of life. During this time, 75 per cent of neurological growth takes place. At birth, the brain weighs about 25 per cent of its adult weight. By the age of two years, it has reached 75 per cent of its adult weight and, by five years, 90 per cent of its adult weight. This increase is mainly due to the increase in the myelination of neurons, as various areas of the brain take on more specialised functions. This development and increasing specialisation is heavily influenced by a genetic blueprint, evolved over many generations (Nelson et al., 2006). However, at birth the brain has a great deal of **plasticity** because this specialisation has not yet taken place. The advantage of this is that the neonatal brain is highly adaptable and can often recover from injury. The disadvantage is that it makes it more vulnerable to damage if exposed to drugs or disease, or if deprived of sensory experiences. However, the process of neurological development is not so highly **canalised** that the environment cannot impact on brain development. Indeed, brain development relies on individual experience to customise its connections and this relationship will be explored in greater detail in the next chapter.

Critical thinking activity

Prenatal learning

Critical thinking focus: analysis and evaluation of written text

Key question: *To what extent does current evidence fit the claims of those advocating prenatal learning?*

Do a literature search using an academic search engine such as PsycINFO to find further up-to-date evidence (post-1990) about prenatal learning and post-natal preferences. Choose one or two of the papers you have found to answer this key question.

Use the following prompts to guide your reading and response to the question.

- Identify the aim of the piece of writing

- What is the author's point of view?

- What assumptions have been made?

- Which concepts and principles have been used in arguing the case?

- Summarise the key information given.

- Do you agree with the inferences and conclusions made?

Worked example

Literature example: Krueger, C, Holditch-Davis, D, Quint, S and DeCasper, A (2004). Recurring auditory experience in the 28- to 34-week-old fetus. *Infant Behavior and Development*, 27: 537–43.

- *Identify the aim of the piece of writing.* This report outlines a descriptive study that looked at changes in foetal heart rate in response to maternal speech at 28–34 weeks' gestation.

- *What is the authors' point of view?* The authors believes that prenatal recognition of speech and language is likely to begin relatively early in gestation (notably before the foetus is viable) and that both the timing of this language experience and its quantity are important for later language acquisition.

- *What assumptions have been made?* It seems to be assumed that prenatal exposure to maternal speech is necessary for post-natal language development; it is clear that the authors believe that language acquisition is primarily experiential and so, in the same vein, it is also assumed that '**motherese**' is essential for language learning.

- *Which concepts and principles have been used in arguing the case?* The study is based on traditional experimental models in this area of psychology. Thus, it is argued that a small deceleration in foetal heart beat (1–5 bpm) is an orienting or attentional response designed to enhance stimulus intake. A deceleration in foetal heartbeat in response to an auditory stimulus is therefore taken to demonstrate recognition of that stimulus. A heart rate acceleration of 1–5 bpm, however, is seen as a defensive response that limits stimulus intake.

- *Summarise the key information given.* Sixteen women expecting their first baby were asked to recite a nursery rhyme aloud each day, three times in the morning and three times in the evening. Mothers were randomly assigned to one of two groups; mothers in Group 1 recited the verse from the twenty-eighth to the thirty-fourth week of gestation, while those in Group 2 only began reciting the rhyme at 32 weeks. Both groups were tested weekly for foetal reactions to a recording of the rhyme from the twenty-eighth to the thirty-fourth week of gestation. The women were asked to eat approximately one hour before reciting and to perform the recitation while sitting in a quiet room. They were to begin reciting only after they felt no foetal movement for at least one minute, to ensure that the foetus was in a quiet state. The mothers were also taught to recite the verse in motherese. The recording was provided by a female drama student and also used motherese. The nursery rhyme was not a common verse, making it unlikely that the foetuses would be spontaneously exposed to it. At 32 weeks' gestation, no response to the rhyme was noted for either group; at 33 weeks' gestation, Group 1 approached significance for detection of a cardiac orienting response, while Group 2 responded with a cardiac acceleration. At 34 weeks' gestation, both groups demonstrated a cardiac orienting response to the rhyme. Furthermore, those foetuses whose mothers began recitation at 28 weeks' gestation took longer to respond with an orienting response to the rhyme than those who began hearing the rhyme at 32 weeks' gestation. It is therefore concluded that the preterm foetus can recognise language and speech patterns, but that the timing of this language experience and its quantity are also important.

- *Do you agree with the inferences and conclusions made?* In general, this study shows good experimental design and a number of possible extrinsic confounding variables are well controlled, making study conclusions compelling. However, the inclusion of a control group would have strengthened findings. Would a foetus which had not heard the nursery rhyme read by its mother also have paid attention to the recording made by the drama student? Could the foetal attentional response be seen because of the use of an intonation pattern known to be attractive to newborns – and by extension to the unborn infant (motherese) – rather than because the rhyme itself is recognised? Furthermore, this current study does not conclusively tell us whether prenatal language experience is important for later language development, as testing stopped at 34 weeks' gestation. Perhaps prenatal experience is irrelevant to language learning and we are simply hardwired to recognise speech patterns from before birth. This study does not provide any new evidence to support the idea that prenatal education is of benefit to later development.

Critical thinking review

This activity helps develop your skills of analysis and evaluation in relation to a piece of text. This means you are learning to read closely, in a structured way, to be sensitive to the author's perspective and to extract the key information given. These are important skills that will allow you to evaluate and make critical judgements about psychology research and its application to the real world.

Other skills you may have used in this activity include reflection, recall of key principles and ideas, communication (literacy) skills if you write up the activity, independent learning, and information technology if the follow-up literature search is carried out.

Skill builder activity

Influences on prenatal development

Transferable skill focus: organisational skills and visual communication

Key question: Use the information provided in the chapter to create a **concept map** that shows the relationship between the environment and biological aspects of prenatal development.

In order to address this task, you need to decide which biological and environmental factors are important to prenatal development. You should then ask yourself a number of questions about which aspects of development they influence and whether or not they work alone or together.

Skill builder review

The task requires you to extract information from within the text and reorganise it into a visual format. This kind of mapping helps develop creativity, logical thinking and study skills by revealing connections and helping you to see how individual aspects of development, such as environment and genes, work together. There is also evidence that, because concept maps help you make sense of the topic you are learning about, they support more meaningful critical learning processes.

Assignments

1. Critically evaluate the impact of environmental and other agents on the future cognitive and psychological health of the unborn child.

2. Discuss the importance of timing for ameliorating or enhancing the teratogenic effects of maternal disease, drug and alcohol use and environmental agents such as radiation.

3. To what extent does the evidence support the suggestion that prenatal experiences may affect post-natal preferences and behaviours?

Summary: what you have learned

Now you have finished studying this chapter you should:

- be able to describe the three main stages of prenatal development and understand the ways in which factors such as genetic and environmental influences work together to influence development even before birth;

- recognise the vulnerability of the human organism during prenatal development and be able to evaluate the influence of teratogenic agents and other threats to development;

- be able to evaluate critically the evidence concerning prenatal learning and later cognitive development, being especially aware of the importance of prenatal experiences for later language acquisition;

- understand critically the way that culturally based beliefs and values will influence women's experiences of childbirth and determine the practices a society believes are appropriate for providing care;

- be aware of the abilities of the neonate, including reflexes, sensory capacity and early neuro-logical development;

- have developed your ability to analyse and evaluate written text by carrying out a literature search and reviewing one paper about prenatal learning;

- have developed your organisational skills and visual communication by creating a concept map of the influences on prenatal development.

Further reading

Caley, L, Syms, C, Robinson, L, Cederbaum, J, Henry, M and Shipkey, N (2008) What human service professionals know and want to know about fetal alcohol syndrome. *Canadian Journal of Clinical Pharmacology*, 15: e177–e123.

This gives an excellent overview of FAS.

Cordier, S (2008) Evidence for a role of paternal exposures in developmental toxicity. *Basic and Clinical Pharmacology and Toxicology*, 102: 176–81.

This considers the role of paternal exposure to environmental hazards in prenatal development.

Hertz-Picciotto, I, Park, HY and Dostal, M et al. (2008) Prenatal exposure to persistent and non-persistent organic compounds and effects on immune system development. *Basic and Clinical Pharmacology and Toxicology*, 102: 146–54.

This reviews the evidence concerning the impact of environmental hazards such as air pollution on immune system development.

Koenig, JI, Kirkpatrick, B and Lee, P (2002) Glucocorticoid hormones and early brain development in schizophrenia. *Neuropsychopharmacology*, 27: 309–18.

This reviews genes and environment interaction in the development of schizophrenia.

Royal College of Obstetrics and Gynaecology (RCOG) (2010) Clinical Green-top Guideline No. 39: *Management of HIV in Pregnancy* (2nd edn, June 2010). Available online at www.rcog.org.uk/womens-health/clinical-guidance/management-hiv-pregnancy-green-top-39.

Further information on teratogens and papers concerning this issue are also available from the Organisation of Teratology Information Specialists (OTIS) at www.otispregnancy.org.

Chapter 3

Development in infancy

Learning outcomes

By the end of this chapter you should:

- *be able to describe the main sequence of motor skill development;*
- *understand the importance of innate reflexes for psychological development;*
- *be able to evaluate how the development of the object concept progresses;*
- *be aware of the main features of attachment theory;*
- *be able to evaluate critically the evidence concerning aspects of early relationships and later language development;*
- *understand critically the impact of the developmental niche on emerging skills;*
- *have developed your ability to apply theoretical models to real-life scenarios;*
- *have developed your understanding and use of (quantitative) data).*

Introduction

In this chapter we consider human development during the first two years of life. During this period the foundations for psychosocial development established prenatally continue to evolve. Physical and neurological growth progress at an astounding rate and the infant increasingly gains control over physical functioning, in particular **gross and fine motor skills**. This motor control enables the infant to begin to explore their environment, which in turn facilitates the development of cognitive skills. Relationships with others and particularly parents or other carers are essential for the physical survival of the infant because of their continued vulnerability. However, there is also clear evidence that these relationships are necessary for the development of social, psychological and cognitive skills as well.

Physical growth and the development of motor skills

Humans grow from the moment of conception until they attain adult height around the age of 20 years. This process of growth is not regular and one of the periods of most rapid growth is infancy. For example, by the end of the first year of life, a typical infant has achieved around three times his or her birth weight. This increase in weight and height continues through the first few years, before slowing down until puberty, when there is another growth spurt. Increases in overall body size are also accompanied by changes in bodily proportions: in infancy the head accounts for a quarter of body height, but by adulthood this proportion has reduced to one sixth.

However, physical growth is not just about increases in weight and height. It also involves developing control over the muscles of the body and increasing physical coordination. Human motor control is a relatively slow process and, by the end of the first two years of life, infants have achieved mastery of only the basics of mobility and coordination, as shown in Figure 3.1.

Gross motor skill development

Gross motor skills involve the large muscles of the body and include **locomotor functions**, such as sitting upright, walking, kicking and throwing a ball. Gross motor skills depend on both muscle tone and strength. This motor development proceeds from the head down (cephalocaudal) and from the centre outwards (proximodistal). Activities involving the head and upper body therefore

Figure 3.1: The gross motor developments in the first two years

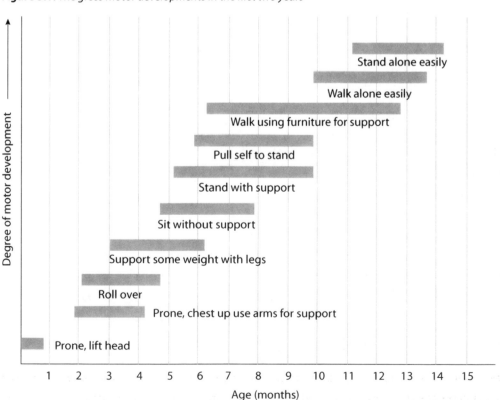

develop before those involving the lower body; and those involving the trunk and shoulders develop before those involving hands and fingers. Motor skills advance in a definite sequence and age *norms* are often used to gauge an infant's developmental progress (Bayley, 1993). This distinct pattern of motor skill development led early theorists to propose that it represents the unfolding of a genetically programmed sequence of events in which the nerves and muscles mature in a downward and outward direction (Shirley, 1933).

Individual variation is, however, common in the development of these skills and the timing of motor skill development may vary by as much as two to four months without being indicative of *atypical development*. In fact, evidence now suggests that environmental factors influence the timing of motor skill development. For example, there is support for the idea that the early motor development often seen in African infants is linked to parenting behaviours (Super, 1976; Cintas, 1989). Parents in African cultures have been shown to help the development of motor skills by providing opportunities for infants to develop muscle tone and strength, for example by placing them in an upright position. Likewise, Jamaican mothers traditionally expect early motor development and work to encourage this by massaging and stretching their baby's limbs (Hopkins, 1991). Jamaican infants born and raised in the traditional way in the UK continue to show this earlier development. However, those not raised in the traditional way show no difference in the age at which they gained these skills when compared to their non-Jamaican peers. This demonstrates clearly that this difference is not genetic, but based on environmental factors such as infant handling.

Infants may also miss out milestones. In the African Mali tribe most infants never crawl (Bril, 1999). Adolph (2002) describes infants in the USA who also bypass the crawling phase, either moving around by rolling or not trying to get around until they are upright. Environmental factors such as parenting behaviours are likely to be important here as well: the reduction in the number of infants crawling coincided with late twentieth-century recommendations to lay babies to sleep on their backs in order to reduce the risk of SIDS (Davis et al., 1998).

Current evidence therefore supports a greater role for the environment in the development of these skills than used to be thought. Maturational processes are believed to place some limits on the age at which an infant will be able to sit up, crawl or walk; however, the experiences and opportunities to practise that each child encounters are very important in influencing the actual age at which these milestones are reached. Modern theories of motor skill development emphasise the interaction between nature and nurture. An important approach here is provided by the dynamic systems theory (Thelen, 1995). This model takes a constructivist approach to motor skill development. It therefore acknowledges the contribution of both nature and nurture to development and also emphasises the active role that the child takes in its own development. According to dynamic systems theory, at first motor actions rely on the innate reflexes described in the previous chapter – for example, grasping, sucking and rooting. Gradually, these reflexes are reorganised into new and more complex actions. Initial motor behaviours are likely to be tentative, disjointed and uncoordinated; however, they are progressively modified and refined until the components fit together, resulting in smooth well-coordinated 'action systems'. In this way, new motor skills are constructed by infants as they actively reorganise existing behaviours into new and more complex actions. Development is seen as a self-organising system: the infant is driven by curiosity about the world around them to develop more complex motor skills in order to achieve new goals. Interesting sights and sounds in the environment will provide motivation for locomotion, especially where the target is just out of reach. In addition, improving physical strength, increases in neurological connections, sensory stimuli and parenting behaviours all contribute to the development of these motor skills. This theory also integrates action, perception and thought as the infant has to think about how to organise locomotion in order to achieve their goals (von Hofsten, 2007).

Fine motor skill development

Fine motor skills involve the small muscles of the body that enable functions such as grasping and manipulating small objects. Functions such as writing, drawing and fastening clothing rely upon our fine motor skills. These skills involve strength, fine motor control, and dexterity. The ability of the infant to reach out and manipulate objects changes considerably over the first year of life. Voluntary reaching and grasping usually develops at three months of age. Prior to this, infants will take uncoordinated swipes at objects they can see; this rarely results in capture of the object in question. The onset of reaching and grasping marks a significant accomplishment for an infant's capacity for interaction with their environment. By four or five months, infants are able to transfer objects from hand to hand and the reflexive **palmar grasp** is replaced by the voluntary **ulnar grasp**. Clumsy and claw-like, this grip nevertheless provides increased ability to explore objects through touch. Gradually, the ability to manipulate objects increases so that, by the end of the first year of life, infants are able to use the far superior **pincer grasp**. This is a crucial development in terms of dexterity, as this finger and thumb grip provides the basis for our more sophisticated manual skills, such as writing, using scissors and cutlery, turning the pages of a book and so on.

Throughout the second year of life infants become increasingly dexterous and coordinated. At 16 months of age they are able to hold a pencil and make basic scribbles; by the age of 24 months they are able to copy simple vertical or horizontal lines. Building blocks, buttons, dials and other objects can now be manipulated easily. Consistent with dynamic systems theory, infants are gaining control over simple movements and gradually reorganising them into increasingly complex movement systems (Fentress and Mcleaod, 1986).

Focus on: the cephalocaudal principle of motor development

If you have ever observed a young infant of just a few months old, you might have noticed that leg-kicking is a common feature of motor behaviour. These kicking movements present a problem for the cephalocaudal principle of motor development and so are usually dismissed as involuntary movements produced by the central nervous system (Lamb and Yang, 2000). However, new evidence suggests that this belief is mistaken; infants, it seems, gain voluntary control of their legs far earlier than the cephalocaudal rule would predict (Galloway and Thelen, 2004).

Galloway and Thelen (2004) carried out two experiments with infants of two to three months of age and found that infants made contact with an object held within reach with their feet earlier than with their hands; contact was made using feet at 12 weeks and using hands at 16 weeks.

Task —— Read the paper described above (Galloway, JC and Thelen, E (2004) Feet first: object exploration in young infants. *Infant Behavior and Development*, 27: 107–12) and answer the following review questions.

– What methods did the study employ?

– What evidence is provided to support the hypothesis presented by Galloway and Thelen that purposive leg movements are seen in infants of only a few months of age?

– How strong is the evidence against the cephalocaudal principle of motor development? Should we reject this 'rule'? Might the proximodistal principle also be incorrect?

Comment

The study uses a well-controlled experimental design to test infant behaviour. However, the two experiments used only a small number of infants ($n = 6$ and 10 respectively), and we are given no information about the participants other than age, gender and ethnicity. Given what we know about the impact of parenting behaviours on infant motor development, how might this background information be important? Might these infants be atypical in their development? However, even if parenting behaviours were found to have influenced the early development of leg movement, this still seems to be good evidence against the cephalocaudal principle and in favour of the dynamic systems theory of motor development.

Perception, cognition and development of the object concept

As you have just learned, motor skills develop as a response to innate capacity and an infant's response to environmental experiences – a clear example of interaction between nature and nurture during development. Relevant experience is, however, not just related to movement – according to Thelen's dynamic systems theory, infant motor development is supported by perceptual experience and cognitive processes such as motivation as well. It is therefore important to understand exactly what infants perceive and understand about the world around them.

Sensation, perception and cognition

Sensation occurs when information interacts with our sensory receptors – our eyes, ears, tongue, nose and skin. Perception is the interpretation of this sensation and is how we make sense of (and ultimately act upon) our world. Perception involves cognitive processing: in order to perceive objects we need to be able to recognise them and understand about their properties. We therefore need to be able to develop mental representations of the objects we come into contact with. In Chapter 2, it was noted that the sensory abilities of the neonate are well developed in terms of touch, taste, smell and hearing, but less so in terms of vision. But what of the infant's perceptual abilities? We know from studies what an infant can see, hear, smell and so on, but how do they interpret this information? How do they *perceive* the world? Is the infant overwhelmed by all the information he or she receives from the senses and so *feels it all as one great blooming, buzzing confusion* (James, 1890)? Or is sensation organised so that infants have mental representation of objects similar to that of adults? Is this an innate capacity? If not, how and when does this skill develop? These questions are difficult to answer since infants do not have the language capacity to tell us what they see and understand of the world around them. Psychologists have therefore traditionally studied infant behaviours to try to find out what cognitive skills infants have; implications about infant perception and cognition are usually made from observing an infant's response to an object.

Understanding objects

As you saw in Chapter 1, Piaget believed that infants gradually develop an understanding of the world through their interactions with the environment. Much like modern dynamic systems theory, he believed that development results from an infant's active and motivated exploration of the world. Early cognitive development, according to Piaget, depends upon the infant using sensory and motor skills to explore and learn about the world. Indeed, he called the first two years of development the 'sensorimotor stage', which he further subdivided into six sub-stages (Table 3.1). According to Piaget, the most important achievement of this stage of development is

Table 3.1: Sub-stages of the sensorimotor stage of development

Substage (age)	Exploratory actions	Understanding of objects
Reflex schemas (0–6 weeks)	Involuntary responses to stimuli, e.g. sucking	Makes no attempt to locate objects that have disappeared
Primary circular reactions (6 weeks– 4 months)	Attempts to repeat chance pleasurable actions, on or near the body, e.g. bringing thumb to mouth	Makes no attempt to locate objects that have disappeared
Secondary circular reactions (4–8 months)	Attempts to repeat chance pleasurable actions in the environment, e.g. hitting a mobile, picking up a cup	Begins to search for objects that are partially hidden
Coordinated secondary circular reactions (8–12 months)	Can put 'secondary circular reactions' together to solve new problems, e.g. uncover, then grasp	Searches for completely hidden objects – but makes the A-not-B error
Tertiary circular reactions (12–18 months)	Will deliberately vary an action pattern, to discover the consequences, e.g. dropping ball from different heights	Can follow visible displacements of an object
Beginnings of symbolic representation (18–24 months)	Can solve problems using representation, e.g. opening and closing mouth	Can follow invisible displacements of an object

the understanding of objects and the realisation that objects continue to exist even when we cannot see them (**object permanence**).

On the basis of observations and experiments (e.g. Piaget and Inhelder, 1969), Piaget argued that, in the early months of life, infants behaved as if they thought that an object that they could no longer see had ceased to exist. In his experiments, Piaget showed an infant an attractive toy. Once he had gained their attention, the toy was placed on a flat surface within easy reach and covered with a soft cloth. The toy would either be completely covered or only partially covered. Piaget then watched the child's reactions. He found that infants would not search for a toy that was completely hidden until around eight or nine months of age, even though by six to seven months of age they were capable of the actions needed to retrieve the toy, their attention had been focused on it and they had watched it being hidden. According to Piaget, this showed that, for the younger infants, the object had effectively ceased to exist once it was covered over. He believed that infants only gradually developed this knowledge by chance during their exploration of the environment.

However, it is possible that, even though infants under nine months of age can both reach and grasp, it may be difficult for them to produce these actions together. The younger infants may therefore have understood that the toy existed, but could not retrieve it because they could not coordinate the actions necessary to remove the cloth. Experiments using visual gaze and **habitu-ation techniques** to overcome the motor coordination problem confirm this idea, demonstrating that even infants of two and a half months understand about object permanence (Baillargeon et al., 1985; Aguiar and Baillargeon, 2002).

A-not-B error

While the limitations of motor coordination may explain the lack of searching before the age of nine months, it does not explain another phenomenon noted by Piaget and known as the A-not-B error. In a variation of the hidden toy procedure described above, Piaget placed two cloths side by side in front of infants aged nine to 12 months. As before, their attention was attracted to an interesting toy, which was then hidden under one of the cloths (location A). Infants older than nine months typically found the toy. After a number of trials the toy was then hidden under the other cloth (location B). Piaget found that, despite watching the toy being hidden in the new location (B), infants under the age of 12 months would continue to look for the toy under the first cloth (location A). According to Piaget, this was evidence that infants do not understand that objects can exist independently of their own actions. The infant connects the rediscovery of the object in location A with his or her own actions in lifting the cloth. The infant is assumed to reason that 'if I wish to find the toy again I must do what I did before'.

This evidence is clearly incompatible with the findings of researchers such as Baillargeon (2002), which suggest that the understanding that objects continue to exist even when not visible develops in the first few months of life. Why would children aged eight to nine months, who understand that objects still exist when hidden, continue to search for an object in the wrong place when they have watched that object being hidden in a specific location? A number of explanations have been put forward for this intriguing behaviour, including the fragility of infant memory (Harris, 1989), habit perseveration (Diamond, 1985), and changes in neurological func-tioning (Munakata, 1998). However, none of these has been found to explain the A-not-B error adequately. According to Smith et al. (1999), this is because the search for a single causal factor is mistaken. Arguing from a dynamic systems perspective, they assert that this behaviour can only be explained by considering multiple causes. The ability to search for the toy under the correct cloth is the result of a number of skills coming together at once. These different skills, such as knowledge of the task, perceptual and motor abilities, unfold over time at different rates. According to Smith et al. (1999), it is the real-time integration of all these skills that will allow an infant to search in the right place, not the development of a single mental structure such as 'understanding of object permanence'. Indeed, it is the dismissal of the idea of mental structures (such as Piaget's schemas) that represents the fundamental difference between Piagetian and dynamic systems theories.

Focus on: multi-causal explanations of the A-not-B error

In revisiting the A-not-B error, Smith et al. (1999) take a new approach in attempting to explain what infants *do* in the A-not-B task rather than what they cannot do. Their explanation focuses on performance and ultimately raises profound questions about what it means to *know*. The idea of knowledge as an enduring mental structure that exists independently of behaviour dominates in the study of cognitive development. It is this idea of mental structures that gradually develop over time that underpins Piaget's theory of cognitive development. Achieving the A-not-B task has therefore always been taken to represent a qualitative change in infant thinking; the task can only be completed successfully once the infant has developed a new schema – the object concept. Smith et al. (1999) challenge this idea. They argue that, although successful completion of the A-not-B task does suggest a *qualitative* change in infant behaviour, this change in behaviour actually represents a number of *quantitative* changes in a complex dynamic system. The A-not-B error is explained in terms of general processes of goal-directed reaching; the erroneous reach back to A is seen as the result of a number of processes that enable the infant to look, discriminate locations, control their posture and plan a motor response. All these processes are brought together and self-organised by the task of reaching for a particular object in a particular context. In this perspective, behaviour and cognition are not separate and there are no causal mechanisms, such as an object concept, that generate a thought or behaviour. In this model what we commonly call knowledge and concepts are distributed across and embedded in behavioural processes.

Task — This model represents a major shift in thinking. How easy do you think it is to explain human cognition and behaviour with reference to function only? Should we no longer aim to explain psychological functioning by the study of mental structures? Or might it be useful to retain these ideas as a shorthand – a convenient way to describe common human thought and behaviour?

Contexts of development and early relationships

So far in this chapter you have learned about some of the important milestones achieved in infancy in terms of both behavioural and cognitive development. It should also be starting to become clear that it is difficult to separate different aspects of development and that development in all spheres is dependent on environment and experience as well as human genetic potential. Indeed, the environment in which an infant is raised is important not just in terms of the physical setting, but also in terms of the social environment.

Most early development typically takes place in a clearly defined social context – the family. It is in this context that early relationships have traditionally been studied, with most emphasis placed on the parent–child dyad and, in particular, the mother–child relationship. One of the most dominant and enduring theories of parent–child relationships was put forward by Bowlby (1969) in his theory of attachment.

Attachment theory

Bowlby was influenced by ethological theory, which proposed that attachment was an evolutionary mechanism designed to ensure the survival of the vulnerable and dependent infant. He argued that infants and their primary carers are biologically predisposed to form attachments. Infants are born with the ability to elicit attachment behaviour from carers, and carers (usually but not always the mothers) are biologically programmed to respond. Early infant behaviours (including reflexes such as clinging and crying) and later **proximity seeking behaviours** are therefore designed to keep the carer nearby and attentive to the child's needs. In this way, the infant's chances of physical survival are maximised. Although biologically based, attachments are not automatic and **maternal responsiveness** is suggested to be the key to the development of secure attachments. Specific attachments develop gradually as carers become more proficient in interpreting and responding to infant signals and the infant begins to recognise different individuals and their behaviours. Once these specific attachments have developed, infants begin to demonstrate other attachment behaviours such as **fear of strangers** and **separation anxiety**. The distress provoked by strangers and separation from the primary carer is seen at around six months of age, and has often been taken as a sign that a secure attachment has been established.

According to Bowlby, the survival value of attachment is not just physical. A psychoanalyst by training, he believed that attachment provided *lasting psychological connectedness between human beings* (Bowlby, 1969, p194). He also believed that the earliest bonds formed by children with their carers have an impact that continues throughout life, through the development of an **internal working model (IWM)**. The IWM is a central premise of attachment theory and is essentially a mental model of the self, the carer and the relationships between these two (Bowlby, 1969). This internalised set of expectations about how relationships work is thought to influence the child's responses to others, even in adulthood (Bretherton and Mulholland, 2009). Therefore, a child whose IWM is based on maladaptive relationships is likely to repeat this pattern of behaviours throughout life. It is important to note, however, that these relationship templates are not developed solely on the basis of interactions with one carer. Bowlby argued that contact with a greater variety of people with whom infants can form attachments could lead to a more fully developed IWM, which would help the child form relationships with a wide range of people later on in life. He also did not see the IWM as permanently and unalterably fixed during infancy, arguing that it can be modified as the infant develops new types of relationship.

Individual differences in attachment

As with all aspects of psychological development, individual variation has been noted in the development of attachments. The standard method for assessing attachment type in infancy is the **Strange Situation** developed by Ainsworth and Bell (1970). This 20-minute procedure has eight episodes, designed to expose infants to increasing amounts of stress. Carers (typically mothers) and their one-year-old infants are observed in a playroom through a two-way mirror. The child's attachment behaviours around their parents when in an unfamiliar environment are recorded. Observers are particularly interested in four infant behaviours: separation anxiety, willingness to explore, stranger anxiety and response to the mother following separation (reunion behaviour). The infants experience the following situations.

1. The mother and infant enter the room, which looks like a typical GP waiting room with chairs, magazines and some toys.

2. The mother and infant are left alone. The mother sits quietly on a chair, responding if the infant seeks attention. The infant usually plays with available toys.

3. A stranger enters the room, talks to the mother, then gradually approaches the infant with a toy.

4. The mother leaves the stranger alone in the room with the infant. The stranger tries to engage the infant with toys. If the infant becomes distressed the scenario ends here.

5. The mother returns and waits to see how the infant greets her. The stranger leaves quietly and the mother waits until the infant settles, and then she leaves again.

6. The infant is left in the room alone. If the infant becomes distressed the scenario ends here.

7. The stranger returns and again tries to engage the infant with toys.

8. The mother returns, the stranger leaves and the reunion behaviour is noted.

According to attachment theory, infants who have formed a good attachment to their mothers should be able to use them as a **secure base** from which to explore the novel environment. The stranger's entrance should inhibit the infant's exploration and cause them to move a little closer to their mother. When the mother leaves the room, the infant is expected to try to bring her back by crying or searching behaviours. A reduction in exploration of the room and toys is also expected. Following the parent's return, infants should seek to re-engage in interaction. If distressed, they may also want to be cuddled and comforted. The same responses should be seen following the second separation and reunion. Based on their observations, Ainsworth and Bell (1970) found that 66 per cent of infants behaved in this way and so classified them as securely attached.

The remaining infants did not use their mother as a secure base from which to explore, and were classified as insecurely attached. These children reacted in two quite distinct ways.

- **Insecure-avoidant** children showed little concern at their mothers' absence. Instead of greeting their mothers on reunion, they actively avoided interaction and ignored their parents' bids for interaction. These infants comprised 22 per cent of the sample.

- **Insecure-resistant** children were distressed by their mothers' absence, and behaved ambivalently on reunion, both seeking contact and interaction and angrily rejecting it when it was offered. These infants accounted for 12 per cent of the sample.

Later research (Main and Solomon, 1986) added a further category, **insecure-disorganised**, which consisted of children who showed contradictory behaviour patterns and seemed to be confused or apprehensive about approaching their parents. This behaviour has been found to be associated with children who were abused or who had severely depressed mothers. However, the causes of disorganised attachment are still not clear and research continues on this topic.

It has been suggested that, typically, 65 per cent of children can be classified as securely attached, 20 per cent as insecure-avoidant and 15 per cent as insecure-resistant (Main and Solomon, 1990). However, cross-cultural research has highlighted variations in attachment classifications, even in Western cultures (van Ijzendoorn and Kroonenberg, 1988). As demonstrated in Table 3.2, compared to other countries, more German infants are categorised as avoidant, while in Japan more infants are categorised as resistant. However, in each country the majority of attachments are rated secure and this has been demonstrated in other studies (e.g. Thompson, 2006). This is often taken as evidence that the meaning of attachment relationships is universal and cultural variations simply illustrate how different caregiving patterns lead to varying percentages of secure and insecure attachments.

However, another interpretation of this data is that what qualifies as secure or insecure attachment varies across cultures. In Japan, for example, mothers respond differently to their babies when compared to Western mothers (Rothbaum et al., 2000). Japanese mothers usually have much closer contact with their infants and strive to *anticipate* their infants' needs rather than *react* to their infants' cries as Western mothers tend to do. Social routines and independent exploration are given less emphasis than in the West. For Japanese mothers the aim is to promote a state of total

Table 3.2: Cross-cultural patterns of attachment (based on data provided in van Ijzendoorn and Kroonenberg, 1988)

Country	Secure (%)	Insecure-avoidant (%)	Insecure-resistant (%)
USA	65	21	14
Germany	57	35	8
Japan	68	26	27
UK	75	22	3

dependence on the mother and assumption of mother love and indulgence, which is known as *amae* (ah-MY-ay). In Japan this state of total dependence and resistance to separation from the mother is considered healthy secure attachment. This is important, because it sets the stage for the development of culturally valued community orientation in which individuals are interdependent and accommodating to others' needs; cooperation and working towards group goals are of prime importance in Japanese culture (Rothbaum et al., 2000). This suggests that, while attachment is a universal feature of human relationships, the meaning of attachment and what constitutes a healthy relationship is not. The Strange Situation has been criticised for being **ethnocentric** in its approach and assumptions, as it does not take into account the diversity of socialising contexts that exist in the world. Cultural values influence the nature of attachment (Cole and Tan, 2007).

In addition to cultural expectations about infant independence, who provides the care will also influence attachment patterns; in Nigeria, for example, Hausa infants are traditionally cared for by the grandmother and siblings as well as the mother and tend to develop attachments to a large number of carers (Harkness and Super, 1995). In Western cultures, increasing numbers of children spend time being looked after by someone other than the mother – either with relatives or in day care (Hochschild and Machong, 1989). Might this influence their response to maternal separation? What does this then suggest about all those children classified as insecurely attached? Perhaps, rather than trying to aim for a global way of categorising and classifying children's behaviour, more consideration needs to be given to the context in which children's development takes place and to the impact of this **developmental niche** on early relationships.

Early relationships and language development

In addition to providing a basis for social and emotional development, early relationships also have a role to play in the development of cognitive functioning and, in particular, the acquisition of language. There are particular features of early relationships that have been noted to be important precursors to language development. The first of these is something known as **meshing**. This describes the smoothly integrated interactions that are seen when two people get on well together, with each person's contribution to the interaction fitting with that of the other. This feature is particularly seen during conversations where one partner waits until the other has finished speaking before giving their input. In the meantime, their conversational partner takes their turn in the listening role, waiting for their turn to speak to come round again, and so on. In the 1970s, observations of mother–child interactions during infant feeding (breast or bottle) demonstrated that both the baby's and the mother's behaviour are closely meshed (Kaye and Brazelton, 1971). Human infants feed with a 'burst–pause' rhythm, in which they suck for a while, and then pause for a few seconds before starting to suck again. It was found that mothers usually synchronise their own behaviour to this rhythm from the very first feed: they tended to speak to their baby during a pause rather than while the baby was feeding. They also showed a tendency to gently shake, or 'jiggle', their baby during a pause. Mothers typically say that jiggling 'wakes up' their baby and helps to keep them sucking. However, the evidence suggests that jiggling actually lengthens the pause and inhibits sucking behaviours, which only recommence once the jiggling stops (Kaye and Brazelton, 1971). Once the mother stops jiggling, the baby is more likely to start a new burst of sucking. The mother's response is both predictable and contingent on the child's behaviour and, as such, is believed to provide the child's first experiences of relatedness. This experience provides an opportunity for the infant to begin to form not only a representation of the other, but also a representation of how their own behaviour has meaning and is responded to by the other. As you learned in the previous section, this is important for the development of the IWM. In addition, this synchronised turn-taking behaviour produces a very 'conversation-like' interaction between the two during feeding and is often referred to as a **pseudo-dialogue**. Similar turn-taking behaviour has also been observed in other parent–child interactions, such as Peek-a-boo and other face-to-face play (Kaye and Fogel, 1980) and has been suggested to have an important role in the development of language (Bruner, 1985). Initially controlled by the adult, these turn-taking episodes are progressively driven by the infant and their own active, appropriately timed inputs. In this way pseudo-dialogue gradually metamorphoses into **proto-dialogue**, still without the meaningful language content that will come later, but with a clearly defined turn-taking framework.

Another feature of early interactions is the use of a distinctive speech pattern characterised by a lot of repetition, simplified short utterances, raised pitch and exaggerated expression (see Table 3.3). This form of speech has often been referred to as *motherese* (Kuhl, 2000), as it was observed to be characteristic of the type of speech used by mothers when talking to their children. However, during the 1970s it was observed that this speech pattern is used not only by mothers, but also by women who have not had children (Snow, 1972), fathers (Berko Gleason, 1973) and even four-year-old children (Shatz and Gelman, 1973). Thus a more accurate term for this distinctive form of speech is 'child-directed speech' (Matychuk, 2005).

This type of speech is also very widespread and has been identified in a range of cultures, including the Kung Bushmen of the Kalahari, forest dwellers in the Cameroons, the Yanomami of the Amazon Basin and the Eipo of New Guinea (Fernald, 1985). However, it is not a universal feature of language and, in cultures where it is not used, language development follows the same progress although more slowly (Lieven, 1994). This suggests that such speech is useful but not essential for language

Table 3.3: *Features of child-directed speech*

Phonological characteristics	Semantic characteristics
Higher pitch	Limited range of vocabulary
Exaggerated and more varied intonation	'Baby talk' words
Lengthened vowels	More words with concrete referents
Clear enunciation	

development. Child-directed speech is thought to make language learning easier because of the way it simplifies language (Thiessen et al., 2005). Child-directed speech is also more effective than standard speech in getting an infant's attention and studies have shown that infants prefer to listen to this type of speech (Singh et al., 2002). Some researchers (e.g. Bombar and Littig, 1996) also believe that this type of talk is an important part of the emotional bonding process.

Communication is, of course, a two-way process and infants use vocalisations to communicate to their carers long before they are able to produce recognisable speech. Crying, babbling and cooing are all recognised as important precursors to speech (see Table 3.4). Gestures such as pointing, waving and nodding are also seen in the prelinguistic child and, as well as being used for communicating, may aid the development of language (Harris et al., 1995a). Pointing is especially relevant here: it is believed to be the first form of intentional communication used by infants (Colonnesi et al., 2010) and is important as a **joint attention** behaviour.

Joint attention and sharing interactions are key features of early relationships and, according to Bruner (1985), these play a key role in the development of language. To begin with, such interactions might only involve the carer and child, for example playing a game of Peek-a-boo. Simple games such as this mimic the give-and-take features of conversation and so teach the infant about turn-taking and how to take an active part in interactions. Gradually, other objects are introduced into these sharing interactions and the mother creates what Bruner (1985) calls **joint-action formats**. In joint-action formats the mother creates simple, structured activities with objects such as toys so as to teach her infant what the objects are for and how to use them – for example, building blocks into a tower, or using a spoon for feeding. These shared sequences are also talked about by the mother, which encourages the infant to acquire language (Bruner, 1975, 1985, 1993). The joint-action formats provide a mapping activity during which the child learns to link words and phrases with the correct objects and events. Pointing has an important role to play in ensuring joint attention during joint-action formats – for example, when reading picture books with their carers, infants show joint attention to objects shown in the book through pointing, which is usually accompanied by labelling of the object. Furthermore, the adult response to pointing by an infant is usually to label the object pointed at (Hannan, 1992). Research has also shown that blind children are able to label significantly fewer objects than sighted infants

Table 3.4: Developmental sequence of prelinguistic communication skills

Age	Method of communication
Birth	Crying
1–2 months	Cooing begins
6 months	Babbling begins
8–12 months	Use of gestures begins

(Norgate, 1997), which lends further support to the importance of pointing for acquiring object names.

Sequences in joint-action formats are repeated over and over, which reinforces the learning process. Bruner argues that, in this way, the mother (or other carer) provides a social context in which the meaning of language can be learned. This idea that the social context supports language acquisition is supported by evidence that the first words to be understood by an infant are typically the child's own name, the names of other family members and the names of familiar objects such as clock, drink and teddy (Harris et al., 1995a).

Research suggests that most infants begin to understand their first words when they are around eight months old and the total number of words understood grows slowly up to about 12 months of age, when there is a sudden increase in vocabulary (Fenson et al., 1994). Harris et al. (1995b) carried out a longitudinal study in which they found that the age at which infants first showed signs of understanding the names of objects was ten months. This new development in comprehension was highly correlated with the development of pointing – further evidence in support of a role for pointing in language acquisition.

Language production develops after comprehension. Early talkers may produce their first word at around nine or ten months, but many children do not produce their first word until well into their second year. As with comprehension, first words are limited in number and **overextension** and **underextension** are both commonly seen in the use of first words (Woodward and Markman, 1998). Word production increases gradually until around the end of the second year, when there is a vocabulary spurt (Bloom et al., 1985). At around the same time, a qualitative change in language use can be seen as infants begin to use two-word phrases. You will learn more about these changes in language development in the next chapter.

Critical thinking activity

Transactional models of development

Critical thinking focus: reflection (on the application of psychological models to developmental outcomes)

Key question: How do **transactional models** of development explain atypical development?

Traditional attachment theory suggests that the carer's behaviour, in particular their responsiveness to the child's needs, is an important factor in the development of a good relationship. However, as you have seen in this chapter, this is not the only factor involved in relationship development. The socio-cultural context of development, including expectations and beliefs about behaviour, is also relevant. In addition, it is important to remember that relationships by definition involve more than one person and it is essential to ask what influence the child brings to the developing relationship. Sameroff (1991) describes a *transactional model* of development in which the mutual effects that children and adults have on modifying each other's behaviour is emphasised. In this model the dynamic interactions between child and social environment are seen to be at the heart of developmental progression. Furthermore, the response of each individual to the other at a given time point fundamentally changes each individual's future responses. In this way, patterns of interaction develop. Sameroff (1991) provides the following example:

> *A complicated childbirth may have made an otherwise calm mother somewhat anxious. The mother's anxiety during the first months of the child's life may have caused her to be uncertain and inappropriate in her interactions with the child. In response to such inconsistency the infant may have developed some irregularities in feeding and sleeping patterns that give the appearance of a difficult temperament. This difficult temperament decreases the pleasure that the mother obtains from the child and so she tends to spend less time with the child. If there are no adults interacting with the child, and especially speaking to the child, the child may not meet the norms for language development and score poorly on pre-school language tests. In this case the outcome was not determined by the complicated birth nor by the mother's consequent emotional response. If one needed to pick a cause it would be the mother's avoidance of the child, yet one can see that such a view would be a gross oversimplification of a complex developmental sequence.*

(Sameroff, 1991, p174)

Read the following case studies and, drawing on the information presented above, reflect on how the different experiences of the two children's carers may impact on how they respond to their children and how this in turn may have further influenced their children's development.

Case study 1: Anna, aged two years, lives in a three-bedroom semi-detached house with her two parents and her older sister, Laura, who is four years of age. When Anna was born she suffered from severe anoxia as a result of a difficult birth. However, she seemed to show no lasting physical effects and was discharged home with a clean bill of health. Although initially worried, her parents were reassured by the positive attitude of the midwife and hospital consultant. Anna's mum felt that her second-born child initially fussed more than her sister Laura had, but used the same calm, consistent approach that had worked with Laura and found that she was soon able to settle her. Early developmental checks were normal and the family soon forgot about the more alarming aspects of Anna's birth. At the age of two she is able to walk alone, kick and throw a ball. She understands spoken language and is a good communicator, able to use sentences of two to three words. At this stage her preferred activities are 'drawing' (undefined scribbles) and 'reading' (turning the pages in her favourite picture book). Her mother, a part-time florist, takes her to a mother and toddler group twice a week, where she socialises well with the other children. On the days when her mother is working, she is cared for either by her maternal grandmother or by her father, who works shifts in a local factory.

Case study 2: Maria is also two years of age. An only child, she lives in a two-bedroom terraced house with her mother, a single parent. Maria also suffered from severe anoxia at birth, which seemed to show no lasting physical effects. However, Maria seemed to be a difficult, fretful child who was hard to settle. As a small baby she cried frequently, which her mother found very distressing. Maria's mother works full-time to support herself and her child and feels constantly tired. The emotional and physical stress experienced by Maria's mother have made it harder and harder for her to enjoy interacting with Maria – even caring for her physical needs always seems an uphill struggle. When her mother is at work, Maria is cared for by her aunt – a caring but busy mum herself who has three children of her own aged ten months, three years and five years. Maria therefore experiences very little social interaction with adults either at home or with her aunt. Early developmental checks suggested some delayed development and this seems to have continued. At the age of two Maria is not yet walking and her coordination and manual dexterity are poor. The health visitor who did Maria's two-year health check noted that Maria only has a vocabulary of around 20 words, rather than the 50 that would be expected by this stage.

Although the above case studies are hypothetical, they reflect the reality of development following anoxia. For many years it was believed that anoxia at birth caused problems with intellectual development. However, this belief was based on retrospective studies of children with learning difficulties. Prospective studies of children with anoxia found that, in fact, most children who suffer anoxia develop normally. According to Sameroff and Chandler (1975), in most cases, only those anoxic newborns who lived in socio-economically disadvantaged homes, characterised by neglect and a dearth of learning opportunities, tended to perform below average on IQ tests in childhood. The social environment, it seems, is more important than the initial birthing problem.

Critical thinking review

This activity helps develop your ability to apply theoretical models to real-life accounts. This means you are learning to think about and evaluate the materials you read, making critical judgements about psychological theory and its application to the real world.

Other skills you may have used in this activity include reflection, recall of key principles and ideas, and communication (literacy) skills if you write up the activity.

Skill builder activity

Measuring attachment

Transferable skill focus: understanding and using (quantitative) data

Key question: *Use the information provided in Table 3.5 to decide how valid and reliable Ainsworth's Strange Situation is when used in different cultures.*

The data in Table 3.5 show different patterns of attachment types in a number of cultures. What can you say from this table about different patterns of attachment in these different cultures? Thinking back to the earlier discussion of the Strange Situation, what does this data suggest about the reliability of the Strange Situation

Table 3.5: *Cross-cultural patterns of attachment (based on data provided in van Ijzendoorn and Kroonenberg, 1990)*

Country	Secure (%)	Insecure-avoidant (%)	Insecure-resistant (%)
USA	65	21	14
USA	67	21	12
USA	71	17	12
Germany	77	18	5
Germany	42	54	5
Sweden	75	21	4
Japan	70	0	30
Israel – Kibbutz	69	14	17
Israel –Daycare	86	4	11
Netherlands	66	34	0
Netherlands	75	20	5

when used cross-culturally? Is it possible to say anything about the validity of this test on the basis of these figures? What other information would be useful when interpreting these figures?

To find out more about this data set and the use of the Strange Situation cross-culturally, read the paper by van IJzendorn and Kroonenberg (1990), which is freely available from the University of Leiden at https://openaccess.leidenuniv.nl/bit stream/1887/1435/1/168_101.pdf.

Skill builder review

The task requires you to extract data from within the table and reorganise them. You need to reflect on the information learned earlier in the chapter and evaluate the data and their meaning. To do this task fully, you need to think about other information that would help you to interpret these figures. If you follow up on the reading, you will also be learning independently and developing your skills of analysis and evaluation in relation to a piece of text.

Assignments

1. Critically evaluate the dynamic systems theory of human motor development.

2. Discuss the importance of early relationships for later psychological development.

3. To what extent does the evidence support the suggestion that attachment is a universal feature of human development?

Summary: what you have learned

Now you have finished studying this chapter you should:

- be able to describe the main sequence of motor skill development and understand the importance of this physical maturation for psychological development;

- recognise the importance of innate reflexes for this stage of development;

- be able to evaluate critically how understanding of the object concept progresses during this period and which developing cognitive processes this might reflect;

- understand the main features of attachment theory and be able to evaluate critically how specific features of early relationships may influence later language development;

- understand critically the impact of the developmental niche on emerging skills.

- have developed your ability to apply theoretical models to real-life scenarios by reflecting on how the experiences of two sets of parents may have impacted on how they respond to their children.

- have developed your understanding and use of (quantitative) data by interpreting data from published papers using the Strange Situation to assess attachment.

Further reading

Aguiar, A and Baillargeon, R (2002). Developments in young infants' reasoning about occluded objects. *Cognitive Psychology*, 39: 116–57.

Discusses the development of the object concept.

Cole, PM and Tan, PZ (2007) Emotion socialisation from a cultural perspective, in Grusec, JE and Hastings, PD (eds) *Handbook of Socialisation*. New York: Guilford.

Useful article on the cross-cultural perspective of emotional social development.

Munakata, Y (1998) Infant perseveration and implications for object permanence theories: a PDP model of the AB task. *Developmental Science*, 1(2): 161–84.

Presents a parallel distributed processing (PDP) model for understanding object performance.

Ratner, N and Bruner, J (1978) Games, social exchange and the acquisition of language. *Journal of Child Language*, 5: 391–401. Available online at http://web.media.mit.edu/~jorkin/generals/papers/33_ratner_bruner.pdf.

Good background on the theoretical approach of Bruner and the idea of a social support system for language acquisition.

Rothbaum, F, Weisz, J, Pott, M, Miyake, K and Morelli, G (2000) Attachment and culture: security in the United States and Japan. *American Psychologist*, 55: 1093–1104.

Compares Japanese Western patterns of attachment.

Smith, LB, Thelen, E, Titzer, R and McLin, D (1999) Knowing in the context of acting: the task dynamics of the A-not-B error. *Psychological Review*, 106(2): 235–60. Available online at www.indiana.edu/~cogdev/labwork/SmithThelen1999.pdf.

Describes the dynamic systems approach to understanding the development of the object concept.

Chapter 4

Early childhood

Learning outcomes

By the end of this chapter you should:

- *be able to recognise the importance of motor skills for different areas of psychological development in the preschooler;*

- *be aware of the main features of language development in this phase and be able to evaluate critically theories of language acquisition;*

- *be able to evaluate the emergence of symbolic thinking;*

- *understand the importance of play for psychological development;*

- *be able to evaluate critically the evidence concerning the emergence of sense of self;*

- *have developed your ability to analyse and evaluate major themes and theories in developmental psychology;*

- *have developed your IT and independent learning skills.*

Introduction

By the age of two, children are no longer infants or babies. They are entering early childhood, a phase that lasts until the age of five. Throughout this period children grow taller and stronger, and their shape is changing: body fat is decreasing, legs are lengthening and, by the end of this phase, children no longer seem top heavy as they did during infancy. The increased mobility seen in early childhood promotes exploration of the environment and provides new learning experiences. In addition, emotional and social development is enhanced by growing interaction with peers, which is provided through a range of social learning environments, such as mother and toddler groups, play groups and nurseries, which many children of this age attend. Cognitive and language skills are also rapidly improving during this period of life. Language has been described as our most significant cultural tool. It provides an effective medium for children's learning, not only by allowing adults to communicate information to children, but also by enabling children to ask about the world they encounter every day.

Physical development

There are a number of important physical developments taking place during this period of life. Arguably the most important of these from a psychological point of view are the continuing maturation of the brain (Nelson et al., 2006) and the development of fine and gross motor skills. Together these two developments contribute vastly to the child's growing abilities to explore the world around them.

Maturation of the brain

The changes that occur in the brain between the ages of two and five years enable children to plan their actions, pay greater attention to tasks and increase their language skills. The brain does not grow as rapidly during this time period as it did in infancy, but there are still some dramatic anatomical changes that take place (Thompson et al., 2000). Researchers have shown that, during early childhood, children's brains show rapid growth in the prefrontal cortex in particular. The prefrontal cortex is an area of the frontal lobes that is known to be involved in two very important activities: planning and organising new actions, and maintaining attention to tasks (Blumenthal et al., 1999).

Other important changes include an increase in myelination of the cells in the brain. This myelination speeds up the rate at which information travels through the nervous system (Meier et al., 2004). Increases in myelination at this phase of development have been found to be greater in certain areas of the brain and this has been linked to developing skills. For example, myelination of the area of the brain that controls hand–eye coordination is not completed until around four years of age. Brain-imaging studies have shown that children with lower rates of myelination in this area of the brain at four years of age show poorer hand–eye coordination than their peers (Pujol et al., 2004). Hand–eye coordination is, of course, important for good motor skills.

Motor skill development

Between the ages of two and four years, quite impressive gains are seen in the development of gross and fine motor skills (see Table 4.1). By the age of two years, children are much more confident in their ability to get around the environment under their own steam (Edwards and Sarwark, 2005) and this confidence grows over the next few years so that, by the age of five, children are quite self-assured in their ability to run, jump and climb. As you will see later in this chapter, these gross motor skills are very important for play activities.

At the same time, fine motor skills in this age group are becoming more precise. While a three year old finds great pleasure in building a tower of bricks as tall as they can, the four or five year old will

Table 4.1: *Fine and gross motor development in the early years*

Age (years)	Gross motor skills	Fine motor skills
2	Walks well Runs Goes up and down stairs alone Kicks ball	Uses spoon and fork Turns pages of a book Imitates circular stroke Builds tower of six cubes
3	Runs well Marches Rides tricycle Stands on one foot briefly	Feeds self well Puts on shoes and socks Unbuttons and buttons Builds tower of ten cubes
4	Skips Performs standing broad jump Throws ball overhand Has a high motor drive	Draws a person Cuts with scissors (not well) Dresses self well Washes and dries face

be far more interested in the careful placement of the bricks as they build the tower. Indeed, it is likely that just building a tower will no longer be satisfying in itself – by this age children want to build more intricate structures such as bridges and buildings.

Children in this age group also enjoy practising their fine motor skills by activities such as drawing, writing and colouring. It is through these sorts of activities that parents and other carers begin to become aware of whether their child has a preference for using their right or left hand. This 'handedness' or 'hand preference', as it is called, seems to have a strong genetic basis. This idea is based on a range of research, including adoptive studies, which have shown that the handedness of an adopted child is related to the handedness of their biological parents, but not the handedness of their adoptive parents (e.g. Carter-Saltzman, 1980). In addition, prenatal ultrasound scans have shown that the unborn child shows a hand preference when sucking their thumb, with most foetuses showing a preference for their right hand (Hepper et al., 1990). This strongly suggests that handedness develops long before environmental influences, such as cultural and social expectations, can have an effect.

A right-hand preference dominates in all cultures at a rate of approximately nine to one. Handedness has traditionally been thought to have a strong link to brain organisation. Paul Pierre Broca first described language regions in the left hemisphere of right-handers in the nineteenth century and, from then on, it was accepted that the reverse, that is, right-hemisphere language dominance, should be true of left-handers (Knecht et al., 2000). However, in reality the left-hand side of the brain dominates in language processing for most people: around 95 per cent of right-handers process speech predominantly in the left hemisphere (Springer and Deutsch, 1985), as do more than 50 per cent of left-handers (Knecht et al., 2000). According to Knecht et al., left-handedness is *neither a precondition nor a necessary consequence of right-hemisphere language* dominance (Knecht et al., 2000, p2517). However, according to this study, left-handedness does increase the likelihood of right-hemisphere dominance for language processing.

So are there any differences in the abilities of right- and left-handed individuals? Left-handedness is more frequently seen in creative and artistic individuals, such as musicians and artists, than would be expected by chance (Schachter and Ransil, 1996). Famous left-handers in this category include the artists Michelangelo, Leonardo da Vinci and Pablo Picasso; Lewis Carroll, the author of *Alice in Wonderland*; the composer, Johann Sebastian Bach, and Oasis musician, Noel Gallagher. This might be explained by the finding that left-handers tend to have exceptional visual-spatial skills (Holtzen, 2000), meaning that they are better able to recognise and represent shape and form (Ghayas and Adil, 2007). Studies have shown a tendency for left-handers to score highly on intelligence tests (e.g. Bower, 1985; Ghayas and Adil, 2007); however, it has also been noted that left-handers are more likely to have reading problems than right-handers (Natsopuolos et al., 1998), which may be related to the way they process language.

Language development

As you learned in Chapter 2, it seems likely that prenatal learning establishes the basis for later language development. The neonate is born with the ability to recognise acoustic cues and can make distinctions between **phonemes** in any language (Kuhl et al., 2006). Between the ages of six and 12 months, they become better at perceiving the changes in sound in their native language, gradually losing the ability to detect differences that are not important. For example, the sounds *r* and *l* are important in spoken English, distinguishing words such as rake and lake. No such sound distinction exists in Japanese. Iverson et al. (2003) demonstrated that six-month-old infants from English-speaking homes could detect the change from *ra* to *la* and gradually improved in detecting this change over the next few months. In contrast, infants from Japanese-speaking homes were as good as the infants from English language homes at six months, but by 12 months had lost this ability. It is likely that this recognition of distinct sounds and speech patterns develops over the first year of life into the recognition and comprehension of words. As you learned in Chapter 3, understanding of language also begins around the same time that this change from universal linguist to language-specific listener occurs.

You also know that language production develops much later than language comprehension. One reason for the lag between comprehension and production of language is that changes in the anatomy of the vocal tract are necessary for the production of the complex range of movements that speech requires. At birth, the infant vocal tract is very different from that of an adult. It is designed to enable strong piston-like movements that are essential for sucking. The infant's **larynx** is positioned high up, so that the epiglottis nearly touches the soft palate at the back of the mouth. The tongue is large in relation to the size of the mouth, nearly filling the oral cavity, while the **pharynx** is very short compared to that of an adult, allowing little room for manipulation of the back part of the tongue. Once sucking becomes less of a priority at around four months of age, the vocal tract gradually takes on a more adult form. This is accompanied by neural maturation of the related motor areas in the brain. Together, these physical and neurological developments provide infants with control over the fine motor movements that are essential for producing the full range of speech sounds. Thus, both physical and neurological changes are needed for the speech production that begins in infancy and then progresses rapidly in early childhood.

From first words to telegraphic speech

Infants are able to express various meanings simply by altering the intonation of a single word. For example 'milk' could mean 'I want my milk', 'Where is the milk?' and even 'I've spilt my milk!' Interpretation of these single-word sentences, or **holophrases**, also relies on the context in which they are uttered, and in the absence of environmental cues (such as spilt milk) carers may not always get the meaning right first time. The two-word utterance, so-called **telegraphic speech**, which develops around the age of two years (at about the same time that the vocabulary spurt occurs), provides a more effective means of communication and is a universal feature of language development (Boysson-Bardies, 1999). Slobin (1972) identified a range of functions for these telegraphic utterances, as demonstrated in Table 4.2. However, the child still has to rely heavily on gesture, intonation and context for conveying meaning. Once the telegraphic speech stage has been reached, young children move rapidly from producing two-word utterances to create three-, four- and five-word combinations and so begin the transition from simple to complex sentences (Bloom, 1998). As well as getting longer, utterances also become more grammatical and the transition from early word combinations to full-blown grammar is rapid. By the time children reach their fourth birthday, they have mastered an impressive range of grammatical devices. Indeed, they seem to assimilate the structures of their native language without explicit instruction or

Table 4.2: *Functions of early telegraphic utterances*

Utterance	Function
See doggie	Identification
Book there	Location
More milk	Repetition
All gone	Non-existence
My candy	Possession
Big car	Attribution
Mama walk	Agent action
Where ball?	Question

correction (Brown and Hanlon, 1970), which has often been cited as evidence for language acquisition being driven by an innate process.

Theories of language acquisition

One of the predominant debates in theories of language development concerns the question 'Is language innate or learned?' According to the behaviourists, language is learned through a process of reinforcement and imitation. As the infant babbles, it happens to say 'dada' – this is interpreted by the mother as the baby trying to say 'Daddy'. Hugs, kisses and praise given to the child reinforce this behaviour, making it more likely that it will be repeated. Gradually, the infant will learn to associate a particular sound with an object or person. They have begun to learn how to label objects, and what was initially meaningless babbling has become meaningful language. In addition, children are said to learn through imitating the sounds made by others. For example, during play a mother may use the word 'Teddy' to her child, while giving them the teddy. Gradually, the child learns the association between the word and the object and tries to imitate the sounds made by the mother – resulting in reinforcement, repetition and so on.

Nativists such as Noam Chomsky argue that this is too simple an explanation for what is essentially a complex behaviour. In particular, learning theory cannot explain how children are able to construct novel sentences or the ease with which children learn the rules of grammar. There is evidence, for example, that parents do not reinforce or explicitly correct syntax or other grammatical errors (Brown, 1973). Chomsky (1979) argues that there must therefore be an innate mechanism for language learning. He calls this the *language acquisition device (LAD)* (see Chapter 1, page 3). Through the LAD the child is hard-wired to recognise the grammar of whatever language they are exposed to in infancy. This LAD matures over time, allowing the child to use increasingly complex language.

Contemporary theories of language development tend to be less extreme. Both sides have modified their position, so that nativists recognise that the environment has a role to play in language acquisition, and environmentalists accept that imitation and reinforcement are insufficient to explain the child's entry into the complex world of language. Bruner's theory provides a good example of an interactional framework for thinking about language development. He maintains that, while there *may* be an LAD as suggested by Chomsky, there must also be a *language acquisition support system (LASS)* (Bruner, 1983). In this support system he is referring to the features of early relationships described in Chapter 3.

In the last chapter you learned about the way in which adults constantly provide opportunities for children to acquire language. Parents and other carers (unknowingly) provide ritualised scenarios – the ritual of having a bath, eating a meal, getting dressed, or playing a game – in which the phases of interaction are rapidly recognised and predicted by the infant. It is within these social contexts that the child first becomes aware of the way in which language is used. The utterances of the carer are themselves ritualised and accompany the activity in predictable and comprehensible ways. Gradually, the child moves from a passive position to an active one, taking over the movements of the caretaker and, eventually, the language as well.

Bruner cites the example of a well-known childhood game, Peek-a-boo, in which the mother, or other carer, disappears and then reappears. Through this ritual, which at first may be accompanied by simple noises, or 'Bye-bye . . . Hello', and later by lengthier commentaries, the child is both learning about separation and return, and being offered a context within which language, charged with emotive content, may be acquired. It is this reciprocal and affective nature of language that Bruner suggests Chomsky neglects to consider.

The importance of shared activities for language development is supported by current research (e.g. Liebal et al., 2009) and theorists from different schools now agree that social context plays an important role in language development. Dynamic systems theorists (e.g. Evans, 2006; Gershkoff-Stowe and Thelen, 2004) would agree with Bruner's proposition that features of the social environment are important for language development. They would also concur with the idea that development happens as a result of an interaction between this environment and the child's innate predispositions. However, they would disagree with the idea that there is an innate language-specific mechanism; according to this theory, language emerges from the same general processes as all other behaviours. In this way, language and cognitive development are linked rather than separate processes.

Tomasello (2006) describes a similar approach in his usage-based theory, which argues that the essence of language is its symbolic dimension, not its grammatical construction. Language is learned as a specific tool for conversation and communication. Concrete words are learned initially, with no grammatical rules at all. All the child has is a collection of useful concrete speech units, which form the basic building blocks of language. Gradually, the ability to construct longer and more complex utterances emerges. Initially, children do not possess the fully abstract categories and schemas of adult grammar. Children construct these abstractions only gradually and in piecemeal fashion. According to Tomasello, children construct their language using the following general cognitive processes:

- intention-reading (e.g. joint attention), by which they attempt to understand the communicative significance of an utterance;

- pattern-finding (categorisation, schema formation), by which they are able to create the more abstract dimensions of linguistic competence.

This implies that language development follows on from the development of our thinking processes.

Language and thought

This link between thought and language development deserves further consideration. This is another classic debate in psychology: does language merely reflect thought, or do we need to be able to think (e.g. categorise, understand concepts etc.) before language can develop? Piaget claimed that, although language and thought are closely related, language depends on thought for its development. Language is not possible until children are capable of symbolic thought; they must understand that one thing can stand for another before they can use words to represent objects, events and relationships.

Piaget based this claim on a range of evidence, including development in infancy, in which fundamental principles of thought (e.g. understanding concepts) are displayed well before language; and the simultaneous emergence of language and other processes, which are explored later in this chapter, such as **symbolic play**, suggesting that language is just one of a number of outcomes of fundamental changes in cognitive ability.

In contrast, Vygotsky (1986) saw thought as dependent on language. As you learned in Chapter 1, for Vygotsky language is one of our most important cultural tools and the medium through which most (if not all) learning takes place. **Mental operations** are believed to be embodied in the structure of language, and cognitive development results from the internalisation of language. According to Vygotsky, this happens in the following way. Initially thought and language develop as two separate systems. Before the age of about two years, children use words socially – that is, to communicate with others. Up to this point, the child's internal cognition is without language. At around two years of age, thought and language merge. The language that initially accompanied social interaction is internalised to give a language for thought. This internalised language can then guide the child's actions and thinking.

Vygotsky (1930/1978) identified self-talk as a critical part of the child internalising previously external social speech. In early childhood, especially between the ages of three and four, children often talk out loud to themselves. Over time this self-talk seems to disappear. Piaget (1923) called this self-talk **egocentric** speech and suggested that it reflects some of the limitations of young children's cognitive skills, which we discuss in the next section. In contrast, Vygotsky argued that all speech, including self-talk, is 'social' and therefore self-talk did not disappear – it simply becomes internalised. He argued that to believe that self-talk disappears would be like believing that children stop counting when they stop using their fingers to do so. Vygotsky alleged that, even when internalised, self-talk continues to guide a child's actions. This idea is given some support by the way in which the conscious use of self-talk intensifies when children are presented with tasks of increasing difficulty. Perhaps you can even think of examples of adults using self-talk as an aid for learning? It is as a result of this internalising of 'social language' that the social environment becomes embedded in children's mental reasoning. In this way, all our higher mental functions are thought to originate as actual interactions between human individuals (Vygotsky,

1930/1978). This theory therefore gives an important role to the social context for the development of both thinking and language.

Focus on: the relationship between language and thought

Task Read the following newspaper article, which discusses the relationship between thought and language, using spatial knowledge as an exemplar:

O'Connell, S (2002) It's the thought that counts: does language shape our thoughts, or is it the other way around? *The Guardian*, 16 May. Available online at www.guardian. co.uk/science/2002/may/16/languages.medicalscience.

Now answer the following questions.

– To what extent do you think the research cited provides good evidence in support of the idea that thought shapes language rather than the other way around?

– Can all of the findings presented be explained in terms of differences in social context?

– Which developmental theorists does this call to mind?

Comment

Social context is cited by a number of theorists as having a role in cognitive and language development, including Tomasello, Bruner and Vygotsky. In comparison, Piaget placed little emphasis on this issue. Indeed, it is an important criticism of his theory as the next section shows.

Cognitive development

As you have just seen, language acquisition is one of the major gains of early childhood development. At the same time, other cognitive processes, including memory, are also developing rapidly. Children are learning a lot about the world around them and their role in that world. Thinking at this age is also creative, free and fanciful, and imagination seems to run wild.

Theories of cognitive development

Piaget (1923) called his second stage of cognitive development 'preoperational' because children cannot yet perform *mental operations*, although the beginnings of logical reasoning can be seen, especially towards the end of this stage. As you saw with language development, during early childhood children are increasingly able to represent the world symbolically using words; this is also reflected in their use of other images and drawings. Piaget divided this period of early childhood into two sub-stages:

- symbolic functioning (two to four years);

- intuitive thinking (four to seven years).

In this chapter we are concerned primarily with the first of these sub-stages, during which the child develops the ability to represent mentally an object that is not present. This is perhaps most easily demonstrated by considering children's pretend play at this stage. Two- and three-year-old children often engage in what Piaget (1923) called *symbolic play*. In this form of play, children use one object to represent another that they do not have access to at the time, for example a lego block as a hair brush; a chair as a car; a finger as a toothbrush (Boyatzis and Watson, 1993). Having the ability to pretend that a particular object can be something else that is not present shows that they have a mental representation of that object. Gradually, this ability to use symbols becomes more sophisticated, so that by the age of four children no longer need to use an object to symbolise another object that is not present. An imaginary representation can be used; Boyatzis and Watson found that a three or four year old will use their finger as a toothbrush when the object is not present, while a five year old will pretend that he or she is holding a toothbrush.

Piaget (1923) believed that children's mental reasoning at this stage was limited by magical thinking and **animism**. Animism is the belief that objects have lifelike qualities and are therefore capable of having feelings, intentions and emotions. For example, a preoperational child may explain the rain by saying that the clouds are sad and are crying. According to Piaget, this limits children's understanding of how the world works and so reduces their ability to think logically. It also means that they find it difficult to tell the difference between reality and fantasy. Another limitation to logical thinking at this age is egocentrism, the inability to distinguish between your own perspective and someone else's. Piaget and Inhelder (1969) studied children's egocentrism using their 'three mountains task' (see Figure 4.1). In this task the child walks around the model of the mountains in order to familiarise themselves with what the mountains look like from different perspectives. Each of the three mountains has a specific identifying feature such as snow, a house or a church on top, meaning that each viewpoint would be quite different. The child is then seated at the table and a researcher places a doll in different locations around the table. At each location the child is asked to select the doll's view from a number of photos. Piaget found that preschool children are unable to choose the correct photo and cited this as evidence of egocentrism.

One important feature of Piaget's experiments, such as the three mountains task, is that they are reliable – if you were to do exactly what Piaget did, you would get the same results that he did. But as you learned in Chapter 1, that does not necessarily mean that his interpretation of these findings is valid. The important question is, do these results mean what Piaget suggests they do?

***Figure 4.1:** Piaget's three mountains task*

Woolley (1997) disagrees with the idea that children's thinking is more magical than that of adults. Adults have been found to be just as likely as children to engage in magical thinking, especially when they do not have the knowledge to explain phenomena. Adults invent speculation to fill gaps in their knowledge, much as children do. It is probably also worth remembering that many of the fantastical ideas children believe in – Father Christmas, the tooth fairy and the Easter bunny – are all actively encouraged by the adults around them. Why wouldn't children take at face value what they are told by the authority figures in their lives? After all, we expect them to accept much of what we say on trust. It is therefore the social context that determines whether or not adults or children engage in magical thinking.

There is also evidence that the social context has an impact on young children's egocentrism. In a classic experiment, Hughes (1975) repeated the three mountains task using a situation he thought would be more familiar (and therefore more socially relevant) to the child – a 'naughty boy' hiding from a policeman (see Figure 4.2).

In this task, children are shown a board with two barriers. Toy policemen are placed at the end of each barrier and the child is asked to place a model boy in the layout where the policemen can't see him. Hughes found that 90 per cent of children aged three to five could complete the task successfully, concluding that it was lack of understanding of the situation rather than egocentrism that caused the problems for Piaget's participants.

Another criticism of Piagetian theory is provided by information-processing theory. According to this model of cognitive development, preschoolers are limited by their processing skills rather than their logical reasoning. Between the ages of two and four, children are more likely to pay attention to salient characteristics of a task, to the detriment of more relevant ones. Such characteristics distract the child's attention from the task. Young children are also less systematic in their approach to a task. When asked to compare two complex pictures, they do not necessarily consider all the details before making a judgement (Vurpillot, 1968). Finally, preschoolers are

Figure 4.2: Hughes's test of egocentrism

impeded by the accuracy and capacity of their short-term memories. Increased myelination in areas that support memory and planning (e.g. the hippocampus and frontal cortex), which occurs during early childhood, is thought to explain why these areas of processing improve during this phase of development (Pujol et al., 2006). How might the limitations in these processing features explain children's responses in the three mountains task, do you think?

Play

Play also has an integral relationship with early social, cognitive and linguistic development. Much of the contemporary work on this subject, and on *symbolic play* in particular, has been based on the work of Piaget (1962), who maintained that play advances cognitive development. Through play children are able to practise their competencies and skills in a relaxed and pleasurable way. Vygotsky (1962) also saw a value in symbolic play for cognitive development, especially during the preschool years.

However, this is not the only benefit of play. Play also allows children to practise the developing motor skills that you learned about earlier in this chapter. Better control of their bodies allows children to run, skip, ride a tricycle, enjoy the slides and swings in the park, and to draw, colour and construct and make things. Although this play can be a solitary activity, it can also be a social activity, especially in the preschool years.

Types of play

A number of theorists have advanced elaborate classifications of play. Perhaps the most well known is that of Parten (1932). In this model, based on observations of play during the preschool years, Parten describes six different types of play (see Table 4.3).

For many years it was accepted that these categories were developmental – children progressed from solo to more social play. Recent research suggests that this is far from the case. All of these types of play are seen in the preschooler: five year olds spend more time in solitary or parallel play than in cooperative or associative play; and parallel play is as common at five years as it is at three years of age (Rubin et al., 1998). Furthermore, there is evidence that parallel play is not an immature form of play, but a sophisticated strategy for easing your way into an ongoing game; successful integration into cooperative play involves observation of others at play, followed by playing alongside before interacting with other players (Rubin et al., 1998).

It has also been argued that this model is limited by neglecting the cognitive aspects of play (Bergen, 1988). A more useful way of classifying play is to focus on the type of activity rather than the social aspects. Three main activity types emerge from this way of thinking, as shown in Table 4.4. The different levels of social interaction described by Parten can be seen in each of these activity types – solitary play may be functional (e.g. bouncing a ball) or constructive (e.g. building with lego). All these activities are popular throughout early childhood; however, the social play that is seen most often in the preschool years is socio-dramatic play. Indeed, many experts in play consider this period of development the peak time for make-believe or fantasy play (Fein 1986).

Table 4.3: *Classification of play behaviours (Parten, 1932)*

Type of play	Description of play behaviour
Unoccupied play	Child is relatively stationary and appears to be performing random movements with no apparent purpose. A relatively infrequent style of play.
Solitary play	Child is completely engrossed in playing and does not seem to notice other children.
Onlooker play	Child takes an interest in other children's play but does not join in. May ask questions or just talk to other children, but the main activity is simply to watch.
Parallel play	Child mimics other children's play but doesn't actively engage with them. For example, child may use the same toy.
Associative play	Children now more interested in each other than the toys they are using. This is the first category that involves strong social interaction between the children while they play.
Cooperative play	Some organisation enters children's play, for example the playing has some goal and children often adopt roles and act as a group.

Table 4.4: *Types of play activity*

Activity type	Description of play behaviour
Functional play	Physical activities such as bouncing a ball, or rough and tumble.
Constructive play	Building and making things, drawing or colouring.
Socio-dramatic play	Role-play or 'let's pretend'.

Socio-dramatic play and development

Socio-dramatic play is perhaps the most complex form, as it involves sharing a fantasy world with others. Children need to negotiate roles ('I want to be the mummy' – 'No, it's my turn'), agree on the development of the narrative ('My baby is poorly and needs to go to the doctor'), rules ('My power-ranger can jump over houses but yours can't) and symbolism ('The chair is my car'). It requires a sophisticated level of interaction and is thought to foster children's understanding of other minds (Dunn, 1988) because of the opportunities present for discussing thoughts, feelings and motivations, as you shall learn in the next chapter. It also helps children develop a sense of who they are as they practise different social roles and learn about how others see them.

Self-concept

Our sense of self is at the centre of our social, emotional and personal development. It is our self-identity – our understanding of who we are as an individual – and includes awareness of subjective experience and relationships with others. There are two aspects to sense of self, first defined by William James in 1890: the 'I', or the 'self-as-subject', also referred to as the *existential self* (Lewis, 1990) and the 'me', or the 'self-as-object', which is also referred to as the *categorical self* (Lewis, 1990).

The existential self is characterised by subjective experience and the sense of having a continuous identity across situations and through time. The first step on the road to self-understanding is the recognition that 'I' exist as an individual, and have agency (the power to act) and distinct and unique experiences. This awareness is thought to begin to develop in infancy, when babies begin to show understanding that they have agency; that is, they can cause things to happen and have the ability to control objects (Cooley, 1902). Infants learn that, when they let go of something, it drops; when they touch a toy, it moves; when they cry or smile, someone responds to them. In this way a sense of agency emerges at around four months of age and is gradually consolidated. By the time the infant moves into early childhood, this sense of agency is more clearly developed. A two-year-old child is more assertive, demanding and picky than a four-month-old baby. Indeed, the tantrums so often associated with the 'terrible twos' are suggested to reflect the frustration felt by toddlers when attempts to control the world around them fail. However, it is difficult to know to what extent this demonstrates true sense of self. Empirical investigations of the existential self in infants and toddlers are limited and studies tend to be speculative (Damon and Hart, 1988). This is not surprising, as studying self-awareness is difficult at any age; it is difficult to think about or articulate the different aspects of the 'I', and so even more difficult to study them empirically.

Empirical support for the emergence of the categorical self in late infancy/early childhood is provided by an investigation carried out by Lewis and Brooks-Gunn (1979). They used the **rouge test** with infants aged between nine months and two years. In this test, an experimenter surreptitiously places a dot of rouge on the nose of the child, who is then placed in front of a mirror and whose reactions are then monitored. Self-recognition is shown when the child touches their nose or attempts to wipe away the rouge. Lewis and Brooks-Gunn found that self-recognition emerges at around 18–24 months; at 18 months, 50 per cent of the group recognised the reflection in the mirror as their own, and by 20–24 months this increased to 65 per cent. However, it is important to remember that this is only behavioural evidence for awareness; it does not tell us anything about the subjective experience associated with this consciousness.

Children's understanding of themselves as active agents continues to develop in early childhood and can be seen in their attempts to cooperate with others in play. They use their knowledge of their own power to act on their world, when they offer to share a toy or join in pretend play with a friend. It is in these routine relationships and interactions that the child's understanding of him- or herself continues to emerge Dunn (1988). Once children have gained a certain level of awareness of the existential self, they begin to form increasing awareness of their categorical self as they begin to place themselves – and to be placed by others – in different categories (e.g. gender, nationality).

The categorical self is thought to emerge primarily through our interactions with others. Children build up their sense of identity from the reactions of others to them and from the view they believe these others have of them. Cooley (1902) called this the 'looking-glass self'; it is as if other people provide a 'social mirror', and children come to see themselves as they are reflected in others. According to **symbolic interactionist theory**, the self and the social world are inextricably bound together (Mead, 1934). The self is essentially a social structure that can arise only through social experiences. Mead believed that children begin to assume the perceptions that others have of them through their use of language, their games and their play. It is through doing this that they become capable of reflecting on themselves. The child cannot therefore develop a sense of self without the chance to interact with others, in order to begin to understand how these others view the world, including how they view the child. Evidence to support this view comes from cases of extreme social deprivation early in life, for example so-called **feral children** or children such as Genie, a girl who was kept locked in a room for several years by her abusive father (Rymer, 1993). These children have been shown to have poor communication skills and only a limited under-standing of self. Victor, the original and perhaps most famous feral child, showed few of the elements of the categorical self when he was found at the age of 12 years: he was unable to recognise himself in a mirror and had no sense of his own psychological characteristics or of social roles. It is generally believed that he was unable to develop the capacity to reflect on himself, because he did not have others around him whose behaviour he could observe, or who could give him feedback about his own behaviour and characteristics. An alternative explanation is that Victor was abandoned by his family because he was unresponsive socially – nobody knows anything about Victor's development before he was found, so this is as good an explanation as any. Caution is therefore necessary in drawing too many conclusions from this and similar cases.

Other evidence that identity development is linked to social experiences comes from observations of children's play during the preschool years. Clear awareness of different social groupings can be seen in the choices children make regarding their play partners; for example, by the age of three children show a preference for playing with peers of the same ethnicity (Urberg and Kaplan, 1989) and gender (Maccoby, 2002). This suggests that the preschooler has realised that there are different groups in society and has begun to identify with those groups. More is known about how this process happens in relation to the development of **gender identity**, although it seems likely that development follows a similar pattern for all group identities.

Development of gender identity

Once children realise that there are two genders and that they belong to one of them, they begin to show a clear motivation to behave in the ways that a member of that gender 'should'; they dress in the same way, and choose friends, activities and toys to suit this label. Bem (1989) suggests that having labelled themselves as either male or female, the child begins to develop a **gender schema**. This mental model of what males and females 'do' – the **gender role** – is based upon observations of other members of the same group. Children pay more attention to the behaviour of same-gender peers so as to remember more about how their own group behaves and imitate that behaviour (Ruble and Martin, 1998). Behaviours are often highly stereotyped and children's attitudes at this age are frequently sexist – even about their own gender and in the face of contradictory evidence. Children may even show hostility to the other gender (Ruble and Martin, 1998). On the face of it, such extreme behaviour does not seem to provide any developmental advantage. If childhood is preparation for adulthood, don't children need to learn to cooperate with each other, and not segregate themselves by gender? One explanation seems to be that it is only by committing wholeheartedly to a particular social group that the child can develop conceptual coherence – and this includes subscribing to an extreme version of gender-typed behaviour.

An alternative explanation is that the differences we see in male and female behaviour are biologically rather than socially determined. There is evidence to suggest that hormones play a role in behaviours such as aggression, play patterns and attitudes to gender roles (Reiner and Gearhart, 2004). It has also been found that children display preferences for gender-appropriate toys by six months, well before they have knowledge of gender roles (Alexander et al., 2008). This is believed to provide strong evidence for a biological basis to this preference. However, given that the evidence in favour of a role for the environment in the development of gender identity is so strong, it seems unlikely that such differences are based on biology alone. By six months of age, infants have already notched up a lot of experience in the world – perhaps their preferences for particular toys reflect these experiences and the choices made by the adults and others who make up their world. There is, for example, evidence that carers' responses to their children depend in part on whether their child is male or female (Maccoby, 2003), with fathers showing greater differential treatment than mothers (Leaper, 2002). Parents reward gender-appropriate choices and may even make early toy choices for their children that are linked to their child's sex. Social responses to a biological distinction, along with hormonally based differences in behaviour, thus set the scene for later cognitive and emotional development. Once again, biological, social and emotional features are working together to determine a child's development.

Critical thinking activity

Language development

Critical thinking focus: analysing and evaluating major themes and theories

Key question: How do children acquire language?

As you have learned in this chapter, one of the key questions in language development concerns the extent to which this development depends on innate mechanisms.

Read the following chapter by Steven Pinker, in which he describes language as a complex biological adaptation:

Pinker, S (2003) Language as an adaptation to the cognitive niche, in Christiansen, M and Kirby, S (eds) *Language Evolution: States of the art*. New York: Oxford University Press. Available online at http://pinker.wjh.harvard.edu/articles/papers/Language _Evolution.pdf.

While you are reading, you need to think critically about the explanations that Pinker puts forward to explain language development. This may mean reading the chapter several times. There are two things to focus on in particular.

– Do the explanations Pinker gives make sense? Are they credible?

– Can you apply any alternative perspectives and still provide a credible explanation?

For example, Pinker describes how, if children are thrown together without a pre-existing language that can be 'culturally transmitted' to them, they will develop one of their own. According to Pinker, the development of these Creole languages can only be explained by an innate mechanism, given the fact that these languages share many features (such as grammar) in common with established languages. He also gives examples from atypical development to support this viewpoint. Can you think of an alternative explanation for the development of Creole and spontaneous sign language? What would a dynamic systems explanation be for the development of grammatical spontaneous language?

You might also want to take your knowledge of this area further by reading the paper by Tomasello (2006), which is listed in the 'Further reading' for this chapter. Again, try to take a critical approach to Tomasello's paper.

Critical thinking review

This activity helps develop your ability to apply theoretical models to real-life accounts. This means you are learning to think about and evaluate the materials you read, making critical judgements about psychological theory and its application to the real world.

Other skills you may have used in this activity include reflection, recall of key principles and ideas, and communication (literacy) skills if you write up the activity.

Skill builder activity

The importance of play for development

Transferable skill focus: IT and independent learning

Key question: *Using a database such as PsycINFO or Academic Search Complete, carry out a search for papers that address the following issue: 'The impact of gender on type of play activity in preschoolers'.*

Basic steps in using PsycINFO through the EBSCO Host platform

The first stage in any database search is to establish the basic subject you are interested in. This is not always as easy as it sounds if there are a number of terms or different spellings (e.g. American spelling 'pediatric'; UK spelling 'paediatric') covering what is essentially the same topic. At the top of the page there are several links, including *Choose Databases, Search Options, Basic Search, Advanced Search, Visual Search, Search History.*

Basic Search allows you to search the PsycINFO database for specific relevant word(s) and phrases, but it is not a very sophisticated approach as the following example shows.

A good starting place when searching past literature relevant to 'The impact of gender on type of play activity in preschoolers' might be to examine previous studies of play. In the *Search* box provided, type 'play' and click on the *Search* button. You should get details of over 88,000 articles in which the word 'play' appears. Such a large number is far too many even for a dedicated researcher to read. Thus, a more refined search is necessary. There are two ways to refine a search on PsycINFO. The first is to use the *Advanced Search* command, which allows you to search specific fields. The second option is to search several words independently and then combine these via the *Search History* command. We are going to focus on the first option.

Advanced Search offers the opportunity to combine terms using *AND*, *OR* and *NOT* commands. To perform an advanced search, click on the *Advanced Search* tab and type a key word in each of the three boxes provided. Then click either the:

- **AND** button if you want references in which both terms appear;

- **OR** button if you want references in which either term appears; or

- **NOT** button if you want to exclude a particular term.

For example, search for records on play by entering 'play' in the *Search* box. This will find you the same number of records, as was found in the basic search. If you then wanted to exclude all references to play in animals you could type 'animal' in the second box and select the *NOT* button. If you now select *Search*, you should get details of around 80,000 articles in which the term 'play' but not the term 'animal' appears. This suggests that around 8,000 of the publications in the original search referred to animals and play.

So this has still not reduced the number of papers found to a manageable number. Carry out the search again adding the term 'gender' and selecting the *AND* button. Selecting *Search* now gives you 4,000 papers. Better, but still a lot to try to read! If you look down the left-hand side of the screen, you will see that you have selected papers published as far back as 1945. This is fine if you want to look at classic studies in psychology. However, more often than not you need to be searching for contemporary work. So this time you run the search, select *Publication date* and change the limits so that you only search for papers published between 2000 and 2010. This should reduce the number of papers by just over 1,000.

Now try the search one last time entering the terms 'play activity' *NOT* 'animal' *AND* 'gender' and limiting the publication date to 2000–2010. This should give you a manageable 35 articles. Scan through these, reading the abstracts to find relevant papers. One of the papers that you might like to read from your search should be the following:

Kinzie, MB and Joseph, DR (2008) Gender differences in game activity preferences of middle school children: implications for educational game design. *Educational Technology Research and Development*, 56: 643–63.

You might also want to think about other search terms you could have used (what about 'sex' instead of 'gender', for example?). Try the search again using different synonyms and varying your database and see if this gives you any new papers on the topic. Sometimes, researchers run searches on several different databases using a variety of search terms and only come up with one or two new papers on the different search engines. This might seem like a lot of effort for only a little return, but it is the only way to be sure your search is thorough.

Skill builder review

The task requires you to find relevant journal articles using a subject-specific database. Literature searching is an important skill. When you write essays and research reports, you will need to search the literature for relevant papers. PsycINFO is an enormous database, with many ways to search, so you need to know how to extract the information you need. This activity has shown you one way of finding the information you seek. Practise these skills using different databases and remember to use different search terms until you have found all the relevant information you can.

Assignments

1. What is the evidence to support the suggestion that language provides the concepts that we use to organise our thinking and that children therefore cannot think or have knowledge before they learn language?

2. Critically evaluate the role of play in human socio-emotional development.

3. To what extent does the evidence support the emergence of the *self-concept* in early childhood?

Summary: what you have learned

Now you have finished studying this chapter you should:

- be able to recognise the importance of motor skills for different areas of psychological development in the preschooler, including language and play;

- be aware of the main features of language development in this phase and be able critically to evaluate contrasting theories of language acquisition;

- be able to evaluate the emergence of symbolic thinking and its relationship to language and play;

- understand the importance of play for psychological development;

- be able to evaluate critically the evidence concerning the emergence of sense of self;

- have developed your ability to analyse and evaluate major themes and theories in developmental psychology;

- have developed your IT and independent learning skills.

Further reading

Alexander, G, Wilcox, T and Woods, R (2008) Sex differences in infants' visual interest in toys. *Archives of Sexual Behavior*, 38(3): 427–33.

Describes a study investigating infant's visual interest by preferences.

Liebal, K, Behne, T, Carpenter, M and Tomasello, M (2009) Infants use shared experience to interpret pointing gestures. *Developmental Science*, 12(2): 264–71. Available online at http://email.eva.mpg.de/~tomas/pdf/LiebalEtal_SharedExperience_2009.pdf.

Study investigating infant's understanding of pointing gestures.

Tomasello, M (2006) Acquiring linguistic constructions, in Kuhn, D and Siegler, R (eds) *Handbook of Child Psychology, Vol. 2: Cognition, perception, and language* (6th edn). New York: Wiley. Available online at wwwstaff.eva.mpg.de/~tomas/pdf/tomasello_HoCP2005.pdf.

Good overview of Tomasello's theory of language development.

Urberg, KA and Kaplan, MG (1989) An observational study of race-, age-, and sex-heterogeneous interaction in preschoolers. *Journal of Applied Developmental Psychology*, 10: 299–311.

An investigation into preschoolers' choices for playmates at school.

Chapter 5

Middle and late childhood

Learning outcomes

By the end of this chapter you should:

- *be able to evaluate the importance of peer relationships;*

- *be able to discuss critically the mastery of cognitive tasks that takes place in childhood, including early mathematical and scientific thinking;*

- *critically understand the development of reading and writing skills;*

- *understand the possible impact of atypical development on experiences such as schooling;*

- *have developed your ability to reflect on the importance of the socio-cultural context for development;*

- *have developed your problem solving and logical reasoning.*

Introduction

One of the most important changes that happen towards the end of early childhood is the start of formal compulsory schooling. In this chapter we consider children's development during the early school years – from four until 11 years of age. Although many children have already had some experience of social contexts and environments outside the home, starting school is still seen as an important milestone in Western society. Indeed, it opens up a very different set of social, emotional and cognitive experiences for children. While, for many children, these experiences will be negotiated with ease, for others, perhaps most notably those children whose developmental course is atypical, this journey may be much more difficult. Peer relationships become increasingly important during middle and later childhood. The nature and understanding of friendship also changes as children negotiate their place within their peer group. Transformations in cognitive and language skills are reflected in children's understanding of scientific and mathematical thinking, and in their manipulation of symbols as they learn to read and write.

Cognitive development in middle and late childhood

A remarkable transformation in children's cognitive skills can be seen between the ages of four and 11. According to Piaget (1923), this marks a qualitative shift as children make the change from preoperational to operational thinking. However, not everyone agrees with Piaget's assessment of what develops or how these changes occur.

Developing operational thinking

As you learned in the previous chapter, according to Piaget (1923), a key milestone for children in the early part of the preoperational stage (the symbolic functioning sub-stage) is the ability to develop mental representations of an object that is not present. In the later part of the preoperational stage (intuitive thinking), children also begin to use primitive reasoning. However, according to Piaget, children's reasoning is still flawed. The main limitations to thinking at this age are **centration** and a lack of understanding of **reversibility**. These limitations of thinking are best illustrated by **conservation** tasks (Inhelder and Piaget, 1964). Conservation tasks measure awareness that altering an object's appearance does not change its quantitative properties. Probably the most well known of these is the beaker test, in which conservation of liquid is tested (see Figure 5.1). In this task a child is shown two identical beakers each filled to the same level with liquid (Stage 1). They are then asked if these beakers contain the same amount of liquid – a question to which the majority of children aged between four and seven years will say yes. The liquid from one beaker is then poured into a third beaker that is taller and thinner than the first two (Stage 2). The child is then asked if the amount of liquid in the tall thin beaker is the same as in the original beaker that has *not* been altered (Stage 3). Children in the preoperational stage usually say no, and when asked why not, justify their answers by referring to the differing height of the liquid in the two beakers. Children older than seven or eight years who have reached the concrete operational stage usually say yes, the amounts are the same, and can justify their answer in terms of reversibility ('If I poured the liquid back into the first beaker it would still look the same).

Piaget (1923) also tested conservation of number, matter and length (see Figure 5.2), with similar outcomes. So why are young children not able to conserve? According to Piaget, children under the age of seven make two important errors when carrying out this task. First of all, they centre their attention on the most salient characteristic of the task. In the beaker task they focus on the height of the liquid to the exclusion of all other features. They fail to consider characteristics such as the different shapes of the two beakers. In addition, they cannot mentally reverse the action they have just observed – they are unable to make use of the logical reasoning that the liquid must still be the same because it has only been poured from one beaker to another and could easily be poured back. When asked to judge the beakers the second time, the child is unable to make a causal link between the current and original situation. They therefore fall back on making a judgement based on how things look now.

Figure 5.1: *The beaker test (conservation of liquid)*

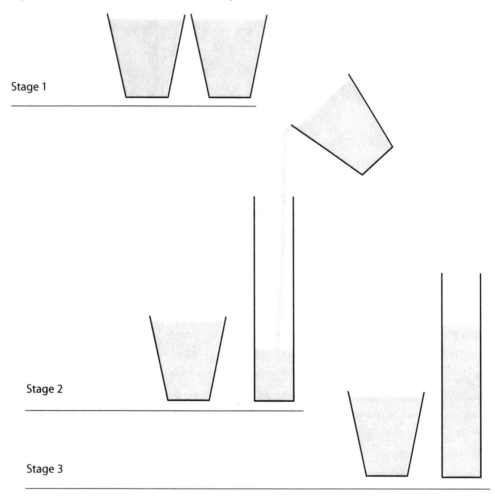

Stage 1

Stage 2

Stage 3

This limited way of thinking can also be seen in Piaget's class inclusion task (Inhelder and Piaget, 1964), which demonstrates a lack of understanding of hierarchical classification. In this task children are shown a picture of a set of objects such as horses and cows and are asked 'Are there more cows or more animals?' Despite knowing that cows are a type of animal and being able to count the number of cows and animals correctly, children aged six or seven will say that there are more cows. According to Piaget, this is because preoperational children can only make one grouping at a time. Once they have put the cows in the class 'cows', they cannot mentally undo that to include the cows in the larger 'animal' class and so are unable to understand the relationship between cows and animals. Without reversible mental operations, the classes 'cow' and 'animal' cannot exist simultaneously in the child's mind.

Children develop reversible mental operations and learn to decentre around the age of seven to eight years. This means that they are able to conserve and answer the class inclusion questions

Figure 5.2: *Conservation tasks in the preoperational stage*

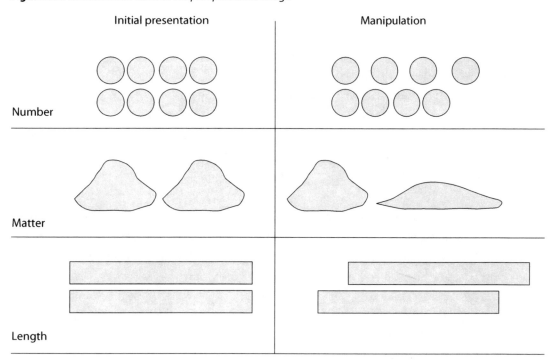

correctly. More importantly, they can give a logical reason for their answers. However, reasoning is still limited between seven and 11 years of age. Piaget (1923) calls this the concrete operational stage because, although children can reason logically and understand about causal relationships, they can only do so if that reasoning is tied to specific concrete examples. They cannot yet make use of hypothetical or abstract reasoning.

Not everyone agrees with Piaget's estimate of when children's ability to conserve and understand hierarchical classifications emerges. As you learned in Chapter 4, Piaget has been criticised for using tasks that are unfamiliar to the child (e.g. Hughes, 1975). Donaldson (1978) also argued that these conservation and class inclusion tasks did not make human sense to the child. Why pour liquid from one beaker to another if it makes no difference? Why ask if there are more cows than animals if we know that cows are animals? Donaldson and others since have shown that, by changing the tasks so that they make sense to the child, even four year olds are able to succeed in conservation and class inclusion tasks. For example, if the class inclusion task is changed so that it only uses cows, some standing, some lying down, and the question asked is 'Are there more cows or more sleeping cows?' (a more sensible question), then three year olds can answer correctly. The logical challenge is the same, but the task makes more sense (Donaldson, 1978).

Donaldson (1978) also criticised the procedural aspect of these tasks. In the classic Piagetian conservation tasks, the same question is usually asked twice in order to test the child's reasoning

– once before any changes are made and then again after the transformation. However, if the children are only asked the question once, after the transformation, more of the younger group get the answer right. According to Donaldson, this is because children learn to make sense of adults' questions in teaching and testing situations. The child is not only trying to work out what the meaning of the task is, but also trying to work out the demands of the social relations in which the task is embedded. A key part of this process is trying to guess what answer the adult expects, and what response will please them most (Donaldson, 1978). Children learn early on that adults do not usually ask a question twice if the correct answer has already been given. In trying to make sense of the social situation and the adult's intention, the child uses the rule of thumb that, when a teacher asks a question twice, it can be taken to mean that they want a different response. Since the only thing that has changed since the question was first asked is something to do with the materials, a plausible guess is that the tester wants the child to say that the amounts are different. According to Donaldson, for the child the implicit social rules of the situation are as much of a problem to be solved as the explicit problem that is being posed. Thus, the social context impacts upon children's ability to solve problems. Wheldall and Poborca (1980) also agreed that the wording of the question prevents the children giving the correct answer to conservation tasks. They therefore used a non-verbal version of the beaker task and found that twice as many children could conserve using this task than in the original approach.

Information-processing models provide a different challenge to Piaget's theory. Donaldson and others criticised Piaget for the tasks he used, suggesting that they did not allow younger children to demonstrate their logical reasoning. However, the assumption was still that human reasoning depends upon having mental structures for logical thinking (what Piaget calls 'operations') – what they did not agree on was the age at which these structures developed. Information-processing models consider this problem from a different angle. They suggest that children cannot do these tasks because of the demands on processes such as memory and attention, which are still developing at this age. In response, supporters of Piaget's theory (**neo-Piagetians**) have taken some of these ideas from information processing and integrated them with Piaget's original theory. For example, it is argued that development through the stages (and changes in logical structures) is made possible by increases in working memory capacity and processing efficiency (Demetriou et al., 2002).

It has also been proposed that younger children's thinking is hindered by a lack of general knowledge. According to Johnson-Laird (1993), problem solving is not based upon existing mental structures of logical thought, but depends instead on factual knowledge and our understanding of the world around us. We construct mental models – mental images of the problems to be solved – that are based on our factual understanding of the world. The difficulty for children is that they have less knowledge and information about the world – the problem is therefore a quantitative, not a qualitative, one. This is an idea that we shall explore in more detail in the next chapter.

The zone of proximal development

Like Piaget, Vygotsky (1930/1998) believed that children develop qualitatively different ways of thinking about the world. However, he had a very different idea about how this happens. As you learned in Chapter 4 (page 80), Vygotsky believed that cognitive development was based on social interactions, not individual exploration of the environment. This belief is reflected in Vygotsky's ideas about how learning takes place within what he calls the *zone of proximal development (ZPD)*. This concept refers to a child's developmental potential. According to Vygotsky, a child's actual developmental level is determined by their independent problem solving, while their potential developmental level is determined by the problem solving they can achieve with instruction from an adult or more knowledgeable peer. The ZPD is the distance between these actual and potential developmental levels. Children develop new ways of thinking and problem solving through working with more knowledgeable others on tasks that are within this zone. If children are to develop new ways of thinking, it is really important that the tasks that children are given are just out of reach of their independent problem-solving abilities, but not so difficult that they cannot do them even with help. Adults teach children new skills gradually through a process known as **scaffolding**. During a learning interaction, the teacher takes the child step by step through the task, varying the level of help given so that it is contingent on the child's needs (Wood et al., 1976). In the early stages of mastering a task, a child may need a lot of help in the form of direct instruction and modelling. As they become more capable at a task, guidance will become less directed as the child takes more control of the activity. This model presents development as an apprenticeship in which the expert (adult or other more skilled individual) teaches the novice (the child) how to succeed. It is important to remember that, for Vygotsky, teaching is something that happens all the time – parents teach children, and older siblings teach younger ones. Teaching is not restricted to formal educational settings. However, you may not be surprised to learn that this theory has been applied to a school setting.

Focus on: cultural variation in starting school

In the UK, school entry usually happens at around the ages of four or five; in other parts of Europe it may be as late as seven years; and in America school entry is usually between the ages of five and six years. There is a lot of debate concerning the 'right' age at which children should start school. The following articles consider this topic from very different angles. One is written from an American and the other a UK perspective. One is a professional academic text, the other a newspaper article. Both are freely available online.

- Stipek, DJ (2003) School entry age, in Tremblay, RE, Peters, RDeV, Boivin, M and Barr, RG (eds) *Encyclopedia on Early Childhood Development*. Montreal: Centre of Excellence for Early Childhood Development. Available online at www.child-encyclopedia.com/documents/ StipekANGxp.pdf.

- Bruton, C (2007) Do we send our children to school too young? *The Times*, 6 September. Available online at http://women.timesonline.co.uk/tol/life_and_style/women/families/article 2392738.ece.

Task — Read the above two articles and then consider the following questions.

– How does the professional article differ from the newspaper account?

Tip: think about the evidence used, the language and tone, and the purpose of the article.

– What can you learn from this comparison?

Comment

Although both articles cite some research evidence, the way this information is presented is very different. The newspaper article is written in a chatty, friendly way. Anecdotal as well as research evidence is cited. The style is deliberately personal and emotive. Newspaper articles are, after all, designed to be not only informative, but also provocative. The professional article is much more objective in style. The evidence presented is based on research, not anecdote. Reading and comparing these two sources of information is important because, as a psychologist, you need to understand that not all evidence is equal. For example, a single case study does not usually provide the defining word on a subject, although it may be a good starting point; causal conclusions cannot be drawn from correlational studies; and you must always consider the source of information and evaluate its credibility. This task is designed to help you develop your skills in this final area and help you to be a wise consumer of information.

School experiences and cognitive development

In Western societies the school provides an important context for children's continuing cognitive development. There is, however, a lot of debate about the best way for schools to help this development. *Traditional teaching methods* relied heavily upon rote learning and the direct transmission of knowledge and information from teacher to child. More *progressive teaching methods* are child-centred and based on the idea that children need to be actively engaged in the learning process. Both Piaget and Vygotsky agreed that learning had to be active. From a Piagetian perspective, this means a child exploring and discovering things for themselves (**discovery learning**). In contrast, the Vygotskian approach emphasises the importance of interaction between the learner and more experienced others. One other important difference between these two approaches for learning concerns not so much how children should be taught, but more *what* can be taught.

According to Piaget (1923), children cannot learn something until they are **cognitively ready**. They need to have developed the appropriate cognitive structures before learning can take place; for example, children cannot learn about conservation until they have reversible mental operations. For Piaget, this meant that in school the teacher's role is to facilitate children's learning rather than provide direct instruction. On the contrary, Vygotsky (1962/1978) believed that a child can be *taught* anything as long as the activity falls within the child's ZPD. The teacher's role is therefore to provide direct instruction. In one sense, Piaget and Vygotsky are both arguing for readiness to learn. However, the important difference is that for Piaget development leads to learning, while for Vygotsky learning results in development.

If Vygotsky is right, could it be possible to teach a skill such as conservation to children who are not yet at the operational stage of development? Indeed, there is evidence that three- and four-year-old preschoolers who are not yet able to conserve can be taught this skill (Field, 1981). However, Field also found that four year olds were better conservers than three year olds and, once taught, were more likely to retain this skill over time. When the children in her study were retested five months after being taught to conserve, the majority of three year olds (70 per cent) had reverted to being non-conservers. In contrast, the majority of older children were more likely to have remained as conservers. The short-term nature of the conservation shown by the younger children suggests that they had not actually learned a new thinking skill, but had simply rote learned the 'correct' answers. By the time of retesting, they had forgotten what the answers were. This is further evidenced by the finding that the children who retained the ability to conserve were those who had shown that they could generalise their conservation skills to untrained quantities. This suggests that Vygotsky was right – new ways of thinking can be taught, but a child has to be ready to learn those skills.

The experiences children are exposed to in school, whether through discovery learning or direct instruction, therefore seem to influence cognitive development. But how does school influence development and is school necessary? In schools across the world children learn about a range of topics – science, maths, history and geography. Although the topic may be the same, the content may not, and variations are seen in terms of the depth and breadth of information that children are expected to cover (NRC, 1996). In maths and science, for example, an international survey found that the content covered was dictated in part by the social and cultural setting in which the child lives and the expectations of that culture (NRC, 1996). Curriculum delivery has also been found to be different within as well as across cultures (NRC, 1996; Moor et al., 2006). There has been a lot of debate in education about the extent to which schooling and curriculum content matter for intellectual development (e.g. Hanushek, 2003; Sammons et al., 2004). Separating learning and development – often expressed as the influence of school versus individual ability – is particularly difficult (Carneiro et al., 2001). It is like trying to answer that age-old question – which comes first, the chicken or the egg? Looking at cross-cultural studies of children who do not experience formal schooling may help solve this conundrum. Cross-cultural studies have shown that cognitive skills develop at different rates and may manifest themselves in different ways depending on the context in which a child lives (Cole, 1990). Nunes et al. (1993) showed, for example, how child street traders in Brazil who had not been exposed to formal schooling had difficulty finding the correct solution to hypothetical mathematical problems when these problems were given to them in written form. However, they did statistically better when the same problem was presented orally. Nunes et al. argue that this demonstrates that the children possess the ability to solve hypothetical problems, but because of a lack of experience and training in written mathematical problems, they fail when these problems are presented as they would be in a formal school setting. So does school really matter for development? Since children are able to develop sophisticated cognitive skills without attending school, the answer would seem to be 'no' – what matters is that children experience a range of learning opportunities. Development of logical thought is not influenced by schooling – it will develop anyway. However, what school does influence is *how* those skills develop and are manifest, by teaching the language and expectations of a specific cultural setting in relation to particular cognitive tasks (Cole, 1990). This happens in two ways. First, children learn the jargon necessary to access academic tests of cognitive ability at school. Second, they learn how to manipulate a new set of linguistic symbols by learning to read and write.

Focus on: atypical development and school experiences

As well as looking at the evidence from cross-cultural research, we can look at research that considers the school experiences of children who are developing atypically. In their paper 'School experiences after treatment for a brain tumour', Upton and Eiser (2006) describe how lengthy school absences can impact upon cognitive performance for school-age brain tumour survivors. They discuss how school absence interacts with a range of other factors, including the social context and the child's brain functioning, to influence the special educational needs of these children.

Task — Read the paper described above (Upton, P and Eiser, C (2006) School experiences after treatment for a brain tumour. *Child: Care, Health and Development*, 32(1): 9–17) and answer the following review questions.

– Could you develop a model to explain the development of these children using dynamic systems theory?

– What factors do you need to consider? Is this just about cognitive development, or is social development also relevant?

Comment

Upton and Eiser also note that long absences from school mean that children fall behind their classmates, and that performance is most affected in subjects such as literacy and numeracy where prior knowledge and skills are vital. This is also true for children with chronic health problems that do not involve neurological difficulties. What does this tell us about performance, ability and school? Does performance on a task necessarily demonstrate ability? Performance on tests is frequently used as a measure of cognitive ability – but what does this really tell us? You know from reading about cross-cultural studies that children may be able to think logically, but cannot demonstrate that skill if the tasks do not make social sense. Is this the same for children who have long school absences due to illness or is a different mechanism at work? Is their cognitive development delayed, disrupted, or is it simply that their knowledge of the language of performance testing is lacking? What other factors might influence cognitive development for these children? Why not use your literature search skills to find out more about this topic. What do studies of children with chronic illness show about their cognitive functioning and school attendance?

Language development in childhood: learning to read and write

Reading and writing are perhaps two of the most significant skills that children learn at school. Vygotsky saw language as an essential cultural tool for learning and he included written language as a necessary part of this. Through language, humans have shared knowledge across generations for centuries. This has often been through the spoken word. The oral tradition is common throughout the world; storytellers such as the griots and dyelli from Africa keep cultural traditions alive, using narrative to transmit cultural history and ancestry to new generations. Written language, however, expands our ability to pass information on to others. First, writing things down creates a shared memory. Second, knowledge can be disseminated much further in a written format than if communication were to be limited to the spoken word. Modern technology – for example, the internet – has created even more opportunities to share knowledge and information through the written word. Stop and think for a minute about how often you make use of the written word to learn something new (reading this book, for instance) or to communicate something to others.

One of the other major advantages of the written word is the way it enhances our cognitive functioning. Writing things down can be a great memory aid; working things out on paper expands our thinking power, allowing us to deal with a larger quantity and complexity of material. In this way, writing is able to enhance our cognitive processes (Menary, 2007). Learning to read and write opens up a whole new world of information to the child. However, it is important not to think of the child as a sponge passively soaking up knowledge. By learning to read and write, the child is also able to become an active participant in the socio-cultural world of which he or she is a member (Nelson, 1996).

Reading

Reading is not automatic. Learning to read involves mastering and integrating a number of separate skills. English and other European languages use an alphabetic script where each symbol (letter) represents a phoneme. In order to learn to read, the child must develop a conscious awareness that the letters on the page represent the sounds of the spoken word. This happens through either a bottom-up or top-down process. In a bottom-up process we learn to spell out each phoneme and build up the word. To read the word 'cat', the word must first be split into its basic phonological elements. This is known as a 'phonics approach' to learning to read. Once the word is in its phonological form, it can be identified and understood. So the word 'cat' is first decoded into its phonological form ('kuh, aah, tuh') and is then identified. In a top-down process the whole word is recognised by its overall visual appearance. This is known as the 'whole-language approach' to teaching reading. There is much debate about which approach is best, but the evidence suggests that children use and benefit from both strategies (Siegler, 1986; Vacca et al., 2006). Once the word is identified, higher-level cognitive functions such as intelligence and vocabulary are applied to understand the word's meaning: in the case of the word 'cat', this might be 'small furry mammal that purrs'.

Many factors can influence how this learning progresses. Often children know a lot about reading before they start school – especially in homes where books are readily available and the children have been read to regularly. These children will understand that books tell stories, that they have a right and a wrong way up and that the writing goes from left to right. They may even copy the act of reading – turning the pages and using the pictures to invent a story or simply repeating a story from memory. Many children may also know the letters of the alphabet when they first start school. These children tend to be more successful in learning to read than those who have not learned the alphabet. However, this probably reflects a general interest in books and reading that has been encouraged at home (Adams, 1990). Knowledge of nursery rhymes and rhyming games also seems to play an important part in developing the understanding that words can be broken down into separate sounds (phonemic awareness). Children with a greater knowledge of nursery rhymes show a much better phonemic awareness (Maclean et al., 1987). It seems that rhymes allow children to discover phonemes.

It is this knowledge that learning to read is not just about what is taught in schools, but is in fact underpinned by activities at home, that underlies the UK Bookstart strategy (www.bookstart. org.uk). This campaign is a national programme that encourages all parents and carers to enjoy books with their children from as early an age as possible. Bookstart offers the gift of free books to all children at three key ages before they start school, the aim being to stimulate a love of reading. Wade and Moore (1993) have shown the programme to have had an impact on a number of reading-related activities in families, including sharing books with young children, the use of libraries and book buying. Support for the long-term advantages of early reading has been provided by the observation that Bookstart children achieve higher scores in English and maths (Wade and Moore, 1998). There is also some evidence that Bookstart enables children to acquire consistently higher levels of language and literacy development (Hines and Brooks, 2005).

Writing

Writing and reading are closely related and, some would say, inseparable. Better writers tend to be better readers, and better readers produce better writing. It makes sense that the strategies children use to read are the same ones they use in order to write. However, in addition to the cognitive and linguistic skills that children need for reading, in order to write, children also need to have developed fine motor skills. Play activities that involve the manipulation of objects, such as art and crafts, play dough, jigsaw puzzles, building blocks and so on, help to develop fine motor skills. However, there is some evidence that motor development has a much wider role to play in the development of cognitive skills, including language. Studies of children with **specific learning difficulties** have highlighted the joint occurrence of motor and language difficulties (Viholainen et al., 2002). Indeed, the observed prevalence of motor problems in children with developmental language problems has been estimated to be somewhere between 60 and 90 per cent (Viholainen et al., 2002). One possible explanation for this **co-morbidity** is that motor and language problems share a common underlying neuro-cognitive system. There is increasing evidence that, structurally, the interface for the integration of cognitive and motor functioning is the cerebellum, a peach-sized structure situated at the base of the brain (see Figure 5.3).

It has been known for a long time that the cerebellum is responsible for coordinating movement, planning, motor activities, and learning and remembering physical skills, and for a long time this was believed to be its only role. In the last 20 years, evidence from **neuro-imaging studies** and studies of patients with cerebellar lesions has shown that the cerebellum also plays an important role in a range of high-level cognitive functions, such as language, previously believed to be under the sole control of the cortex (Booth et al., 2007). According to the cerebellar deficit hypothesis (Nicolson et al., 1995), both literacy and *automaticity* problems can be explained by abnormal cerebellar function. Indeed, there is evidence from both behavioural and neuro-imaging tests that dyslexia is associated with cerebellar impairment in about 80 per cent of cases (Nicholson et al., 2001). It therefore seems that not only does motor development create the opportunity for cognitive functions to develop, as you learned in Chapters 3 and 4, but that the interrelatedness of cognitive and motor development might also be based on shared neural systems (Ojeman, 1984; Diamond, 2000).

Figure 5.3: *A cross-section of the brain, showing the position of the cerebellum*

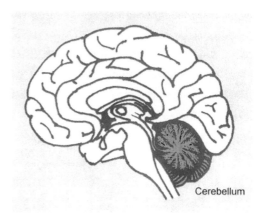

Cerebellum

Theory of mind

An important area of cognitive development that takes place during the school years is children's understanding of mental states; they develop what is known as a **theory of mind**. Theory of mind refers to the understanding that other people may have different thoughts, knowledge, desires, feelings and beliefs (Harris, 2006). Even preschoolers try to attribute knowledge and mental states to others; however, it is not until around the age of four years that children are thought to demonstrate a coherent theory of mind (Gopnik, 1993). Some theorists argue that this ability demonstrates a qualitative shift in children's thinking (e.g. Wellman and Gelman, 1998). However, others disagree, arguing that the tasks used to test for theory of mind underestimate children's abilities (Siegal and Peterson, 1994). This is very similar to the debate about other areas of cognitive development considered earlier in this chapter and, as in that debate, a lot of effort has gone into trying to change the tasks used to make more human sense, thus allowing children to demonstrate their understanding of mind at an earlier age.

The task most commonly used to assess theory of mind is the 'false belief task' (Wimmer and Perner, 1983). There are a number of variations of this task, but probably the most famous is the 'Sally Anne task' (Baron-Cohen et al., 1985). Children are told or shown a story involving two characters, Sally and Anne, who have a basket and a box, respectively (see Figure 5.4). Sally also has a ball, which she places in her basket, and then she leaves to take a walk. While she is out of the room, Anne takes the ball from the basket, eventually putting it in the box. Sally returns, and the child is then asked where Sally will look for the ball. If the child answers that Sally will look in the basket, where *she* put the ball, they have demonstrated understanding of mind; they recognise that Sally has a different mental representation of the situation from theirs – they possess knowledge Sally does not. The results of research using false belief tasks have been fairly consistent: most typically, developing children are unable to pass the tasks until around the age of four. However, it has been suggested that this is because younger children misinterpret the key false belief question – 'Where *will* Sally look?' – to mean 'Where *should* Sally look?' (Siegal and

Figure 5.4: *The Sally Anne task*

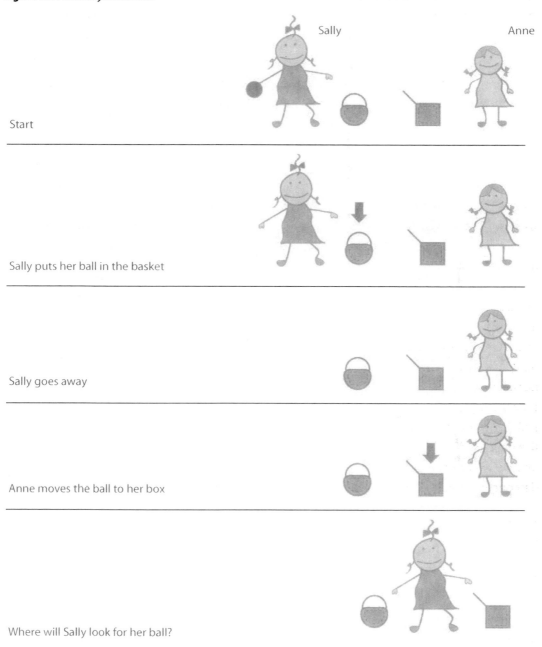

Start

Sally puts her ball in the basket

Sally goes away

Anne moves the ball to her box

Where will Sally look for her ball?

Peterson, 1994). If this is so, their wrong answer is actually correct. Indeed, three year olds have been found to perform better when the question is reworded to a less ambiguous form, for example 'Where should Sally look *first of all*' (Siegal and Beattie, 1991).

It has also been suggested that three year olds are unable to demonstrate their understanding of mind because of the burden that tasks such as these place on immature processing skills, such as memory and reasoning (Flavell and Miller, 1998). This has been tested by the 'false photograph task' (Leslie and Thaiss, 1992), which has the same burden in terms of memory and inference, but does not require children to consider another's mind. In this task, children are shown a doll placed sitting on a box. They are then given an instant camera and asked to take a photo of this. The doll is then moved to a new position such as sitting on a mat. The child is then asked, 'Where will the doll be in the developing photo?' Once again, four year olds are able to answer this question correctly – three year olds are not. This strongly suggests that the three year olds' inability to answer the false belief task is at least partly related to poorer processing skills.

Although clearly a cognitive skill, theory of mind is also a social skill that plays an important role in our ability to get on with others (Liddle and Nettle, 2006). If you have theory of mind, you are able to put yourself in somebody else's shoes, to imagine what it is they are feeling. In this way, theory of mind is a part of empathy – our ability to understand and identify with another person's feelings. Empathy is also believed to play an important role in fostering pro-social behaviour and social competence (Eisenberg and Fabes, 1998; Hoffman, 2000), both of which are important for good peer relationships during the school years.

Developing peer relationships

It has been estimated that, in middle childhood, 30 per cent of a child's social interactions involve peers – three times more than in early childhood (Rubin et al., 1998). There is evidence that these school playground experiences have both an educational and a social value for child development (Blatchford et al., 2002). However, not all peer interactions are positive and there is also evidence that the incidence of bullying and aggression in the playground is sufficiently widespread to cause serious concern (e.g. Whitney and Smith, 1993), and racist and sexist teasing and fighting has been observed (e.g. Kelly, 1994; Short, 1999). There is evidence that, in both the US and the UK, there has been a move to reduce the time allocated for the lunch break in order to tackle unnecessarily aggressive and aimless behaviour, bullying and peer rejection (Blatchford et al., 2002).

However, this may not be helpful – and may even exacerbate the very behaviour it wishes to eliminate. Blatchford et al. (1990) suggested that a child-governed break-time culture from which adults are excluded exists in the playground. While this culture is not always a benign one, it is nevertheless extremely important to children, because of the freedom from adults that it affords. The developmental advantage of this is that, without adult intervention, children have to learn to regulate playground games and space themselves. They must also discover how to manage teasing and bullying. In so doing, Blatchford argues, they are able to develop a sophisticated set of social understandings.

Popularity

During middle childhood, some children seem to have many friends, while others only have a few. Indeed, a central concern of most school-age children is popularity, also known as social status. Popularity is defined by the majority of peer interaction researchers as the number of children who name a target child as 'liked', 'disliked', 'friend' or 'best friend' (Newcomb et al., 1993). Using these nominations, the extent of children's popularity can be classified into one of four groups: children with the most 'liked' nominations are popular; children with the most 'disliked' nominations are rejected; children with very few (or even no) nominations are neglected; and children are considered controversial if they are both nominated frequently by some and actively disliked by others. A relationship has been found between children's popularity levels and their social behaviours as follows.

- *Popular children*: demonstrate high levels of positive social behaviour and cognitive ability and low levels of aggression and withdrawal compared with average children.

- *Rejected children*: are more aggressive and withdrawn and less sociable and cognitively skilled than average children. They tend to be perceived as 'different' by their peers.

- *Neglected children*: demonstrate less social interaction and disruptive behaviour but more withdrawal than average children.

- *Controversial children*: are less compliant and more aggressive than average children.

The important thing to consider is whether popular children's array of competencies makes them the recipients of positive peer nominations as Newcomb et al. believe, or whether the increased opportunities for interaction with others that popularity affords leads to an increase in social skills. Peer acceptance may, for instance, influence friendships by determining the amount of choice that children have for making friends (Azmitia et al., 1998).

Friendship

Middle childhood brings clear changes in the understanding of friendship. In early childhood, friendships are transient in nature and are often related to the availability of the other person. A friend is defined as someone you play with or with whom you share some other activity. In middle childhood, children's relationships still tend to be with others who are similar to themselves; this is partly because children are more likely to come into proximity because of similarities in age, socio-economic status, ethnicity, etc. However, there is also evidence that children also become increasingly similar to their friends as they interact (Hartup, 1996).

It is during middle childhood, however, that children begin to identify the special features of friendship that supersede mere proximity. During this period of development, children begin to recognise that friendships provide companionship, help, protection and support (Azmitia et al., 1998), are reciprocal (Selman, 1980), demand trust and loyalty (Bigelow, 1977) and last over time (Parker and Seal, 1996). That is not to say that friendships made in middle childhood endure for long periods. School-age children often have what have been called 'fair-weather friends', because friendships at this age are often unable to survive periods of conflict or disagreement (Rubin et al., 1998). There also appear to be gender differences in the time it takes to mend broken friendships. Azmitia et al. (1998) observed that, following friendship conflict, boys would typically work it through and renew the friendship in one day, whereas girls would take about two weeks. This may be because triads are more common in the friendships of school-age girls than in those of boys, causing one member of the group to feel left out. By the end of middle childhood, friendships are becoming intimate, and are characterised by an enduring sense of trust in each other. The ability to engage in mutual role-taking and collaborative negotiation develops throughout this period, leading to greater loyalty, trust and social support. For example, Azmitia et al. (1998) found that girls' expectations that friends would keep secrets rose from 25 per cent in eight to nine year olds, to 72 per cent in 11 to 12 year olds. However, this expectation developed slightly later in boys. Thus, the ability to form close, intimate friendships becomes increasingly important as children move towards early adolescence (Buhrmester, 1990).

Critical thinking activity

Developing scientific thinking

Critical thinking focus: reflection on the importance of context for development

Key question: How do children come to understand scientific explanations of floating and sinking?

Science, especially in primary school, is often presented as a set of facts to be learned. However, knowledge of science is much more to do with knowing how to think appropriately about a problem, and current evidence shows that children have to undergo a process of conceptual change in order to truly understand about science. Piaget argued that children cannot understand scientific reasoning until they have reached the formal operational stage of development, which usually happens in adolescence. However, many educators and psychologists now agree that children begin to understand about the natural world and how it works from an early age (Duschl et al., 2007). The evidence suggests that they construct their own theories of how the world around them works based on their everyday experiences. While a rudimentary understanding of scientific phenomena such as density has even been demonstrated in preschoolers (Kohn, 1993), it must be remembered that these naive theories are often imperfect and may include misconceptions. Piaget (1923) argues that this is because young children do not have the cognitive structures to enable them to understand the scientific theory. According to Piaget, early misconceptions must be replaced by more accurate understanding as the child's cognitive abilities mature. However, contemporary evidence suggests that, rather than dismissing children's early theories, this knowledge should be used as a building block for scientific thinking.

Read the following paper:

Pine, KJ, Messer, DJ and St John, K (2001) Children's misconceptions in primary science: a survey of teachers' views. *Research in Science and Technology Education*, 19(1): 79–96. Available online at https://uhra.herts.ac.uk/dspace/bitstream/2299/613/1/103202.pdf.

This paper gives a clear insight into the factors that might affect the development of scientific thinking. This includes children's experiences at home, as well as the teacher knowledge and approach to topics. Pine et al. consider two science topics – balance and curvilinear motion. How might you apply some of the ideas expressed here to explain children's understanding of another scientific concept – floating and sinking? Consider the following questions.

- What activities do children routinely engage in at home that may influence naive theories of floating and sinking?

- Can you apply Karmiloff-Smith's representational redescription model (described in the paper) to this understanding?

- What do you understand about why objects float and sink and where did you get this knowledge from? Do you think yours is a sophisticated view or might it include some misconceptions? Compare your ideas to the developmental progression provided by Deakin University: www.deakin.edu.au/arts-ed/education/sci-enviro-ed/early-years/pdfs/floating-sink.pdf. Do you think all adults understand the Archimedes Principle as described here? How important is it for primary school teachers to understand this fundamental physics concept?

Now read the following paper:

Hardy, I, Jonen, A, Möller, K and Stern, E (2006) Effects of instructional support within constructivist learning environments for elementary school students' understanding of 'floating and sinking'. *Journal of Educational Psychology*, 98: 307–26.

To what extent does the approach described here help overcome some of the problems raised by Pine et al.? What are the pros and cons of this method of teaching science?

You might also find the following paper, which considers how a teacher dealt with children's misconceptions of temperature and heat, of interest: www. exploratorium.edu/ifi/resources/workshops/teachingforconcept.html.

Critical thinking review

This activity helps you understand how children develop scientific ways of think-ing and how school experiences are designed to nurture this understanding. Reflecting upon the influence of everyday experiences of children at home, as well as at school, should increase your awareness of the importance of different contexts for development. This also helps consolidate your understanding of key models of development, such as social constructivism.

Other skills you may have used in this activity include applying theory to real developmental contexts, and the recall of key principles and ideas.

Skill builder activity

The importance of context for logical reasoning

Transferable skill focus: problem solving – logical reasoning

Key question: *Try these two puzzles. Write down your answer to the first puzzle before moving on to the second.*

Puzzle 1

There are four cards, labelled either X or Y on one side and either 1 or 2 on the other. They are laid out like this:

X	Y	1	2

A rule states: 'If X is on one side then there must be a 1 on the other.' Which two cards do you need to turn over to find out if this rule is true?

Puzzle 2

As you walk into a wine bar you see a sign stating that 'You must be over 18 to drink alcohol here.' There are four people in the bar. You know the ages of two of them, and can see what the other two are drinking. The situation is:

- Rosie is drinking red wine;

- Gabe is drinking Coke;

- Dominic is 42 years old;

- Francesca is 17 years old.

Which two people would you need to talk to in order to check that the 'over-18 rule' for drinking alcohol is being followed?

Skill builder review

The focus of this task is the way social context can affect reasoning skills – even for adults. These two problems/puzzles require the same set of reasoning skills. However, the first of the puzzles is given in abstract terms, while the other is related to a common social situation, which makes it easier to solve. You should see from this activity how the social and cultural knowledge we have influences our learning and, therefore, how we apply and demonstrate our logical reasoning skills. How did you get on with these tasks? The solutions and their justification are given below.

Puzzle 1: The answer is X and 2, but people often answer X and 1. Turning the X over lets you check that there is a 1 on the other side of that card. You also need to check that the 2 does not have an X on the other side, as that would break the rule that X must have 1 on the other side. Turning the 1 card over will not help you because the rule only states what should be on the other side of an X card; it does not say that cards labelled with a 1 must have an X on the back. However, people often make this (logically false) assumption.

Puzzle 2: This puzzle requires exactly the same reasoning, but you are likely to find this one easier to solve. This is because the problem is embedded in a familiar social situation – and uses a well-known cultural rule. The correct solution is to ask Francesca what she is drinking, and ask Rosie her age. Your knowledge of the social situation means that you are less likely to make the same kind of mistake that you

> did in Puzzle 1 – the equivalent error in this problem would be to assume that the rule implies that, if you are over 18, you must be drinking alcohol – and so you would ask Dominic what he is drinking. In the context of this puzzle, such a suggestion seems illogical, because of what we know and understand of the cultural rules and expectations surrounding behaviour in bars.

Assignments

1. 'Peer group relationships are essential for psycho-social development in middle childhood.' Critically evaluate this statement.

2. Critically discuss the extent to which primary age children's thinking is limited by under-developed cognitive structures.

3. To what extent does learning to read and write depend upon oral language skills?

Summary: what you have learned

Now you have finished studying this chapter you should:

- be able to evaluate the importance of peer relationships and recognise their importance for psycho-social development in childhood;

- be able to discuss critically the mastery of cognitive tasks that takes place in childhood, and have some understanding of how the social context may influence children's ability to demonstrate their skills, using early mathematical thinking as an exemplar;

- critically understand the development of reading and writing skills, and how this might link to general language development;

- understand the possible impact of atypical development on experiences such as schooling;

- have developed your ability to reflect on the importance of the socio-cultural context for development by considering how children's everyday and school experiences influence the development of scientific thinking;

- have developed your problem solving and logical reasoning by engaging in and reflecting on the tasks presented in the chapter.

Further reading

Blatchford, P, Pellegrini, T, Baines, E and Kentaro, K (2002) *Playground Games: Their social context in elementary/junior school*. Final report to the Spencer Foundation. Available online at www.break time.org.uk/SpencerFinalReport02.pdf.

A very useful description of children's play activities at school.

National Research Council (NRC) (1996) *Mathematics and Science Education Around the World: What can we learn from the Survey of Mathematics and Science Opportunities (SMSO) and the Third International Mathematics and Science Study (TIMSS)?* Washington, DC: National Academy Press.

Identifies clearly the differences in curriculum around the globe.

Nunes, T, Schliemann, AD and Carraher, DW (1993) *Street Mathematics and School Mathematics*. New York: Cambridge University Press.

Insightful description of the way in which learning is embedded on social and cultural contexts.

Stipek, DJ (2003) School entry age, in Tremblay, RE, Peters, RDeV, Boivin, M and Barr, RG (eds) *Encyclopedia on Early Childhood Development*. Montreal: Centre of Excellence for Early Childhood Development. Available online at www.child-encyclopedia.com/documents/StipekANGxp.pdf.

Discusses the differences in school starting age cross-culturally.

Upton, P and Eiser, C (2006) School experiences after treatment for a brain tumour. *Child: Care, Health and Development*, 32(1): 9–17.

Describes a study looking at children's cognitive preference following long school absences due to chronic illness.

A number of studies assessing the effectiveness of Bookstart are available from the following website, including the study carried out in Sheffield by Hines and Brooks (2005): www.bookstart. org.uk/about-us/research.

Chapter 6

Adolescence

Learning outcomes

By the end of this chapter you should:

- *understand the main developmental tasks of adolescence;*

- *be able to evaluate the development of sense of self;*

- *be able critically to discuss storm and stress theory;*

- *critically understand the increasing importance of peer relationships;*

- *have developed your critical and creative thinking skills;*

- *have developed your ability to understand and use qualitative data.*

Introduction

Adolescence is the period of transition between childhood and adulthood. Important physical and hormonal developments take place during adolescence, leading to increasing **sexual dimorphism**. It is the entry into this period of intense physical change (*puberty*) that is usually recognised as the start of adolescence. However, adolescence is about more than physical maturation. It is also a period of significant social and emotional development, characterised by increasing independence from family, a clearer sense of self and greater emphasis on peer group relationships. In the light of this, it is perhaps not surprising that, traditionally, adolescence has been seen as a tumultuous period of development characterised by three key features: conflict with parents, mood disruptions and risky behaviour. However, as this chapter shows, current evidence suggests that 'storm and stress' does not describe the typical experience of an adolescent.

Biological and physical changes in adolescence

Puberty is a period of rapid physical change, involving hormonal and bodily changes. However, it is not a single sudden event, but rather an extended set of changes that take place over time (Dorn et al., 2006). These changes include increases in height and weight, and reaching sexual maturity. The specific changes are different for boys and girls, as are the timings at which such changes occur. In general, girls enter puberty approximately two years before boys. Initial changes are associated with increased height and weight. On average, for girls this growth spurt begins at the age of nine years, while for boys this is closer to 11 years of age. The peak of this growth spurt happens approximately three years later, so girls are growing fastest between 12 and 13 years of age, while boys are growing fastest between the ages of 14 and 15 years. During the growth peak, girls grow by around 9cm a year and boys by 10cm, which is why, by about 14 years of age, boys have overtaken girls in terms of height. Girls also end their growth spurt earlier when they are around 18 years of age, while boys need another two years before they finish growing at the age of 20 years.

The adolescent growth spurt starts on the outside of the body and works inwards, so the hands and feet are the first to expand, followed by arms and legs, which then grow longer. Following this the spine elongates. The last expansion is a broadening of the chest and shoulders in boys, and a widening of the hips and pelvis in girls.

This growth spurt is triggered by a flood of hormonal changes, which is set off by the **hypothalamus** and **pituitary gland**. The main hormones associated with pubertal changes are **testosterone** and **oestrodiol**. Both of these chemicals are present in the hormonal make-up of both boys and girls, but testosterone dominates in male pubertal changes and oestrodiol in female pubertal changes. In boys, increases in testosterone are associated with an increase in height, a deepening of the voice and genital development. For girls, increasing levels of oestrodiol are linked to breast, uterine and skeletal development (e.g. widening of the hips).

It has been suggested that these same hormones may contribute to psychological development in adolescence (Rapkin et al., 2006). For example, studies have shown links between testosterone levels and perceived social competence in boys (Nottelmann et al., 1987), and between oestrodiol levels and the emotional responses of girls (Inoff-Germain et al., 1988). However, the relationship between hormones and behaviour is a complex one; there is evidence that the link between behaviour and hormones may work in the opposite direction as well, since behaviour and mood have been found to influence hormone levels (Susman, 2006). Indeed, it seems unlikely that hormones alone can account for the psychological changes that occur in adolescence (Rowe et al., 2004).

Physical changes and psychological well-being

One of the first major tasks of adolescence is to adjust to the huge physical changes that are taking place. How easily adolescents deal with this will depend partly on how closely their bodies match the well-defined stereotypes of the 'perfect' body for young women and young men that are promoted by the society in which they live. In general, however, it seems that all adolescents show some body dissatisfaction during puberty (Graber and Brooks-Gunn, 2001). The evidence suggests that girls tend to become increasingly dissatisfied as they move through puberty, while boys become increasingly satisfied. It is likely that this is linked to the natural increases that occur in body fat in girls and in muscle mass in boys; indeed, when adolescents try to change their physique, girls are more likely to try to lose weight, while boys will try to increase muscle tone (McCabe et al., 2002). Adolescents who do not match the stereotype may well need more social support from adults and peers to improve their feelings of self-worth regarding their body type.

For girls, this issue is further confounded by the timing of entry into puberty, the effects of which appear to be different for males and females. At 11 to 12 years of age, early-maturing girls tend to have greater satisfaction with their body shape than late-maturing girls. However, this changes as girls reach 15 to 16 years of age, when late-maturing girls start to report greater satisfaction with their body shape (Simmons and Blyth, 1987). Interestingly, this change in body satisfaction may reflect differing body shapes at the end of puberty – early-maturing girls stop growing earlier and so tend to be shorter and stockier in comparison to their taller, thinner, late-maturing peers (Brooks-Gunn et al. 1985).

Early-maturing girls have also been found to be more vulnerable to emotional and behavioural problems, including depression, eating disorders and engaging in risky health behaviours such as smoking, drinking and drug taking, and early sexual behaviours (Wiesner and Ittel, 2002). These girls are also more likely to have lower educational and occupational attainments (Stattin and Magnusson, 1990). It seems that girls who physically mature at a younger age spend more time with their older peers and are easily drawn into problem behaviours, because they do not have the emotional maturity to recognise the long-term effects of such behaviours on their development (Sarigiani and Petersen, 2000). However, there is evidence to suggest that the negative psychosocial consequences of early puberty may not last into later adolescence or adulthood (Blumstein Posner, 2006).

Thus, it seems that, for girls, the advantages lie in later maturity. In contrast, the evidence suggests that, for boys, the advantage lies in early maturity. There is evidence, for example, that early-maturing boys have more successful peer relationships than their late-maturing counterparts (Simmons and Blyth, 1987). There is, however, some disagreement about whether or not this remains an advantage across the lifespan (Brooks-Gunn et al., 1985). Nonetheless, what is becoming more evident is that the link between an adolescent's beliefs about their appearance and their sense of self-worth – which is an important aspect of an individual's identity – should not be underestimated (Frisen and Holmqvist, 2010).

Developing a sense of self

One of the developmental tasks that has been seen to dominate in adolescence is developing a sense of who we are, what we believe and what our values are: in other words, establishing our sense of self. It has been suggested that sense of self follows a set developmental sequence in which younger children define themselves in terms of concrete characteristics, while adolescents increasingly come to define themselves in terms of more abstract inner or psychological characteristics. This idea is based primarily on research that has shown that children's self-descriptions change with age from observable and physical descriptions such as 'I am tall' to more psychological traits such as 'I am friendly' as, for example, in the classic study carried out by Rosenberg (1979). It has been suggested that this developmental trend reflects children's growing ability to distinguish themselves psychologically from others as they get older (Bannister and Agnew, 1977; Leavitt and Hall, 2004).

Focus on: Rosenberg's study of self-descriptions

Arguably one of the most important studies of the development of sense of self was carried out by Rosenberg (1979). He conducted open-ended interviews with individual children to find out about their self-perceptions. He interviewed a sample of 8–18 year olds about various aspects of their sense of self. The children were selected at random from 25 schools in Baltimore, USA. Many of his questions explored aspects of the children's categorical selves that went beyond the simple self-description ('Who am I?') to include feelings of pride and shame in aspects of their selves ('What are my best things/weak points?'); their sense of distinctiveness as separate individuals ('In what ways am I the same as/different from other children?'); and feelings about an ideal self ('What kind of person would I like to become?').

Rosenberg's first aim was to find a way of sorting the children's replies into meaningful categories. His second aim was to search for any patterns in the kinds of replies that were given by particular age groups. He was interested in looking for anything that might suggest a developmental progression in children's sense of self. He was able to categorise the children's replies into a series of broad groups of self-descriptions as follows.

Physical: descriptions of self that could be observed or identified or potentially be described by others; they are mainly about physical features or physical activities such as:

- objective facts – e.g. 'I am eight years old'; overt achievements – e.g. 'I can swim 25 metres';

- manifested preferences – e.g. 'I like milk';

- possessions – e.g. 'I've got a blue bike';

- physical attributes – e.g. 'I've got brown hair and blue eyes';

- membership categories – e.g. 'I am a girl'.

Character: descriptions of self that refer to personal characteristics or traits: personality, emotional characteristics and emotional control. These qualities could still be inferred by others from the behaviour of an individual but only the individual can have direct access to them, for example:

- qualities of character – e.g. 'I am a brave person and I think that I am honest;

- emotional characteristics – e.g. 'I am generally happy and cheerful';

- emotional control – e.g. 'I don't get into fights', 'I lose my temper easily'.

Relationships: descriptions of self that refer to interpersonal traits or to relationships with others, such as:

- interpersonal traits – e.g. 'I am friendly and sociable', 'I am shy and retiring';

- relationship to others – e.g. 'I am well liked by other children', 'Other people find me difficult to get on with'.

Inner: descriptions of self that refer to an individual's more private inner world of emotions, attitudes, wishes, beliefs and secrets, such as self-knowledge – for example, rather than simply describing a personal trait such as shyness, they would tend to qualify this with explanations of the circumstances in which they felt shy, why they thought that they were shy, how it affected them and how they coped with being shy.

Rosenberg (1979) found that the majority of the descriptions given by younger children were about physical activity and physical characteristics. The older children were more likely to use character traits to define the self. Rosenberg also found increasing reference to relationships. For example, when questioned about points of pride and shame, only 9 per cent of the eight year olds' responses consisted of interpersonal traits (e.g. 'friendly', 'shy'), as opposed to 17 per cent of the 14 year olds' and 28 per cent of the 16 year olds' responses. Likewise, when asked about what kind of person they would like to become, 36 per cent of the eight year olds' responses were to do with interpersonal traits, as opposed to 69 per cent of the 14 to 16 year olds' answers.

The oldest children (those aged around 18 years of age) made far more use of inner qualities, knowledge of which was only available to the individual. These descriptions were concerned with their emotions, attitudes, motivations, wishes and secrets. Rosenberg also found that older children are much more likely to refer to self-control when describing themselves, for example 'I don't show my feelings'. When questioned about points of shame, only 14 per cent of the eight year olds' responses related to self-control, while 32 per cent of 14 year olds' responses referred to the ability to hide self and feelings from others.

Task — Answer the following review questions.

– How robust is the evidence presented here by Rosenberg? How reliable and valid do you think these findings are?

– What developmental changes other than sense of self might Rosenberg's findings reflect?

Comment

Rosenberg's study seems to give a definitive picture of changing sense of self from childhood to adolescence. The sample size was robust and representative of the children in Baltimore. In many ways, the idea of a shift from the concrete to the abstract makes sense and mirrors other theorists' ideas in developmental psychology, including Piaget's theory of cognitive development. However, there are a number of things to consider in terms of the validity of this study. First, this was a cross-sectional study, so while differences may well have been observed in terms of the self-descriptions given by children at different ages, it is difficult to be absolutely certain that these differences reflect developmental change – only a longitudinal study could really confirm this interpretation. Second, even if these changing descriptions do reflect a developmental change, how can we be sure that the developmental change is actually about understanding of self? Self-descriptions necessarily rely on linguistic ability – perhaps the developmental change that is reflected is in terms of increasing sophistication in language ability. It is quite possible that verbal language skills limited the younger children's ability to communicate their knowledge of self.

Identity development

An important aspect of our sense of self is our personal identity. Identity has a number of different aspects, some of which are shown in Table 6.1. The importance of these different aspects of our personal identity may change across time and place. Intellectual identity may, for example, be felt more strongly during the school years; religion may be an important part of an individual's identity at home, but not at work.

The notion that identity is the key to adolescent development comes from Erikson's theory, which you learned about in Chapter 1. According to Erikson (1950), during adolescence, young people are faced with an overwhelming number of choices about who they are and where they are going in life. For Erikson, this is the crisis that has to be resolved at this developmental stage; if adolescents are not able to answer this question adequately they will suffer from identity confusion, which will delay their development in the later stages of life. The search for identity is supported by what Erikson calls a psychosocial moratorium. What he means is that adolescents are relatively free of responsibility, which enables them to have the space to try out (and discard) different identities. They are able to experiment with different roles and personalities until they find the ones that best suit them. Marcia (1987) suggested that this development is a staged process and he identified four different identity statuses.

- *Identity diffusion* refers to the individual who has not yet experienced a crisis or made any commitments. They are undecided about future roles and have not shown any interest in such matters.

Table 6.1: *Aspects of identity*

Aspect of identity	Components
Vocational identity	Career choice and aspirations; current or intended occupation
Intellectual identity	Academic aspirations and achievements
Political ideology	Political beliefs, values and ideals; may include membership of political groups
Spiritual/religious identity	Religious beliefs, attitudes to religion and spirituality; religious practices and behaviours; may relate to a specific moral and ethical code
Relationship identity	This may refer to intimate relationships and be defined by whether you are single, married, divorced etc; or to social relationships such as friend, colleague etc; or to family relationships – mother, daughter etc.
Sexual identity	Sexual orientation – heterosexual, homosexual, bisexual
Cultural identity	Where you were born and/or raised and how intensely you identify with the cultural heritage/practices linked to this part of the world; may also include language preference
Ethnic identity	The extent to which you feel a sense of belonging to a particular ethnic group; the ethnic group tends to be one to which you can claim heritage and the beliefs of the group may influence your thinking, perceptions, feelings and behaviour
Physical identity	Body image and beliefs about your appearance
Personality	Characteristics that define patterns of behaviour, such as being shy, friendly, gregarious, anxious etc.

- *Identity foreclosure* describes individuals who have made a commitment to an identity without experiencing a crisis. They may, for example, have simply followed the ideologies and aspirations of their parents.

- *Identity moratorium* is the term used to describe individuals experiencing an identity crisis and whose commitments have not yet been strongly defined.

- *Identity achievement* is reached once individuals have undergone a crisis and made a commitment to their identity.

According to Marcia (1993), young adolescents are usually described by one of the first three statuses. However, there is increasing evidence that identity development is not solely a task of adolescence. Indeed, some aspects of identity are already well on the way to being established before adolescence. Gender, for example, is one aspect of identity that is a key aspect of development at an early age, but continues to be built on as more complex understandings of what it means to be male or female are negotiated. Likewise, some of the most important changes in identity occur after adolescence, taking place during early adulthood (Waterman, 1992). It has even been argued that identity is not stable and the identity we achieve in adolescence is not necessarily the one we will keep for life (Marcia, 2002). Personal experiences and changes in society are likely to lead us to question our beliefs and who we are throughout the life span. Perhaps the healthiest identity is one that is flexible, adaptive and open to change.

Focus on: identity development

There is continuing debate about the value of the identity status approach. How well do you think this theory explains identity development?

Task — In order to explore the question above, think about your own exploration and commitment to different aspects of identity by answering the following questions.

– Would you describe yourself as diffused, foreclosed, in moratorium or as having achieved identity following a crisis?

– Is this approach more useful for some aspects of identity than others?

– Do you agree that foreclosure is a limitation to identity development?

Completing the following chart will help you focus on some of the relevant issues.

Identity component	Identity status			
	Diffused	Foreclosed	Moratorium	Achieved
Vocational				
Political				
Religious				
Relationships				
Achievement				
Sexual				
Gender				
Ethnic/cultural				
Physical				
Personality				

Self-esteem

Linked into all these different identities is another aspect of our overall sense of self – our **self-esteem**. Self-esteem refers to a general feeling of self-worth and, as such, encompasses all the evaluations we make of our skills and abilities in different domains of life, such as our physical appearance, athletic ability and intellectual skills. In a sense, it is a value judgement we make about how 'good' we are and, as such, is influenced by the domain-specific or *self-concept* evaluations we make. It is important to recognise that self-esteem reflects perceptions that do not always match reality (Baumiester et al., 2003). We tend to make judgements about our abilities in different aspects of our lives based on our successes or failures. However, failure does not automatically lead to low self-esteem. The impact of any failures – or successes – on our global self-esteem depends to a great extent on the importance we place on that aspect of our lives. Thus, for the adolescent who places little value on their athletic identity, but a great deal on their intellectual identity, coming last in the 200m hurdles is unlikely to have much impact on self-esteem. By the same token, coming bottom of the class in a test may well have an important negative impact on their feelings of self-worth.

As with other aspects of sense of self such as identity, it seems likely that self-esteem develops and changes as the child moves into adolescence. Given what we know about gender differences in adolescent perceptions of pubertal body changes and the importance of appearance to adolescent identity, it is perhaps not surprising that there is some evidence that self-esteem declines in adolescence – considerably more for girls than for boys (Robins et al., 2002).

Individuality and connectedness

In many ways this developing sense of self can be seen as an important step on the road to adult independence since, in Western society, the goal of self-development is to establish our individuality or a sense of our own uniqueness and separateness from others. Indeed, in Western society the word 'identity' is often taken to be the same thing as uniqueness and individuality; you might test this out by looking in a thesaurus for synonyms of the word 'identity'. The extent to which this search for individuality is a universal goal of development has, however, been questioned (Guisinger and Blatt, 1994). Studies from **anthropology** have suggested that this Western view, with its emphasis on the distinctiveness of the individual from others, differs from that of other cultures. There is evidence that non-Western cultures have a more socially centred ideal of the person that plays down, rather than draws attention to, the distinction between the self and others (Kim and Berry, 1993). This has led some psychologists to challenge the tradition of emphasising the importance of the development of the self, and of identity over the development of social relations (Guisinger and Blatt, 1994). Indeed, there is evidence that connectedness in the form of family relationships and friendships can enhance the search for identity in adolescence (Kamptner, 1988).

Developing peer relationships

During adolescence the development of peer relationships continues the trends started in childhood. In particular, the trend towards spending increasing amounts of time with peers persists in adolescence. It has been estimated that, in late adolescence, excluding time spent in the classroom, teens spend almost a third (29 per cent) of their waking hours with peers, more than double the amount spent with parents and other adults (13 per cent) (Csikszentmihalyi and Larson, 1984). Adolescent peer interaction also takes place with less adult supervision than in childhood.

Friendships are also gradually becoming more stable during this period (Epstein, 1986), although they may be disrupted by transitions such as changing class or school (Wargo Aikins et al., 2005). However, high-quality friendships, which are marked by intimacy, openness and warmth, are more likely to be maintained despite such transitions (Wargo Aikins et al., 2005). Indeed, there is an increased emphasis on intimacy and self-disclosure throughout adolescence (Zarbatany et al., 2000), although there is some evidence to suggest that greater levels of intimacy are reported by girls than by boys (Buhrmester, 1996). This increasing intimacy and self-disclosure has been suggested to be fundamentally important for the adolescent's developing sense of self, as well as for the understanding of relationships (Parker and Gottman, 1989).

Sense of self is also thought to be influenced by adolescent involvement in **cliques and crowds**. According to Erikson (1950), community membership is central to the achievement of identity as it requires solidarity with a group's ideals. Identification with cliques and crowds is argued to help adolescents defend themselves against the loss of identity that may be provoked by the identity crisis. Thus, adolescents deal with the difficulties they experience in committing to adult identities (the identity crisis) by making exaggerated commitments to certain style groups and by separating themselves from other style groups. They may use particular kinds of clothes and music to indicate their unique style and how it differentiates them from other groups. These cliques and crowds, clearly identified by their own set of style, values and norms, are what we often now refer to as 'youth culture'. According to Miles et al. (1998), identifying with youth culture gives adolescents some power over their identity in a rapidly changing world. Paradoxically, by playing the conformity game, adolescents become more able to feel unique and different.

Youth culture is a relatively modern phenomenon thought to be brought about by a specific historical and economic context. As the school-leaving age (for compulsory education) increased during the second half of the twentieth century, so the transition period between childhood and adulthood lengthened. At the same time, young people had increasingly larger financial resources available to them, which gave them consumer power. Recently, studies of youth culture have suggested that such consumption is central to the construction of adolescent identities (Phoenix, 2005). Many such studies have focused on the links between consumption, style and identity, and have concluded that style provides an essential way of defining and sustaining group boundaries

(Croghan et al., 2006). Milner (2004) proposes that adolescents use their consumer power to gain a sense of acceptance and belonging with their peer group. However, the flip side of this is that failing to maintain such an identity can lead to problems such teasing, social exclusion and loss of status (Blatchford, 1998; Croghan et al., 2006). Given that such consumption is often linked to particular brands, an important issue to consider here is how economic disadvantage might make a difference to adolescent popularity. Some evidence suggests that not having enough money to afford the 'right' brands can lead to social exclusion, as brand items serve as markers of group inclusion that have to be genuine and could not be faked (Croghan et al. 2006). Adolescents in this study saw cheap versions of designer goods as a sign of style error, making group membership expensive. Other studies (e.g. Milner, 2004) suggest that, rather than engaging in conflicts around style, young people may express solidarity with these cliques by modelling themselves on the popular groups, but resisting the consumption of brand-name goods, thereby establishing a new, less high-status group.

There is some evidence that this conformity and conflict over style groups become less marked after the age of about 16 years, with older adolescents claiming they no longer felt pressured into buying and wearing particular kinds of things (Miles, 2000). Miles suggests that this is part of maturing as a teenager, which may imply a developmental progression in thinking and identity formation. An alternative explanation is that, at this age, young people in the UK are leaving compulsory education, which brings with it a change in social status and context. This is as true for the young person who goes on to further education as it is for the one who takes the step into the workplace. The organisation of the sixth form, whether at school or at college, is very different from the education system experienced by 11–16 year olds: both the workplace and the sixth form college give more responsibility and independence to the young person themselves. Milner (2004) suggests that young people's relative powerlessness at school makes them particularly prone to focus on status hierarchies that are highly dependent on consumption. It may be that the age-related change in focus on consumption happens at the same time as a change in how young people are organised in the education system, as well as being a developmental shift.

Cognitive skills in adolescence

There is a lot of evidence to suggest that thinking changes during adolescence. The main shift seems to be in the ability to engage in more abstract thought and logical thinking. According to Piaget (1923), this reflects a qualitative change in thinking as the adolescent moves from the concrete to the formal operational stage. There is also evidence that changing cognitive skills reflect ongoing structural and functional brain development. Structural MRI (magnetic resonance imaging) studies, for example, have demonstrated that the brain undergoes considerable development during adolescence, particularly in the prefrontal cortex (e.g. Huttenlocher et al., 1983). It is thought that the production of synapses in the prefrontal cortex continues up until puberty, followed by synaptic pruning during adolescence. This is accompanied by an increase in myelination in this area of the cortex. These structural changes are believed to represent the fine-tuning of this brain circuitry, so increasing the efficiency of the cognitive systems it serves (Blakemore and Choudhury, 2006). There is also some suggestion that functioning in the frontal cortex increases with age (e.g. Rubia et al., 2000), although this has been challenged by some researchers (e.g. Durston et al., 2006). What seems most likely is that whether or not frontal activity increases depends on the function being investigated. The frontal lobes are involved in a range of tasks, including motor function, problem solving, spontaneity, memory, language, initiation, judgement, impulse control, and social and sexual behaviour. They are also sometimes considered to be our emotional control centre. Changes in frontal lobe functioning might therefore help explain many of the cognitive, social and emotional developments seen in adolescence.

Formal operational thinking and adolescent egocentrism

Cognitive skills become more logical in adolescents. While children tend to solve problems in a trial and error fashion, adolescents are more likely to develop plans to solve problems, testing possible solutions in a systematic and organised way. In addition, the ability to engage in abstract reasoning also increases; adolescent thinking is no longer tied to specific concrete examples as it was during late childhood, meaning that they can engage in **hypothetical-deductive reasoning**. This change in cognitive skills is reflected in the growing ability of adolescents to handle increasingly complex scientific and mathematical concepts.

This new way of thinking also underlies the ability of the adolescent to engage in introspection and self-reflection, which, according to some theorists, results in heightened self-consciousness (Elkind, 1978). Elkind called this phenomenon *adolescent egocentrism*, suggesting that this governs the way in which adolescents think about social matters. According to this theory, adolescents believe that others are as interested in them as they are in themselves and in their sense of personal uniqueness. Two aspects of **adolescent egocentrism** have been described.

- *The imaginary audience*: this is where adolescents believe themselves to be 'at centre stage'. Everyone else's attention is riveted on them.

- *The personal fable*: this underpins the adolescent sense of personal uniqueness and invincibility. No one else can possibly understand how they really feel; furthermore, although others may be vulnerable to misfortune, they are not.

An important aspect of the personal fable – a sense of invulnerability – is suggested to be the cause of adolescent risk taking: drug use, smoking, unprotected sex, drinking and so on (Alberts et al., 2007). According to Arnett (1992), risky behaviour in adolescence may well result from a combination of cognitive factors: a feeling of invincibility combined with flawed probability reasoning – the idea that 'It will never happen to me.'

Moral development

Another important aspect of cognitive development that is thought to reach maturity in adolescence is our understanding of morality or what is right or wrong. According to Piaget (1923), understanding of right and wrong reflects increasing sophistication in a child's thinking processes: children under four years of age have no understanding of morality; between the ages of four and seven years, children believe that rules and justice are unchangeable and beyond the control of the individual, and they also judge whether an action is right or wrong by its consequences (**heteronomous morality**); from seven to ten years of age, children are in transition, showing some features of heteronomous morality and **autonomous morality**; finally, at around the ages of ten to 12 years, children's understanding shifts to autonomous morality, recognising that rules are created by people and that intentions are as important as consequences. Piaget believed that, in addition to increasing cognitive abilities, moral development relies on peer relationships. Through the give and take of social interactions and playing games, children experience disagreements that have to be solved, and learn to negotiate the rules of a game, which teaches them to recognise that rules are man-made rather than handed down from a greater authority.

Piaget's theory of moral development was developed further by Lawrence Kohlberg during the 1950s (Kohlberg, 1958). According to Kohlberg, there are three universal levels of moral development, each divided into two stages (see Table 6.2). Initially, children make judgements about right or wrong based solely on how actions will affect them. However, over time they recognise that they may need to take others' needs into account when determining what is right or wrong. Finally, it is recognised that morality concerns a set of standards and principles that account for human rights, not individual needs. Kohlberg suggested that most adolescents reach level II and most of us stay at this level of reasoning during adulthood. Only a few individuals reach the post-conventional level of reasoning; indeed, Kohlberg found stage 6 to be so rare that it has since been removed from the theory.

Evidence supports the view that children and adolescents progress through the stages Kohlberg suggested, even if they may not reach the level of post-conventional reasoning (Flavell et al., 1993; Walker, 1989). Cross-cultural studies also provide some evidence for the universality of Kohlberg's first four stages (Snarey et al., 1985). However, this theory is not without its critics and Kohlberg's model has been accused of both cultural and gender biases.

It has been suggested that Kohlberg's theory is culturally biased because it emphasises ideals such as individual rights and social justice, which are found mainly in Western cultures (Shweder, 1994). Miller and Bersoff (1992) showed that Americans placed greater value on a justice orientation (stage 4) than Indians. In contrast, Indians placed a greater weight on interpersonal responsibilities, such as upholding one's obligations to others and being responsive to other people's needs (stage 3). In the same way, it has been noted that women are more likely to use stage 3 than stage 4 reasoning. According to Gilligan (1982, 1996), the ordering of the stages therefore reflects

Table 6.2: Kohlberg's stages of moral development

Level and stage		Description
Level I: preconventional reasoning	Stage 1: heteronomous morality	Moral behaviour is tied to punishment. Whatever is rewarded is good; whatever is punished is bad. Children obey because they fear punishment.
	Stage 2: individualism, instrumental purpose and exchange	Pursuit of individual interests is seen as the right thing to do. Behaviour is therefore judged good when it serves personal needs or interests. Reciprocity is viewed as a necessity: I'll do something good for you if you do something good for me. Fairness means treating everyone the same.
Level II: conventional reasoning	Stage 3: mutual interpersonal expectations, relationships and interpersonal conformity	Trust, caring and loyalty are valued and seen as the basis for moral judgements. Children and adolescents may adopt the moral standards of their parents in order to be seen as 'good' boys or girls.
	Stage 4: social systems morality	Good is defined by the laws of society, by doing one's duty. A law should be obeyed even if it's not fair. Rules and laws are obeyed because they are needed to maintain social order. Justice must be seen to be done.
Level III: post-conventional reasoning	Stage 5: social contract and individual rights	Values, rights and principles transcend the law. Good is understood in terms of the values and principles that the society has agreed upon. The validity of laws is evaluated and it is believed that these should be changed if they do not preserve and protect fundamental human rights and values.
	Stage 6: universal ethical principles	At this stage the individual has developed an internal moral code based on universal values and human rights that takes precedence over social rules and laws. When faced with a conflict between law and conscience, conscience will be followed even though this may involve personal risk.

a gender bias. Placing abstract principles of justice (stage 4) above relationships and concern for others (stage 3) is based on a male **norm** and reflects the fact that most of Kohlberg's research used male participants. Gilligan therefore argues that these orientations are indeed different, but that one is not necessarily better than the other. However, there is some debate about the extent of the evidence to support Gilligan's claims of gender differences in moral reasoning; a **meta-analysis** of the evidence by Jaffee and Hyde (2000) found that gender differences in reasoning were small and usually better explained by the nature of the dilemma than by gender. The evidence now seems to suggest that care-based reasoning is used by both males and females to evaluate interpersonal dilemmas, while justice reasoning is applied to societal dilemmas.

Kohlberg has also been criticised for not differentiating reasoning about morality from reasoning about social conventions. In his **domain theory**, Turiel (1983) argues that the child's concepts of morality and social convention develop from the recognition that certain actions or behaviours are intrinsically harmful and that these are therefore different from other actions that have social consequences only. For example, hitting another person has intrinsic effects (the harm that is caused) on the well-being of the other person. Such intrinsic effects occur regardless of any social rules that may or may not be in place concerning hitting. The core features of moral cognition are therefore centred around thinking about the impact of actions on well-being, and morality is structured by concepts of harm, welfare and fairness. In contrast, actions that are matters of social convention have no intrinsic interpersonal consequences. For example, in school, children usually address their teacher using their title and surname (e.g. 'Mr Smith'). However, there is no intrinsic reason that this is any better than addressing the teacher by their first name (e.g. 'Joe'). Only social convention – a rule agreed by society – makes 'Mr Smith' more appropriate than 'Joe'. These conventions are arbitrary in the sense that they have no intrinsic status, but are important to the smooth functioning of the social group as they provide a way for members of society to coordinate their social exchanges. Understanding of convention is therefore linked to the child's understanding of social organisation. Recent research into children's beliefs about social exclusion suggests that children are able to separate these two aspects of moral reasoning, but that their ability to tell the difference between morality and social convention increases during adolescence (Killen and Stangor, 2001; Killen, 2007).

Storm and stress

Traditionally, adolescence has been depicted as a tumultuous period, full of chaos and confusion caused by the 'raging hormones' brought about by puberty (Hall, 1904). Indeed, as you learned earlier in this chapter, adolescence involves major physical transitions that include growth spurts, sexual maturation, hormonal changes and neurological development, in particular in the frontal lobes, an area of the brain linked to impulse control. It has also been argued that, for adolescents in Western cultures, there is a disjunction between biology and society that has the potential to create a difficult transitional period: even when adolescents are physically mature enough to perform adult functions such as work and childbearing, they lack not only the psychological maturity, but also the social status and financial resources to perform those functions responsibly. This is because of the extended dependency brought about by social conventions such as the school-leaving age. Indeed, Anna Freud regarded any adolescent who did not experience emotional upheaval as 'abnormal' (Freud, 1958).

However, this image of the troubled or delinquent teenager was challenged as early as 1928 by Margaret Mead, who presented an account of the coming of age for Samoan adolescents that showed a very gradual and smooth transition from childhood to adulthood. The debate about storm and stress in adolescents is frequently mentioned in the literature (e.g., Arnett, 1999); however, it seems that very few developmental psychologists still support this view. The consensus is that most of us negotiate adolescence with few serious personal or social problems. Coleman (1978) proposed a focal theory of adolescence, which suggests that each of the many personal and social issues that have to be dealt with in adolescence come to the teenager's attention at different times. In this way, adolescents do not have to cope with many issues at once. They are able to deal with issues of identity individually and the task is therefore a manageable one. It is only where issues come to a head all at one time that there will be a crisis in adolescence. There is evidence that, for a minority of adolescents, this developmental period can indeed be very troubling. However, it is important to recognise that those children who do have an emotional time in adolescence usually have some pre-existing emotional problem (Graham and Rutter, 1985; White et al., 1990). Likewise, delinquent teenagers are likely to have had behavioural problems as children (Bates, 2003). All of which perhaps points to adolescence intensifying existing predispositions, not creating new ones.

Critical thinking activity

Developing scientific thinking

Critical thinking focus: critical and creative thinking

Key question: *What are the main developmental tasks of adolescence?*

As you learned in this chapter, the changes that confront individuals beginning their second decade of life are complex. Adolescence is marked by a number of changes – biological, physical, intellectual and emotional. These tasks are challenging, but not impossible, even though to the adolescent they may at times feel overwhelming. What do you think are the main developmental tasks of adolescence? Using both the information, in this chapter and any of the reading you have done around this topic, produce a detailed list of the problems teenagers might face. Using this information create a brief guide for parents on 'How to support your teenager'. This can be in any format, from a leaflet to a website, but must be written with the audience in mind.

Critical thinking review

This activity helps you understand the main developments that take place in adolescence and the importance of social context – including family relationships – for that development. Reflecting on the role that parents can play in ameliorating the impact of adolescent changes requires you to think critically about the evidence that we have to support different theoretical views of development. This task demands that you then put this knowledge into a format that enables other people who have no psychology training to access that information. Doing this successfully requires a creative approach – you need to inform without either patronising or going over the heads of your audience. Communicating what you know to others also helps consolidate your understanding of key periods of development such as adolescence.

Other skills you may have used in this activity include recall of key principles and ideas, applying theory to real-life contexts, communication and (depending on the format chosen) presentation skills.

Skill builder activity

The development of self-concept

Transferable skill focus: understanding and using (qualitative) data

Key question: *Read the following written descriptions of self from individuals of different ages. Once you have read these extracts, try to decide from the information given what age group the writer is in – are they an adult, adolescent or child? Now try applying Rosenberg's identity categories (see pages 115–16, including Table 6.2) to this data. Does this alter your perception of the writer at all? Can you see a developmental progression in the understanding of self mirrored by the self-descriptions provided here? Which writer gave the most physical description and which gave the most character-based description?*

Extract A

I am a sister and I am big. I am Indian and English. I like playing football with Johan. I like doing work stuff because learn things are good. I'm really good at maths but get stuck on telling the time. I like reading and doing jigsaws. My hobby is making models. I get most everything that I need. I've lots of friends, because at my school we are all friendly. I love playing schools; it is my favourite game because I can teach children how to do things. I've got pets and I have to look after them. I love animals. I love rabbits and guinea pigs and dogs most of all.

Extract B

I am generally a happy go lucky person. I try and always look on the positives of life – my glass is always half full. In that way I am very different to other members of my family. My sister for example is very pessimistic, always anticipating the worst. She says she just a realist, but sometimes I think you can make your own luck up to a point. I don't really have many hobbies – I'm not very sporty but I do like swimming. I suppose I'm just not a very competitive person. What I real like to do is settle down with a good book and I can spend hour reading if it's a good story line that really gets me hooked. Like with Harry Potter – I just didn't want to put it down. Just wanted to finish it all in one go. Not that I am anti-social. I do like to go out with friends as well – we might go to the cinema or shopping, or sometimes we just hang out at someone's house – that's my favourite pastime, spending an afternoon catching up with friends. Gossiping my boyfriend calls it. I guess it's just a girl thing!

Extract C

I enjoy playing sport, in particular cricket, tennis and hockey. I also quite like to walk and cycle and I like to relax with a good fantasy or sci-fi book or listen to some music. I occasionally listen to something quiet and classical, but I prefer rock. I follow a football team heavily and I listen to any match or buy any books on the subject. I tend to take life as it comes rather than plan ahead which makes me a bit disorganised – as other people keep telling me! I am quite committed at things when I want to be. Overall I tend to be happy, but at times I can get frustrated with my other people and get depressed. I have one very close best friend and a few other good friends. Over the last few years my personality has changed drastically and although I am happier with my new 'image' than I was before I still feel the need to find my true personality, if this is possible, and to define myself. It is difficult not to do this by fitting into a stereotype, as I see many people doing, where the way they dress, their way of talking and even their values are defined by something as immaterial as their taste in music. I think quite deeply about my personality. From talking to my friends I think I am fairly unusual in this. Most people seem to take the way they are for granted whereas I see myself as having to work at myself to find a state in which I am happy.

Skill builder review

The focus of this task is the way in which self-descriptions might reflect inner beliefs about self. There are, however, a number of things to consider when evaluating the data provided above. First, what impact might the media (written self-report) have had on the descriptions that are given by these individuals? What advantages and disadvantages are there in using written self-report? What other mode of data collection (e.g. verbal report or interview) might have been used and would this have overcome any of the problems you thought were associated with written reports? Second, the use of a predefined scheme can feel very artificial when coding qualitative data. Another approach might have been to have looked to see what themes came out of each report. You might want to try reanalysing the data at some point using this method. It is possible that some of the themes that emerge from the data are similar to those identified by Rosenberg; however, it is also likely that you will be able to think of new ways of representing this data as well.

Assignments

1. Critically evaluate the theory that adolescence is a time of storm and stress.

2. Critically discuss the Kohlberg's theory of moral development.

3. To what extent does the evidence support the idea that identity development must take place in adolescence?

Summary: what you have learned

Now you have finished studying this chapter you should:

- demonstrate understanding of the main developmental tasks of adolescence;

- be able to evaluate critically theories concerning the development of sense of self, and understand the relationship between self-esteem, identity and relationships with others;

- be able to use your knowledge of adolescent development to discuss critically storm and stress theory;

- have developed your critical and creative thinking skills by applying your knowledge of adolescent development to an applied task;

- have developed your ability to understand and use qualitative data by applying a simple coding scheme to a set of written self-reports and reflecting on other approaches to such data collection and analysis.

Further reading

Arnett, J (1999) Adolescent storm and stress, reconsidered. *American Psychologist*, 54: 317–26. Available online at http://uncenglishmat.weebly.com/uploads/1/4/3/4/1434319/arnett.pdf.

Discusses traditional views of adolescence.

Casey,BJ, Giedd, JN and Thomas, KM (2000) Structural and functional brain development and its relation to cognitive development. *Biological Psychology*, 54, 241–57. Available online at www.med info.hacettepe.edu.tr/tebad/umut_docs/interests/fmr/aging/MAIN_structural_fonctional.pdf.

Considers links between neurological structures, brain function and cognitive skills.

Miles, S, Cliff, D and Burr, V (1998) 'Fitting in and sticking out': consumption, consumer meanings and the construction of young people's identities, *Journal of Youth Studies*, 1: 81–91.

Good discussion of the relationship between consumerism and identity development in adolescence.

Phoenix, A (2005) Young people and consumption: commonalities and differences in the construction of identities, in Tufte, B, Rasmussen, J and Christensen LB (eds) *Frontrunners or Copycats?* Copenhagen: Copenhagen Business School Press, pp79–95.

This also looks at consumption identity, but from a very British perspective.

Turiel, E (2008) The development of children's orientations toward moral, social, and personal orders: more than a sequence in development. *Human Development*, 51: 21–39. Available online at http://jpkc.ecnu.edu.cn/fzxlx/jiaoxue/The%20Development%20of%20Children%E2%80%99s%20Orientations.pdf.

Describes Turiel's theory of moral development.

Chapter 7

Adulthood

Learning outcomes

By the end of this chapter you should:

- *understand the way in which cognitive abilities change across adulthood;*
- *be able to evaluate the idea that midlife crisis is inevitable;*
- *be able to discuss critically the relationship between physical ageing and psychological well-being in adulthood;*
- *critically understand the impact of social and cultural beliefs on adult experiences;*
- *have developed your critical and creative thinking skills;*
- *have developed your problem solving and communication.*

Introduction

Developmental psychologists usually agree that, in Western industrialised societies, young people enter adulthood between the ages of 18 and 20 years. Unlike adolescence, which is usually heralded by the onset of puberty, adulthood has no obvious physical marker to announce its arrival. However, most people reach their final height at this age and our organs and body systems have also reached maturity (Wold, 2004). In addition, there are cultural, social and psychological markers that help determine the shift to adulthood, as you shall learn later in this chapter, and these may differ across cultures.

For many years, middle adulthood has been described in the literature as beginning at 40 years of age. Indeed, current average life expectancy in the UK is 80 years (ONS, 2010), making 40 years the midpoint of life. However, life expectancy in the UK has almost doubled over the past century and attitudes towards ageing have changed considerably, meaning that identifying middle age in social and psychological terms is becoming much harder. For example, a recent UK survey (Abrams et al., 2009) found that, while most people (71 per cent) agreed that youth ends at 45 years, individuals aged 50–60 years were less likely to identify with their age groups than younger and older people. You are probably aware of the attention that middle age gets in the popular press, with discussions about midlife crisis and whether or not celebrities such as Madonna are middle-aged at 50 years. However, in terms of research, middle age is a relatively neglected period of the lifespan, although this is starting to change (Brim et al., 2004). One reason for the increased interest in middle age is the fact that one of the largest *cohorts* in European and North American history – the post-war baby boomers born between 1946 and 1964 – are now in their forties, fifties and sixties, meaning that there are more middle-aged people in Europe, the UK and the USA than ever before. In addition, this is the best-educated, richest and fittest cohort to pass through middle age (Martin and Willis, 2005; Metz and Underwood, 2005).

Older adulthood is usually described as beginning at approximately 65 years of age, although, once again, attitudes to ageing are changing as people live longer: Abrams et al. (2009) found that, on average, old age was defined as starting at 63 years; however, older individuals, in particular women, were more likely to say that old age started later than this, placing it at over 70 years. This chapter explores the age-related changes that can be seen across adulthood in all areas of functioning, including physical, cognitive, social and emotional well-being. However, it begins by considering the social and cultural factors that surround the transition from adolescence to adulthood.

Emerging adulthood

The process of moving from adolescence to adulthood is marked by continuity for most individuals: well-adjusted adolescents continue to be well-adjusted as adults and troubled adolescents become troubled adults (Schulenberg et al., 2006). However, for some people, the move to adulthood is less straightforward and the increased responsibility and independence of adulthood prove to be difficult to cope with; for others, this shift is a positive one that provides them with the opportunity to get their lives together (Schulenberg et al., 2004). It is now increasingly recognised that the transition into adulthood is a critical point in the lifespan (Arnett, 2004, 2006). This, coupled with a growing trend for young people to delay their entry into the adult world, has led to the introduction of the term 'emerging adulthood' to describe the period between adolescence and adulthood (Arnett, 2004, 2006).

This period is usually described as ranging from 18 to 25 years of age and is characterised by exploration and experimentation with identity, lifestyle and career (Arnett, 2006). Arnett also describes emerging adults as able to be self-focused because they have few duties or commitments to others (for example, no children or ageing parents to look after). Emerging adulthood is an age of possibilities, with many young people optimistic about their plans for the future (Arnett, 2006). Furthermore, the changes associated with emerging adulthood present many young people with the opportunity to turn their lives around and follow a more positive course (Schulenberg and Zarrett, 2006). Most young people of this age do not see themselves as fully fledged adults – however, they do not feel like adolescents either (Arnett, 2000). So why do so many young people feel like 'in-betweeners'?

According to Kefalas et al. (2005), the idea that adolescence can bridge the gap between childhood and adulthood no longer works in modern society, where the timing and sequencing of traditional experiences that represent the process of becoming an adult, such as leaving home, finishing school, starting work and getting married/ having children, are more flexible than they used to be. Social norms and expectations in relation to all these processes have changed dramatically since the post-war years. In the UK, for example, there is an expectation that more young people will stay in education for longer and this is encouraged by government policy that aims to promote post-16 education (DfES, 2007). This social change is in response to economic changes in the nature of available employment, in turn influenced by changes in the labour market; increasing technologies have, for example, changed the emphasis in the skills needed for jobs in the UK in the twenty-first century (Friedberc, 2008). This need for longer education has meant that many young people delay their entry into the economic market, which leads in turn to financial independence being delayed until their early or mid-twenties for many young people today (Cohen et al., 2003).

This often means that young people are still living in the family home in their early twenties (Heath, 2008). This increased dependency on parents for housing is a well-recognised feature of emerging adulthood. However, the reason for this dependency is not just financial. There appear to be a number of demographic factors that influence this dependency, including gender and social class. Males are much more likely to be still living at home in their early twenties than females: in the UK in 2006, for example, 58 per cent of young men aged 20–24 years and 39 per cent of young women of the same age were still living with their parents (Heath, 2008). According to Heath (2008), young people from middle-class families also tend to leave home at a younger age than their peers from working-class families, usually because they are more likely to go to university at the age of 18, although many return once they have completed their studies (Ford et al., 2002). Even if they do go to university, students from working-class backgrounds are more likely than their middle-class peers to remain living at home with their parents (Patiniotis and Holdsworth, 2005).

It does seem from this that practical issues such as financial independence are an important part of feeling like an adult. However, other more cognitive factors, such as the ability to make independent decisions, have also been identified (Shulman and Ben-Artzi, 2003). Sassler et al. (2008) interviewed young adults who had recently returned to live in the family home and found that adulthood was perceived as a psychological state. According to this view, adulthood is reached once an individual feels able to assume responsibility for their actions and feels capable of interacting with other adults (especially their parents) as equals (Sassler et al., 2008).

Entering adulthood is therefore about much more than physical maturity or reaching a specific chronological age. Becoming an adult means being independent in psychological as well as economic terms. The point at which a young person enters adulthood will therefore be determined by choices about whether or not to go on to college or university, as well as individual differences in psychological development. Cultural expectations and beliefs about adulthood are also going to be important: in developing countries marriage is often a marker of entry into adulthood and this often occurs much earlier than in Western societies (Arnett, 2004).

Biological and physical changes in adulthood

It is easy to imagine that physical changes in adulthood are all about decline rather than development. However, this is not inevitable and when and if deterioration of physical abilities takes place depends on a number of factors other than biological age. These include lifestyle choices and demographic factors such as socio-economic status, job type and gender.

Typical physical changes

Young adults are in generally at the peak of physical fitness. Their bodies are at their strongest and healthiest with organ function at its prime. However, the ageing process has already begun. Indeed, the body has been ageing since birth – yet it is not until middle age that we begin to see the effects. Only minor physical changes are seen in the twenties and thirties, but many people begin to notice physical changes in their forties, one of the most noticeable of which is a loss of elasticity in the skin, especially in the face. This results in the lines and wrinkles that are seen as one of the first signs of ageing. Both genders may experience greying of the hair or the hair may thin. Weight changes typically seen across the lifespan include weight gain in middle age, followed by weight loss when people reach their sixties (Whitbourne, 2005).

Ageing involves a decline in efficiency in most bodily systems from the twenties onwards. Strength and flexibility begin to wane in both genders in middle age (Samson et al., 2000), motor performance slows (Newell et al., 2006) and reaction times decrease. However, it seems likely that avoiding a sedentary lifestyle will make such deterioration less marked (Earles and Salthouse, 1995). Research has found that moderate exercise and a healthy diet can protect against stroke, heart disease and late-onset dabetes (Yung et al., 2009). Women also experience the **menopause** – the hormonal changes that result in the loss of the ability to reproduce in middle to late adulthood. An increase in the incidence of chronic disease, such as osteoarthritis, hypertension and heart disease, is also seen in older adults.

Individual differences in ageing

Individual differences in physical functioning increase with age (Harris, 1992). Thus, measurements such as aerobic capacity, strength and reaction times vary more widely among 70 year olds than among 20 year olds. This is in part due to lifestyle choices – for example, physically active older adults are more likely to retain strength (Amara et al., 2003). This is perhaps not so surprising given that muscles atrophy if not used and the heart functions less well if the individual leads a sedentary life style (Rosenbloom and Bahns, 2006). Health problems may also contribute to differences in decline; a classic study in the 1960s showed how deterioration in physical and psychological functioning in men aged 65–91 was linked to **sub-clinical disease** (Birren et al., 1963). Socio-economic status is also often reported to make a difference to health and disability; studies using self-reported measures of health demonstrate greater problems among older people in dis-advantaged socio-economic groups (Marmot et al., 2001). This is usually believed to demonstrate the advantages of having greater material resources and opportunities to promote a healthy lifestyle.

The psychological impact of physical ageing

There are many negative stereotypes associated with ageing in our society. 'Old' is often associated with 'unattractive', meaning that adults of retirement age may see themselves as 'past it' or as a drain on society. There is an increasing drive to maintain physical looks through interventions such as cosmetic surgery (Rohrich, 2000), although, as Grossbart and Sarwer (2003) note, it is likely that cosmetic surgery patients are looking for more than changes in their physical appearance. What happens if these procedures do not lead to improvements in body satisfaction, self-esteem or quality of life? Interestingly, there is evidence that cultural attitudes towards the physical changes of ageing can influence the way in which these are experienced. The female menopause is a universal phenomenon, for example, but there are differences in how this is experienced; hot flushes are more likely to be reported and viewed as a negative experience in Western cultures, where the menopause is viewed as a loss, than in cultures where the menopause represents a healthy, positive life stage (Flint, 1982; McMaster et al., 1997; Gold et al., 2000). Indeed, attitudes towards the menopause help explain individual differences in the experience of the menopause in Western society; while some view this as a medical condition to be treated by medication, others see it as a normal transition (Alder et al., 2000).

The majority of people have some kind of chronic physical health problem by the time they reach 65. However, there is enormous variability in terms of the impact that such health problems have on individual functioning. While the level of chronicity will influence this, there is also evidence that individual differences such as personality and attitude can mediate the impact of these illnesses on feelings of well-being. For example, optimistic individuals with a positive outlook on life have been found to live longer (Snowdon, 2002).

Relationships and psychological adjustment to physical health

In early adulthood, an individual is concerned with developing the ability to share intimacy, seeking to form relationships and find intimate love. Not surprisingly, the trend towards greater intimacy with the opposite sex that began in adolescence continues in early adulthood (Reis et al., 1993). Long-term relationships are formed, and often marriage (or cohabitation) and children result. Young adults tend to have more friends than middle-aged or older adults. As adults marry, have children and take on increasing responsibilities in other areas of life as well, so their social networks shrink (Fischer et al., 1989). This has been suggested to be a choice made by older adults to fulfil an emotional need (Carstensen, 1992). According to socio-emotional selectivity theory, the realisation that life is decreasing prompts adults to narrow their choice of social partners to those who bring most emotional pleasure, usually family and close friends (Carstensen, 1992). However, friendships do remain important across the lifespan, even if greater selectivity is shown. Indeed, the quality of friendships is closely related to well-being in adulthood (Pinquart and Sorensen, 2000) and the importance of a supportive social network for physical as well as psychological health has been noted (Charles and Mavandadi, 2004). Indeed, there is evidence to link having a small harmonious group of friends with better cardiovascular, endocrine and immune systems.

How might having good friends and happy family relationships keep blood pressure in the normal range and improve the body's ability to deal with stress (Uchino et al., 1996)? According to Charles and Mavandadi (2004), emotional and social functioning are closely linked, even in infancy, and the two are codependent. Social relationships affect health and well-being through the effects they have on emotional regulation. Negative features such as separation from caregivers, abuse and emotional deprivation raise stress levels in infants, which disrupts neural development, making these individuals more susceptible to stress in later life (Gunnar and Quevedo, 2007). In contrast, warm, responsive parenting helps infants cope with stressful events and, in the same way, close relations in later life help people keep their emotions in check and avoid stress-related illness (Charles and Mavandadi, 2004).

Cognitive changes in adulthood

Post-formal thought

Piaget's theory of cognitive development focused very clearly on the years of childhood and adolescence. However, we now recognise that cognitive development goes beyond this and a fourth stage of cognitive development has been suggested by a number of theorists (e.g. Commons et al., 1984; Simmott, 1994; Yan and Arlin, 1995). Called 'post-formal thought', this stage has been suggested to be typified by **relativistic thinking**, whereby adults recognise that knowledge depends on the subjective perspective of each individual and that there is, therefore, no absolute truth; problems can be viewed in different ways and there may be more than one solution to a problem.

Perry (1970) studied cognitive growth in college students and found that there was a shift from the initial assumption when entering college that there was an absolute truth to be found, to a gradual recognition that questions might have many answers. This led to the confusion of not knowing which was the 'right answer'. Eventually, however, many understood that some opinions are better supported than others and were able to commit to one position by choosing among the relative perspectives. Thus, we move from absolutist to relativist thinking and, according to some theorists, this results in the use of a greater variety of thinking styles (Zhang, 2002). Furthermore, it is suggested that advanced thinkers relish the challenge of finding the paradoxes and inconsistencies in ideas so as to attempt to reconcile them (Basseches, 1984).

There is therefore evidence to suggest that our thinking may develop beyond the stages outlined by Piaget. However, the extent to which this is a developmental sequence is subject to debate. This type of thinking has only been demonstrated in a minority of adults – particularly those who have experienced higher education – suggesting an important role for experience in developing adult thinking skills (Sinnott, 1996). However, the predominance of this type of thinking in those individuals experiencing higher education does not mean that only an educated few are able to engage in higher-level reasoning. It may be that sophisticated reasoning manifests itself in different ways and that these studies are only demonstrating one type of advanced thinking, linked to a particular set of experiences. Indeed, the evidence supports an important role for context in adult cognitive development that goes beyond the formal educational setting. Adults have been shown to function cognitively at their highest in areas in which they have developed some expertise (Byrnes, 1996). Indeed, 'experts' not only know and remember more about their specialist areas, they are also more effective and efficient thinkers (Proffitt et al., 2000). It may therefore be that a university education simply trains graduates to be experts in relativistic thinking.

Focus on: post-formal thought

Task — Read the following paper:

Kitchener, KS, Lynch, CL, Fischer, KW and Wood, PK (1993) Developmental range of reflective judgment: the effect of contextual support and practice on developmental stage. *Developmental Psychology*, 29: 893–906. Available online at https://gseweb. harvard.edu/~ddl/articlesCopy/Kitchener-etal1993DevRangeReflectJudgem.pdf.

Kitchener and colleagues, like many other theorists working in this area, suggest that an age-related trend can be seen in the development of reflective judgement, a skill thought to be linked to relativistic thinking. However, as Kitchener notes, in this study age may in fact be confounded by experience.

- How strong do you think the evidence provided in this paper is for a developmental progression in reflective judgement and relativistic thinking?

- What other factors do Kitchener and colleagues suggest might influence this change in thinking?

- Are any of these suggestions ones that should be given greater consideration?

Comment

The difficulty with this study is the relationship between age and educational experience. A correlation between increasing age and increasing higher educational experience is clear, making it impossible to say definitively that increasing relativistic thinking is linked to age. It would be necessary to study young adults not engaged in higher education to see if this really is an age-related change. Furthermore, the authors state that their findings have implications for the teaching of reflective skills and suggest that certain skills cannot be taught until the early twenties, implying a need for 'cognitive readiness'. This seems a giant leap, given the need for caution concerning the potential role for experience in the development of relativistic thinking.

Ageing and cognitive skills

There is some evidence to support the suggestion that mental abilities decline with age; elderly adults have been found to perform more poorly than younger adults on Piagetian cognitive tasks, for example (Blackburn and Papalia, 1992). However, there is some debate about the extent to which this decline is an inevitable part of ageing. It has been proposed, for example, that this difference is actually caused by a cohort effect, brought about because the older adults who participated in these studies generally had less formal schooling than most younger adults today. The reason for these findings is therefore suggested to lie in the cross-sectional design of the study. Indeed, other studies that have taken a longitudinal approach have found that cognitive skills either stay stable or improve over time (Salthouse, 2009). This idea is also supported by studies that have shown that older adults in college perform as well as their younger classmates on cognitive tests (Blackburn, 1985). However, it has also been suggested that cognitive decline actually begins in early adulthood (Salthouse, 2009), although not all aspects of cognitive functioning are thought to show early age-related declines.

Salthouse (2009) argues that longitudinal studies also suffer from a methodological problem – practice effects. According to Salthouse, the very fact that an individual has already been tested on a cognitive task could change their performance the next time they are tested – they have learned how to do the task and so will find it easier and perform better. If Salthouse is right, the age trends seen in longitudinal comparisons are misleading: we do not actually get better at cognitive tasks as we age, but because of learning and experience. According to Salthouse, this makes cross-sectional comparisons better measures of age-related change because they do not involve testing the same individuals again. This demonstrates very clearly the way in which the method chosen by a researcher can influence the outcomes of a study. As you learned in Chapter 1, there is often more than one way of designing a study and there is rarely a 'right' way. Usually a researcher has to decide which method will give the best answer to a question by considering which variables are most important to control for and what margin of error they are prepared to accept. Which approach do you think is best in this case? Is it better to risk the influence of practice by carrying out a longitudinal study in which the same people repeat the same measures over time? The advantage of this is, of course, that participants act as their own control and any between-subject external factors such as differences in gender, socio-economic status and educational experience are eliminated. Or is it more important to ensure that the effects of practice are controlled by using a cross-sectional design, which holds the possibility of cohort effects?

Salthouse (2009) is right to raise the possibility of practice effects as they are certainly a possibility with longitudinal studies. However, does that really mean that the findings of longitudinal studies are of no value? Possibly not, as what this actually suggests is that practice might have a protective role for cognitive functioning. This is given further support by cognitive training studies, which have shown that cognitive decline in older people can be reversed in many cases (Blaskewicz Boron et al., 2007). Perhaps cognitive decline is caused by a lack of use? This is what Bielak (2010) calls the 'use it or lose it' hypothesis of cognitive ageing.

If Salthouse (2009) is right and our cognitive skills do decline over time, it is important to know when that decline begins so that appropriate interventions can be put in place. If he is right that decline begins quite early in adulthood, perhaps programmes need to be preventative. It is also important to know what declines: according to Salthouse, functioning based on accumulated knowledge, such as performance on tests of vocabulary or general information (known as **crystallised abilities**) are consistently found to increase until at least the age of 60.

One of the largest studies of age-related changes in functioning, the Seattle Longitudinal Study (e.g. Schaie, 2006; Willis and Schaie, 2006), has suggested that there is no uniform pattern of age-related changes across all intellectual abilities. The study findings suggest that both cohort and age effects are important in determining changes in cognitive ability across the lifespan. This body of work also confirms the trend observed by Salthouse (2009) that, in general, crystallised abilities tend to decline later than **fluid abilities** in intelligence. However, Willis and Schaie describe a number of cohort factors that complicate matters. For example, gender difference trends suggest that women decline earlier on active abilities, while men decline earlier on passive abilities.

Furthermore, changes in decline have been noted with different cohorts, highlighting the importance of the social (and historical) context for cognitive functioning (Schaie, 2006).

A number of factors have also been shown to reduce the risk of cognitive decline in old age, including the absence of cardiovascular and other chronic diseases (Wendell et al., 2009); higher socio-economic status (Fotenos et al., 2008); and involvement in a complex and intellectually stimulating environment (Valenzuela et al., 2007). It has also been suggested that the modern sedentary lifestyle may increase the ageing process; evidence from the British cohort study has shown that maintaining an active lifestyle can help to slow the process of cognitive decline linked to ageing (Richards et al., 2003).

Language and memory

Research on language development tends to focus on the changes that take place in infancy and childhood. The belief is that, in adulthood, language skills are maintained (Thornton and Light, 2006). However, there is evidence that language development continues even into late adulthood: vocabulary increases (Willis and Schaie, 2006) and older adults often maintain or even improve their knowledge of words and what they mean (Burke and Shafto, 2004).

However, some decline in language abilities may appear in late adulthood. This could link to physiological changes that take place in old age, such as hearing difficulties, which can lead to problems in distinguishing speech sounds (Gordon-Salant et al., 2006). Loss of memory skills may also result in problems with word retrieval; for example, the tip of the tongue phenomenon, which is typified by feeling confident that a word is known but is just out of reach (Thornton and Light, 2006). This decline is often compensated for by using very familiar words and much shorter sentences (Burke and Shafto, 2008). It may also explain the greater reliance on filled pauses, which is often seen in older adults (for example, saying 'um' or 'er'), which may provide a means of 'buying time' to retrieve the correct word.

The factors responsible for declining language skills in older people are likely to be general cognitive processing skills rather than language-specific ones (Obler, 2005). These include a decrease in information-processing speed and a decline in working memory that are often seen as people age (Waters and Caplan, 2005). It is easy to see how slower processing would increase the time taken to retrieve information from long-term memory, while poorer working memory would make it more difficult to keep information in mind while processing.

Ageing and the brain

Between the ages of 20 and 90, the brain shrinks, losing 5–10 per cent of its weight (Enzinger et al., 2005). A decrease in volume has also been observed; in one study the volume of the brains of older adults was around 15 per cent less than that of younger adults (Shan et al., 2005). In one study it was found that brain volume reduces by 0.22 per cent every year between the ages of 20 and 65, then by 0.40 per cent per year from 65 to 80 years of age (Fotenos et al., 2008). This is thought to be because of a combination of loss of dendrites, damage to myelin and the death of brain cells. Some areas of the brain shrink more than others as we age: the prefrontal cortex is one area that reduces in size and this has been linked to a decrease in cognitive function such as working memory (Grady et al., 2006).

Recent evidence has supported the idea that it is the structural changes in the brain that cause the loss of functioning (Fan et al., 2008). However, we do not really know whether brain shrinkage leads to cognitive decline or vice versa. It is possible that this cause and effect model is too simplistic, as it fails to consider a number of environmental factors that may influence the impact of any biologically based changes in brain structure. Fotenos et al. (2008) have found, for example, that there is a complex relationship between socio-economic status, structural changes in the brain and cognitive decline. Fotenos and colleagues carried out a large-scale neuro-imaging study in which adults aged between 20 and 80 underwent MRI scans and cognitive testing at the start of the study, then were retested and scanned three years later. The study found that, in older adults with no cognitive decline, those of higher socio-economic status showed more loss of brain volume when compared to individuals of lower socio-economic status. This does not mean that high socio-economic status is related to greater loss of brain volume, but rather that older adults from higher socio-economic groups respond differently to the same loss of brain volume than individuals from lower socio-economic backgrounds.

Normally, it is expected that high levels of loss of volume are linked to serious functional problems, such as those associated with **dementia**. Indeed, that is exactly the relationship seen in individuals of low to moderate socio-econiomic status. However, in individuals of higher socio-economic status, the same structural decline seems to be better tolerated – that is, it does not affect functioning. It has therefore been concluded that higher socio-economic status protects against cognitive decline. It is thought that one of the protective factors is a higher level of education. This is probably true: highly educated individuals are probably more likely to take part in complex intellectual activities even after retirement age and, as you have already learned, using cognitive functions protects against their loss. What other advantages might there be of having a higher socio-economic status that protects against cognitive decline, in particular the loss associated with dementia?

Dementia

Dementia is an umbrella term that is used to refer to any brain disorder in which the main symptoms include deterioration of mental functioning. Individuals with dementia often lose the ability to look after themselves. They may also no longer recognise familiar places or people, including close family members such as their children or a spouse (Clark, 2006). The most common form of dementia, accounting for between 50 and 70 per cent of all dementia, is Alzheimer's disease. Alzheimer's is progressive, meaning that it involves a gradual decline in skills. It is also irreversible. The disease is characterised by a gradual deterioration in memory, reasoning, language and eventually physical functioning. Most people with Alzheimer's are 65 and older, making it predominantly a disease of old age. However, up to 5 per cent of people with the disease have what is known as early-onset Alzheimer's: this form of the disease often appears when someone is in their forties or fifties. Many of the risk factors for Alzheimer's are ones we cannot change, such as age and genetics. However, it is now commonly believed that Alzheimer's disease occurs as a result of complex interactions among genes and other risk factors such as diet and lifestyle choices. This is another example of the diathesis-stress model discussed in Chapter 2 (page 32). This means that, in individuals with the genetic potential for Alzheimer's disease, certain environmental factors such as lifestyle choices may trigger the disease. Without those triggers the individual might not develop dementia; for example, it has been found that there is a link between obesity and Alzheimer's disease. Kivipelto et al. (2005, 2006) found obesity in middle age to be associated with an increased risk of dementia and Alzheimer's disease later in life. Other studies have suggested that health problems in middle age, such as high blood pressure and type 2 diabetes, also increase the risk for dementia, including Alzheimer's disease. Obesity, high blood pressure and diabetes are all health problems that can affect the heart and blood vessels and it is thought that, if the vessels in the brain are affected, this can result in dementia. It has also been found that older adults with Alzheimer's disease are more likely to have heart disease than individuals without Alzheimer's (Hayden et al., 2006). It therefore makes sense that avoiding the risk factors associated with heart disease, such as smoking, obesity and a sedentary lifestyle, might also protect against dementia.

Psychosocial development

Levinson's four seasons and the crisis of midlife

According to Levinson (1986, 1996), the lifespan can be divided into four seasons: pre-adulthood, early adulthood, middle adulthood and late adulthood (see Table 7.1). Each season or era lasts 20–25 years and has a distinct character. Thus, the transition between eras requires a basic change in the character of a person's life. This transition may take between three and six years to complete. Within the broad eras are periods of development, each of which is characterised by a set of tasks – for example, in the early adult transition period the two primary tasks are to move out of the pre-adult world and to make a preliminary step into the adult world. A major theme throughout the various periods is the existence of 'the dream' – a vision of life's goals. Levinson proposed that

Table 7.1: Levinson's stages of development

Stage	Age	Season	Characteristics
Pre-adulthood	0–17	**Spring**	Childhood and adolescence. During this time one usually lives with the family, which provides protection, socialisation, and support of growth.
Early adult transition	17–21		A period of questioning. Young people make the transition from adolescence to early adulthood and explore the possibilities for an adult identity. They form 'the dream' – a vision of their life goals.
Entering the adult world	22–28	**Summer**	Adults build their first life structure, often by making and testing a career choice and by getting married or forming a stable relationship. They work to succeed, find a supportive partner and/or mentor and do not question their lives much.
Age 30 transition	28–33		A period of questioning. Adults ask whether their life choices and relationships are what they want. If not, they may make small adjustments in their life structures or plan major changes such as a career change, divorce or return to education.
Settling down	33–40		This is a time for building and living a new and often different life and for 'making it' or realising 'the dream'. An adult may outgrow the need for a mentor and become his or her own person. Adults at this stage tend to be ambitious, task-oriented and unreflective.
Midlife transition	40–45	**Autumn**	This is a major period of questioning. Successful adults ask whether the dreams they formulated as young adults were worth achieving. If they have not achieved their dreams, they face the reality that they may never achieve them and may again make major changes in their life structure, terminate early adulthood and initiate middle adulthood.
Entering middle adulthood	45–50		Although a person's physical and mental powers are somewhat diminished after 40, they are normally still ample for 'an active, full life' throughout middle adulthood. If conditions for development are reasonably favourable, middle adulthood can be an era of personal fulfilment and social contribution. This requires that a person comes to terms with the three major developmental tasks of the midlife transition: (1) reviewing life in early adulthood and reappraising what he or she has done with it; (2) modifying the negative elements of the present Me structure and testing new choices; and (3) dealing with the polarities in his or her life.

Table 7.1: Continued

Stage	Age	Season	Characteristics
Age 50 transition	50–55		A period of questioning. A crisis is possible, especially if none occurred during the midlife transition.
Culmination of middle adulthood	55–60		A satisfying era (similar to the earlier settling down stage) if the person has adjusted to role changes.
Late adult transition	60–65	**Winter**	Time to prepare for retirement and coming physical decline, making this a major turning point.
Late adulthood	65–?		The person now creates a new life structure for retirement and ageing.

adults go through a repeated process of building a life structure, then assessing and altering it during transition periods. For Levinson, the transition from ages 40–45 is an especially significant time of life – a time of midlife crisis when a person questions his or her entire life structure, raising unsettling questions about where they have been and where they are heading. Levinson based his theory on a series of in-depth interviews and characterised 80 per cent of the men he studied as experiencing intense inner struggles and disturbing realisations in their early forties. Women, however, experience significant crisis during the transition at age 30, as well as in the transition to middle age. This theory is important because of the clear focus on adult development – along with Erikson, Levinson is perhaps the major theorist of this time period. But to what extent is his image of midlife crisis supported by the evidence?

Work, career and retirement

Levinson (1986, 1996) was correct in thinking that early adulthood is the time that we explore vocational possibilities. The evidence supports a process of making tentative commitments and revising them as necessary before establishing yourself in what you hope will be a suitable occupation (Super et al., 1996). Indeed, more than twice as many tentative and exploratory vocational decisions are seen at age 21 than at 36, and this is true for both men (Philips, 1982) and women (Jenkins, 1989). Careers tend to peak during the forties (Simonton, 1990), when there is a tendency for adults to define themselves in terms of their work. However, factors such as personality and gender seem to mediate career success; conscientiousness, extraversion and emotional stability are all associated with job performance (Ozer and Benet-Martinez, 2006) and, even at the start of the twenty-first century, many women still subordinate career goals to family ones (Kirchmeyer, 2006).

There is much less evidence to support Levinson's suggestion of a midlife crisis. Many studies support the idea that midlife is a time of self-reflection, and even a time when goals may change (Hermans and Oles, 1999). However, the image of the adult experiencing a crisis during midlife remains largely unsubstantiated (Hedlund and Ebersole, 1983).

As they age, many people show increased satisfaction with their jobs, are more involved in their work and are less interested in seeking out new jobs (Rhodes, 1983). This is in complete contrast to the image that many people have that, as adults age, they become less able to work. Indeed, the evidence suggests that older adults are as capable as their younger co-workers (Hansson et al., 1997). It is thought that this may well reflect the expertise acquired through 'on-the-job' experience (Hansson et al., 1997).

Ultimately, though, there comes a time at which all men and women are ready to leave behind their careers and retire. It has been suggested that adults progress through a series of phases as they make the transition from worker to retiree (Atchley, 1976). An important part of this process includes information gathering and planning for the future (Ekerdt et al., 2000). Retirement is thought to include a number of different phases as it develops. Initially, there is a honeymoon period during which the retiree enjoys their new freedom from routine to the full – taking up new hobbies or rediscovering old ones, generally doing all those things they could not do when working full time. This may be followed by a disenchantment phase, when the novelty wears off and the retiree may even feel aimless or unhappy. Finally, they move to a reorientation phase during which they develop a sustainable and satisfying lifestyle (Ekerdt et al., 1985). Successful retirement seems to be associated with a number of factors, including retiring voluntarily and having sufficient financial resources, good health and a strong social support network. An optimistic attitude also seems to help – individuals with positive expectations are more likely to be well adjusted in retirement (van Solinge and Henkens, 2005).

Critical thinking activity

A midlife crisis?

Critical thinking focus: critical and creative thinking

Key question: *What are the strengths and weaknesses of Levinson's studies of middle-aged adults?*

Read the following summary of Levinson's studies of midlife carried out in the Boston and New York regions of the USA.

What do you think are the three main positives of this piece of work?

What do you think the three biggest limitations are?

You might want to think about issues such as the era in which the studies were carried out, the methods used and the characteristics of the participants who were interviewed. If you were to replicate this work what changes would you make to the studies?

Summary of Levinson's research

Levinson based his theory of adult development on a series of in-depth interviews with 40 adult males between 35 and 45 years of age at the time the interviews were carried out during the late 1960s (Levinson, 1986). He was motivated to carry out this study because he wanted to try to make sense of his own midlife transition. A clinical psychologist trained in psychoanalysis, Levinson called the interviews 'biographical', explaining to participants that the primary task was to construct the story of a man's life. The aim was to cover the entire life sequence from childhood to the present time in each person's life. Through his study, Levinson claims to have discovered that the life cycle evolves through a sequence that may be expressed in terms of age, eras and seasons of life, as described earlier in this chapter. The men that Levinson interviewed worked either as biology professors, novelists, business executives or industrial labourers. The biographical interviews lasted one or two hours and from six to ten interviews were carried out with each participant. The questions asked focused on the individuals' accounts of their own experiences in their post-adolescent years, focusing on topics such as the men's background (education, income etc.) and beliefs about issues such as religion and politics. The men were also asked about major events or turning points in their lives. Over half of the men Levinson spoke to described midlife as the last chance to reach their personal goals. These goals were linked to key events such as reaching a particular level of income, or to career points such as being a supervisor or full professor. These men described their lives as stressful but manageable. The remaining men felt negatively about their lives because they were in dead-end or pointless jobs. Some of them felt this way despite a good income. A very small number of these men had decided to do something about this 'flawed life structure' and had started to rebuild their lives or careers.

In the 1980s, Levinson interviewed 45 women of the same age (Levinson, 1996). The sample comprised equal numbers of women who were either homemakers, college instructors or businesswomen. He found that, in general, women go through the same type of life cycles that men do. However, they were less likely to enter adulthood with specific goals and, as a result, were less likely to define success in terms of key career events. Rather than focusing on external events, women usually sought changes in personal identity in midlife. For example, they might become more independent or self-reliant in middle age. Often such changes were closely linked to the family life cycle. It is notable that the homemakers found traditional patterns difficult to sustain and often paid a big price in restrictions on self-development, while career women experienced considerable stress and difficulty in breaking down barriers in formerly 'male' occupations and in pushing for a more equitable division of housework.

Thus, according to Levinson, an individual's life structure is shaped by the social and physical environment. Many individuals' life structures primarily involve family and work, although other variables such as religion, race and economic status may also be important.

Critical thinking review

This activity helps you understand how one of the most influential theories of adult development has evolved. There are a number of possible limitations with this theory, starting with the midlife crisis that provoked Levinson's study. While it is good that Levinson acknowledged this personal interest, you might wonder whether this influenced his interpretation of the findings. You might also argue that the biographical interview is not very objective and that Levinson's sample is not very representative. Of course, on the plus side, you might also feel that such rich qualitative data presented a good way to explore the experiences of midlifers. While the retrospective accounts of early adulthood may well be flawed, the first-hand accounts of middle age represent a valid exploration of human perception and experience. Furthermore, it has been suggested that Levinson possesses great insight into the human mind, especially given his knowledge of psychoanalysis, sociology and related disciplines. You might have noted that the men who were interviewed for Levinson's studies would have been born between 1924 and 1934. They were therefore raised in the 1930s and 1940s. Women and men who grew up during this time were gender-typed to a much greater extent than males and females are today. What other differences do you think there were in terms of education, goals, values and statuses for Levinson's interviewees? Do Levinson's findings really apply to the current generation of midlifers? Men who have grown up in the last few decades may well have had to deal with less stable families due to high divorce rates, as well as having to deal with a different kind of economy. What about the women interviewed in the 1980s? How different would their upbringing, aims and expectations have been compared to those of today's 35–45-year-old women? Finally, although his original theory was based exclusively on male accounts, Levinson did try to address this limitation with the interviews carried out with a group of women 20 years later.

Skill builder activity

Psychological well-being in adulthood

Transferable skill focus: problem solving and communication

Key question: *read the following scenario. Can you help this friend improve her well-being? What advice might you give and what practical solutions can you devise?*

Annabel, a close friend, is teetering on the verge of a midlife crisis. There are only six months left until her fortieth birthday and she's not happy at waving goodbye to her thirties. Your friend turns uncharacteristically quiet when the subject turns to her milestone birthday. She has told you that she is really dreading this birthday and her fear is getting worse as the big day draws closer. On deeper probing you find out that she feels she has not really achieved anything worthwhile in her life and is starting to feel resentful about her own situation. A mother of three children, she has devoted the past ten years to bringing up her family and supporting her husband as he climbs the career ladder.

Annabel once had her own promising career in marketing, but didn't feel she could balance the demands of full-time work and having a young family. While she loves her children dearly and doesn't regret the time spent with them, she feels that her own life has been on hold and, as she reaches her fortieth birthday, she is starting to wonder if she has left it too late to make her mark on the commercial world. She is confused and uncertain about what to do next. Is it too late to go back to marketing given her time out of the workplace? Should she try to develop a new career? Or should she just accept her status as 'home maker' – after all, her husband has a secure, well-paid job so she has no financial reason to work. Annabel admits that, in many ways, she is very lucky: the family lives in a five-bedroom house in a pleasant part of town, the children are in good schools, everyone is healthy and happy, and she has a good relationship with her husband. Yet she can't quite get rid of the nagging feeling that there should be more to life.

Skill builder review

The focus of this task is the self-evaluation that we go through at different points of the life cycle. Not everyone feels like Annabel at 40 – we can feel unfulfilled at any point in life. Likewise, for those who are satisfied with their life's course, there will be no midlife crisis. However, for those who find that they had dreams and expectations that were never realised, a midlife crisis is a real possibility. Negotiating such life events might mean reframing our life goals, sense of self and beliefs about our place in society. The social support provided by good friends can help support this reframing. Annabel will need to define her concerns and list possible solutions, consider the practicalities, and pros and cons of each solution, and so on. Friends can help talk through some of these issues and provide a different perspective. However, it is important to remember that, ultimately, Annabel has to determine her life choices for herself if she is to negotiate successfully what she sees as an important age-related milestone.

Assignments

1. Critically evaluate gender differences in ageing.

2. Critically discuss Levinson's theory of adult development.

3. To what extent does the evidence support the idea that the midlife crisis is an inevitable stage of adulthood?

Summary: what you have learned

Now you have finished studying this chapter you should:

- understand how cognitive abilities might change in adulthood and the current debate about when such changes occur;

- be able to evaluate the idea that midlife crisis is an inevitable and universal part of adult development;

- be able to discuss critically the relationship between physical ageing and psychological well-being in adulthood;

- critically understand the impact that social and cultural factors such as beliefs about ageing might have on adult experiences;

- have developed your critical and creative thinking skills through considering Levinson's theory of adult development;

- have developed your problem solving and communication by helping someone improve their well-being.

Further reading

Breeze, E, Fletcher, A, Leon, D, Marmot, M, Clarke, R and Shipley, M (2001) Do socioeconomic disadvantages persist into old age? *American Journal of Public Health*, 91(2): 277–83.http://ajph. aphapublications.org/cgi/reprint/91/2/277.pdf

Describes a survey of men aged 40–69 which considers the relationship between health and income in retirement.

Kitchener, KS, Lynch, CL, Fischer, KW and Wood, PK (1993) Developmental range of reflective judgment: the effect of contextual support and practice on developmental stage. *Developmental Psychology*, 29: 893–906. Available online at https://gseweb.harvard.edu/~ddl/articlesCopy/ Kitchener-etal1993DevRangeReflectJudgem.pdf.

Considers age-related changes in reflective judgement.

Levinson, D (1986) A conception of adult development. *American Psychologist*, 41: 3–13. Available online at http://www.imamu.edu.sa/topics/IT/IT%206/A%20Conception%20of%20Adult%20 Development.pdf.

Provides an overview of Levinson's theory of development across the life cycle.

Population Reference Bureau (2008) Socioeconomic status and health disparities in old age. *Today's Research on Aging*, 11 (June). Available online at www.prb.org/pdf08/TodaysResearch Aging11.pdf.

This review summarises research concerning factors influencing health status in the ageing population.

Salthouse, TA (2009). When does age-related cognitive decline begin? *Neurobiology of Aging*, 30(4): 507–14.Available online at http://faculty.virginia.edu/cogage/links/publications/.

Excellent discussion of factors influencing cognitive skills in later life.

Chapter 8

Death, dying and bereavement

Learning outcomes

By the end of this chapter you should:

- understand the way in which the age of the individual may impact on feelings of loss;

- be able to evaluate the impact of social and cultural factors on grief and loss.

- be able to discuss critically the role of the community and family in providing end-of-life care;

- recognise the role of the hospice and other specialist services;

- critically understand ethical issues concerning quality of life and the right to die;

- have developed your skills relating to analysis and evaluation of data;

- have developed your decision making skills.

Introduction

The final stage of the lifespan is death. As famously noted by Benjamin Franklin, death is one of life's certainties. It might seem that death, like birth, is a straightforward biological process. However, there is much confusion in our society about when life begins and when it ends. For example, proponents and opponents of abortion argue about when human life actually begins: is the developing embryo a human being or merely an organism with the potential for life? In the same way that there are different views about when life actually begins, so too there are debates about when life actually ends: is a person in an irreversible coma truly alive, for example? Finally, there are the debates about an individual's right to die: should a terminally ill patient in agonising pain be kept alive or allowed to die naturally if that is their wish?

Death can come at any time in the life cycle, although there is a tendency to believe that death in old age is the most natural. Two hundred years or so ago it was much more common for individuals to die before reaching old age; indeed, many died in infancy. Today, however, death occurs most often among older adults. Life expectancy in the UK has increased over the past 200 years, with the greatest increase resulting from survival at birth. Life expectancy at birth in the UK has reached its highest level on record for both males and females (ONS, 2010). In the UK in 2010, life expectancy for a newborn baby boy was 77.7 years and for a newborn baby girl 81.9 years. Females continue to live longer than males, but the gap is closing and has narrowed from a difference of six years to 4.2 years over the past 27 years (see Figure 8.1).

One reason for the increasing lifespan in Western society is the advances made in combating disease over the past 200 years. Some of the most important factors include things such as better diet, cleaner drinking water and improved sanitation (Wegman, 2001). Improvements in medical care, such as the introduction of vaccinations, also did much to help eradicate diseases such as smallpox, which was once responsible for around one in seven childhood deaths in Europe (Fenner et al., 1988). Modern medicine is also much better at overcoming diseases that were once thought to be incurable. This means that the main causes of death have changed in our society, from infectious disease to chronic illness. It has also meant that death has become more medicalised and distanced from our daily lives.

Causes of death over the lifespan

Death can occur at any point in development – even prenatally through miscarriage or stillbirth. Death can also happen during the birth process or in the first few days of life. This is usually because of a birth defect or because of incomplete development in the prenatal period. However, one of the most common causes of death in infancy in developed countries such as the UK is sudden infant death syndrome or SIDS (Kurinczuk et al., 2009). SIDS is a condition in which an infant stops breathing, usually in the middle of the night, and dies without apparent cause (Hunt and Hauck, 2006). The risk of SIDS is highest at four to six weeks of age (Matthews et al., 2003);

Figure 8. 1: *Life expectancy 1980–2007 (ONS, www.statistics.gov.uk, ONS licensed under the open government licence v 1.0)*

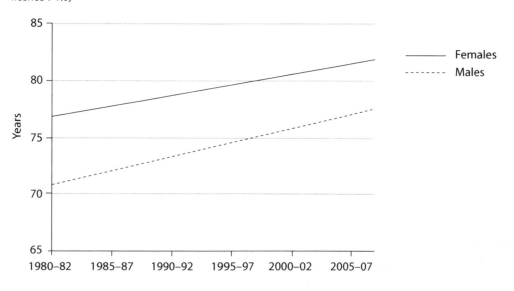

however, advice by the Department of Health in the 1990s to put babies to sleep on their backs has led to a dramatic reduction in the number of SIDS deaths (Hiley and Morley, 1995).

The leading cause of death in preschoolers and school-age children is accident or unintentional injury, such as poisoning, a fall from a high place, a house fire or a car accident. Major illness also accounts for a number of childhood deaths and includes conditions such as congenital heart disease, cancer and birth defects. In contrast, adolescents and young adults are more at risk from murder, suicide or accident. Car accidents are probably the most common kind of accident involving young adults. Older adults are more likely to die from chronic conditions than from accidents. These diseases often incapacitate before they kill, which produces a course of dying that leads slowly to death. Cancer is the leading killer for middle-aged adults, followed by heart disease, while heart disease tops the list for older adults, followed by cancer and stroke.

Biological death

The actual point of death can be hard to define, as it is not a single event but a process and different body systems die at different rates. A hundred or so years ago, defining death was not so complicated a process; death was believed to have occurred once the heart stopped beating. However, advances in medicine mean that some individuals who lack a pulse or are not breathing, who at other times in history would have been declared dead, can now be revived before their brains cease to function. They can then be kept alive by artificial life-support systems. The UK, unlike many countries, does not have a legal definition of death. Guidelines for the diagnosis and confirmation of death are purely medical and are provided by the Academy of Medical Royal Colleges (AOMRC, 2008). This medical definition focuses primarily on irreversible brain stem damage and states that, in the absence of neurological functioning, *the patient is dead even though respiration and circulation can be artificially maintained successfully for a limited period of time* (AOMRC, 2008, p13). This definition is applied to children as well as adults.

These guidelines are clearly concerned with confirmation of death in hospital and in circumstances where the diagnosis of death may be more difficult (patients on ventilators, for example), and it has been argued that the current emphasis on brain death is at least in part driven by the need to harvest (healthy) organs for transplant (Doyle et al., 2004). A diagnosis of brain death is made using observation of such factors as fixed and dilated pupils, lack of eye movement and the absence of respiratory reflexes. However, it is not based on whether or not the heart is still beating and, while in most cases this body function will stop once withdrawal of life support systems occurs, many people still see a beating heart as indicative of life. Kellehear and O'Connor (2008) therefore argue that any decisions made about whether or not someone should be considered to have died ought to include a more social element in order to ease the burden on the family of the dying.

Social meanings of death

As Kellehear and O'Connor (2008) have noted, death is not just a biological process – it is also a psychological and social one. The social meaning attached to death has changed across the course of history (Aries, 1981). In contrast to the Middle Ages, when individuals were encouraged to recognise their own mortality and prepare for death with dignity, in Western society today most people engage in a denial of death. Death has been removed from the home in the UK, and familiarity with death has decreased considerably since the 1900s, when most people died in their own homes (Thorpe, 1993). Two hundred years ago, the death rate was such that half of all children died before the age of ten years and one parent usually died before a child grew up. Nowadays, many people do not experience the death of someone close to them until they are well into midlife (Department of Health, 2008). It is perhaps not so surprising then that, as a society, death and dying is a subject that is not openly discussed in the UK (Kellehear, 2005). Surveys have shown that, given the opportunity and support, most people would prefer to die at home, yet in practice only a minority are able to do so (Department of Health, 2008). Indeed, many people (58 per cent) die in acute hospital settings, which are often not their preferred place for end-of-life care. Much of the responsibility for such care is given over to **hospice** and **palliative care** services (Kellehear, 2005).

Hospice care

The term 'hospice' is rooted in the idea of offering 'hospitality', such as shelter and a place to rest, to sick and weary travellers. The term was originally applied to specialised care for dying patients in 1967 by Dame Cicely Saunders at St Christopher's Hospice in London. Hospice care treats the patient, not the disease, and focuses on quality rather than quantity of life. However, this does not mean that there is ever any intention to shorten life; *euthanasia* is not promoted by the hospice movement. Support is also provided for family members as they go through the grieving process.

Hospice staff can provide direct care to the patient or teach the family to care for the patient between visits if care is provided in the patient's home. However, the focus is not just on prevention and relief of symptoms; social issues, such as ensuring that the patient designates a surrogate decision maker and makes advance plans, and the preparation of patient and family for the time near death, are also undertaken by hospice staff (Lynn, 2001). There are many positive aspects to the hospice movement. The philosophy is one of caring rather than curing, and the aim of this care is to help people find meaning in death (Saunders, 2002). This is just one difference between hospice and hospital care. Other features of hospice care include:

- the individual and their family, not the experts, deciding what support they need;

- care being kept as normal as possible (preferably in the patient's own home);

- an emphasis on pain control;

- the provision of **bereavement** counselling before as well as after death.

Research suggests that the benefits of hospice care include less pain at the end of life, fewer medical interventions and care more aligned to individual emotional needs (Seale, 1991). There also appear to be benefits for the family, including better well-being and fewer symptoms of **grief** (Ragow-O'Brien et al., 2000).

Community care for the dying

According to Kellehear (2005), the type of care provided by the hospice movement emphasises people as individuals, and therefore the focus is placed on providing services to them as patients within these institutions or as patients at home. For Kellehear, a more appropriate approach to care would be to emphasise the person as a member of a social community. Kellehear argues that, even in dying, a person must be seen not just as an individual, but also as a social being, intricately connected to a community of friends, family and co-workers. This philosophy underpins the health-promoting palliative care movement, which emphasises community-based care for people with life-threatening illnesses (Mitchell, 2008). **Compassionate communities** is a movement within the UK that believes that the special needs of those living with life-threatening illness and those living with loss should be met through a supportive community rather than the provision of centralised services. Individuals within a community are provided with an opportunity to work together alongside healthcare professionals. This works to create more unity within the community, empowering the community to support themselves using the resources available to them, and increasing social capacity and resilience towards experiences of dying, death and loss (Kellehear, 2005). This movement has already had some success in Australia, where it originated, and the approach is currently being explored in some regions of the UK as a viable means of working towards quality in end-of-life care.

Bereavement, grief and loss

Bereavement is the loss, through death, of loved ones and can occur at any stage of life. Grief is the psychological and bodily reaction that occurs in people who suffer bereavement and the observable expression of this grief is called **mourning**. However, it is important to recognise that this grief can begin before the actual death, and that those who are dying can also grieve for their own loss.

Grief is the emotional response to loss. This reaction can be displayed physically, emotionally, cognitively and socially. Physical reactions include eating and sleeping problems. Mental reactions can include anxiety, sadness and despair. Social reactions include readjusting to life without the deceased, or readjusting to life after the diagnosis of a terminal illness. The actual grieving process that individuals experience and the response that they have is dependent on a number of factors, such as the relationship with the person (was it a close, happy relationship, or a distant and difficult one?), factors surrounding the loss (for example, whether the death was sudden or expected), as well as unresolved issues with the deceased (not having a chance to say goodbye, for example).

All of these factors will influence whether a person will go through a 'normal' or 'abnormal' grieving process. For example, death resulting from an accident increases the likelihood of there being an abnormal grieving pattern compared to when a death results from a long terminal illness. This is because diagnosis of a terminal illness allows family and friends to prepare for the loss.

Models of grief

According to Archer (1999), a widely held belief is that grief follows an orderly series of stages or phases with distinct features. Traditional models have one main commonality – the need for grief work – which is described as *an effortful process that we must go through entailing confrontation of the reality of loss and gradual acceptance of the world without the loved one* (Stroebe, 1998).

Models of grief and loss emphasise the idea that all individuals will experience particular emotional and physical states but that the amount of time that is spent at each stage will vary. All models emphasise the need to experience all of these stages in order to reach an acceptance of the loss that has been experienced. Grief work models can be applied to the grief process that either adults or children will go through before reaching acceptance, although, as the next section shows, age will impact on how grief is displayed. Parkes's (1972, 1986) four-stage model describes the phases of bereavement and, in turn, the grief work that an individual faces (Table 8.1). According to this model, an individual has to work through the stages of grief in order to reach acceptance and move forward in life.

According to the World Health Organization (WHO, 1990), the need to offer family and significant others support, not only during the patient's terminal illness but also in bereavement, is important.

Table 8.1: Parkes's four-stage model of grief work (Parkes, 1986)

Name of phase	Reactions, emotions in each phase
Phase One	Initial reaction: shock, numbness or disbelief
Phase Two	Pangs of grief, searching, anger, guilt, sadness and fear
Phase Three	Despair
Phase Four	Acceptance/adjustment; gaining a new identity

This need also underlies the main philosophy of palliative care (WHO, 1990). Research suggests that bereaved individuals are most helped by those who say they are sorry for their loss, make themselves available to serve as confidants and let the bereaved express their painful feelings freely when they are ready to do so (Herkert, 2000). Telling people how they should feel and cope is less useful than simply asking how they are and how they are coping. Emphasising the positives may also seem a good approach, but comments such as 'At least he had a good innings' or 'At least he is no longer suffering' may be well intentioned, but are often not well received by those dealing with loss.

Focus on: grief work

Task — Read the scenario provided below and answer the following question:

— Does the staff nurse help or hinder grief work?

Jim, his wife Rose and their three children were overjoyed at the news that Rose was expecting a baby. A couple of months into the pregnancy, Rose was unexpectedly taken into hospital with severe abdominal pains and bleeding. A few hours later, the couple had their worst nightmare confirmed: Rose had had a miscarriage. Both were shocked by the news. The senior staff nurse noticed that both Rose and Jim were finding it difficult to come to terms with the miscarriage and decided to help the couple with their grief, so that coming to terms with the miscarriage would be easier for both of them. The senior staff nurse introduced herself and said how sorry she was for the couple's loss. Rose looked back at the nurse with a blank expression, while Jim replied that they would be fine and that they could do nothing about it now. Rose was kept in hospital for a couple of days until her health became more stable. During her stay, the senior staff nurse and others encouraged Rose to talk about her feelings, but Rose did not reveal any of her emotions. Three days later, Rose's physical health had improved and she was prepared for discharge. Knowing that Rose would be discharged, the nurse decided to talk to Jim and explain her concerns that Rose had shown no emotion. She gave Jim a leaflet listing organisations offering further support for Rose. When Jim then became tearful, the nurse reassured him that the grieving process would become easier over time. She further emphasised the positive things in life that they needed to focus on, such as their three children, comparing their situation to those of others who had miscarried but had no children. Jim was beginning to feel guilty about being upset and thanked the nurse for her help and concern.

Comment

A number of issues come to light in this case study. First, both Rose and Jim have been hindered with their grieving. In such a case, shock is a common initial response and features in the majority of models as the first stage of grief. The initial shock experienced by Rose resulted in the senior staff nurse being more proactive in her attempts to help. However, comparing other cases of miscarriage with that of Jim and Rose was risky, simply because the family circumstances were unknown. What if the three children at home were from Rose's first marriage? What implications would there be had the unborn child been the first one that Rose and Jim had conceived together? The last comment the nurse in the case study made, to the effect that they should think about the three children at home, as some do not even have them, resulted in Jim feeling guilty about grieving. Thus, even though the nurse had good intentions, her actions actually facilitated bad grief. Making Jim feel guilty will result in a delay in the grieving process. The longer this is delayed, the more problems Jim and Rose will have later on when attempting to accept their loss. What might have been a better approach?

Understanding death and grief responses across the lifespan

There are enormous differences in children's understanding of loss and how they cope with bereavement. This has often been understood in terms of the children's cognitive development. Table 8.2 shows the different grief reactions a child may show at different ages.

Most researchers believe that infants have no understanding of death, but as infants develop an attachment to a carer they can experience loss or separation. Very young children do not experience time in the same way that adults do and It is possible that even brief separations may be experienced as a total loss. However, we know very little about infants' actual experience of bereavement and, as they cannot tell us what they experience, it is unlikely that this gap in our knowledge will be filled in the near future.

Between the ages of three and five, children have little idea of what death is. They may confuse death and sleep, and believe that the dead can be brought back to life. Because they do not understand what death is and why it happens, they may blame themselves for the death of someone close to them, which can make the grieving process much harder. In middle to late childhood, understanding about death becomes more realistic. However, research suggests that it is not until nine years and over that children really understand the finality of death (Cuddy-Casey and Orvaschel, 1997). Kastenbaum (2000) suggests that the confusion and misunderstanding about death that has been observed in children simply reflects their attempts to try to come to terms with and fully understand what death is and what it means. It has also been observed that children begin to develop a more logical understanding of what death is through experience – for example, when a grandparent or even a much-loved pet dies (Hayslip and Hansson, 2003). If this

Table 8.2: *Grief and developmental stages (partly adapted from National Cancer Institute, US National Institutes of Health, 2010)*

Age	Understanding of death	Behaviour/expression of grief
Infant	Does not recognise death. Feelings of loss and separation are part of developing an awareness of death.	Separated from mother – sluggish, quiet and unresponsive to a smile or a coo. Physical changes include weight loss, being less active, sleeping less.
2–6 years	Confuses death with sleep. Begins to experience anxiety by age of three.	Asks many questions. May have problems with eating, sleeping, and bladder and bowel control. Fear of abandonment. Tantrums.
3–6 years	Still confuses death with sleep, i.e. person is alive but only in a limited way. Death is temporary, not final. The dead person can come back to life.	Even though they saw the deceased buried, they still ask questions. Magical thinking based on lack of knowledge – his or her thoughts may cause someone to die. Under fives may have trouble with eating, sleeping, and bladder and bowel control. Afraid of the dark.
6–9 years	Curious about death. Death is thought of as a person or spirit (skeleton, ghost, bogeyman). Death is final and frightening. Death happens to others; it won't happen to me.	Asks specific questions. May have exaggerated fears. May have aggressive behaviours (especially boys). Some concerns about imaginary illnesses. May feel abandoned.
9+ years	Everyone will die. Death is final and cannot be changed. Even I will die.	Heightened emotions – guilt, anger, shame. Increased anxiety over own death. Mood swings. Fear of rejection, not wanting to be different from peers. Changes in eating habits. Sleeping problems. Regressive behaviours (loss of interest in outside activities). Impulsive behaviours. Feels guilty about being alive (especially related to death of a parent, sibling or peer).

is true, Kellehear (2005) is right to be concerned about the distancing of death and dying from the family and community: if children are not exposed to death, how can they learn from experience what death is and what it means?

Adolescents have a much clearer understanding of death and are more likely than younger children to recognise it as an inevitable biological process. However, despite this knowledge, there is evidence that many adults and adolescents share the belief commonly held by children that psychological functions such as knowing and thinking continue even when biological functions have stopped (Bering and Bjorklund, 2004). In other words, they believe in an afterlife.

Adolescents tend to grieve in much the same way that adults do, but may be reluctant to express their grief for fear of seeming abnormal or lacking control. They may therefore express their anguish through delinquent behaviour and somatic ailments (Clark et al., 1994).

The experience of dying

Kubler-Ross (1969) was one of the first researchers to study patients and their families from the diagnosis of a terminal illness up until death. This research resulted in more emphasis being given to palliative care and quality of life even if it is inevitable that a patient will die. Kubler-Ross suggested a five-stage model for the experience of dying, which has provided a framework for those working with individuals experiencing personal loss (see Table 8.3).

It is often assumed that terminally ill young children are unaware that they will die and are better off remaining that way. However, the evidence shows that even preschool children with life-threatening illnesses such as leukaemia come to understand that they will die and that death is irreversible (Bluebond-Langner, 1977). Over time, terminally ill children stop thinking about the future and focus on the here and now. Indeed, children experience the same emotions in death as adults – fear, anger, sadness and finally acceptance. Preschool children may not talk about dying, but they can reveal their fears through temper tantrums. School-age children are better able to talk about their fears and there is evidence that talking to a child about their death can be beneficial for both the child and the parents, if the child shows the desire to do so (Faulkner, 1997). School-age children often show a desire to continue with everyday activities such as going to school as long as possible, so as to feel 'normal'.

The response of the adolescent to becoming terminally ill clearly reflects the developmental tasks of this period (Stevens and Dunsmore, 1996). In this age group, the focus is often on body image, meaning that body changes such as weight gain or loss of hair will provoke feelings of distress. In the same way, a loss of identity can be felt when new-found independence is taken away due to the reliance on parents and healthcare professionals that illness may bring.

There is no evidence that a special orientation to death develops in adulthood. However, increasing awareness of death may develop as people acknowledge that they are ageing, and this is thought to be especially acute in middle age. Indeed, there is evidence that middle-aged adults fear death far more than younger and older adults (Kalish and Reynolds, 1976), although older adults are most likely to think and talk about death. Younger adults who are dying often feel more cheated than older adults (Kalish, 1987). They may feel that they have not had enough time to do all the things they wanted to, and that their future hopes and aspirations have been stolen.

Table 8.3: *The five-stage model (Kubler-Ross, 1969)*

Stage	Example	Explanation
Denial and isolation	'No, not me' or 'It can't be me – you must have the results mixed up.'	During this stage there is constant denial of the new status a patient or family are prescribed. Denial acts as a buffer system, allowing the patient to develop other coping mechanisms. It can also bring isolation and the patient may fear rejection and abandonment in suffering and feel that nobody understands what the suffering is like.
Anger	'It's not fair – why me?'	This is the stage where anger is taken out on practitioners such as nurses (and also doctors, relatives or other healthy people). Typical reactions are: 'Because of you (the nurse), I can't go home and pick my children up from school'; 'Because of you (the nurse) I have to take time out so you administer pain to me'; or 'It's okay for you, you can go home at the end of the day.' Also there is a shift from the first stage, from 'No, it can't be me, it must be a mistake', to 'Oh yes, it is me, it was not a mistake.'
Bargaining	'Please God, let me . . .'	This is an attempt to postpone death by doing a deal with God/fate/the hospital. At this stage, people who are enduring a terminal illness and looking for a cure, or 'a bit more time', will pay any price and will often be manipulated. It is not uncommon for patients who have never been religious to now turn to religion – almost bargaining again: 'If I pray, you will grant me another extra couple of days.' The problem is that, even when the couple of extra days are granted, these are never enough; the patient wants more.
Depression	'How can I leave all of this behind?'	This time is very much a quiet, dark and reflective time, very much similar to someone actually experiencing depression. During this stage, the dying patient does not want reassurance from a nurse, but at the same time does not want to be ignored. During this time family members of the dying patient begin the five-stage model, so are very much attempting to be proactive, i.e. in denial that the family member is going to die. They may even become angry at the patient for 'giving up'. The dying patient, during this stage, would like people around them to be quiet, and this is where nurses can make a difference. All they want is someone to be present, who does not question and is not angry. There will be questions the patient will ask and they need to be answered honestly (especially because they don't have to pretend to be strong away from the family). In addition to this, the patient during this stage would also like the nurse to anticipate questions.

Table 8.3: *Continued*

Stage	Example	Explanation
Acceptance	'Leave me be, I am ready to die.'	This is a stage where the individual is neither depressed nor angry. The individual has worked through feelings of loss and has found some peace. During this stage the patient has let go and is ready to go. Also within this stage, family members are very much angry or questioning why the patient is at peace when they still want to change the status of the patient. The patient, however, has begun the process of letting go during the depression stage and has finished this process during acceptance. They are ready to move on.

Cultural differences in grieving

Sometimes a distinction is made between grief and *mourning*; grief is seen as a subjective state – a set of feelings that arise spontaneously after a significant death, whereas mourning describes the way in which grief is displayed. Mourning is often constrained by the rituals or behaviours prescribed by a culture. The Western approach to bereavement is not universal and displays of grief and mourning take different forms across the world. These rituals are often heavily influenced by religion (Chachkes and Jennings, 1994); for example, funerals may be an occasion for avoiding people or for holding a party (Matcalf and Huntington, 1991). Most societies have some concept of spiritual immortality, yet even here there are cultural differences, ranging from the idea of reincarnation to the concept of ancestral ghosts who meddle in the lives of the living (Rosenblatt, 1993). Some cultures, especially those in Latin America, believe that mourning involves the display of intense hysterical emotions that should be shared with the community (Cook and Dworkin, 1992), while others, such as the British, restrain their grief so as not to burden others.

Quality of life and the right to die

The letters DNR written on a patient's file indicate that a doctor is not required to resuscitate a patient if the latter's heart stops. Standing for 'Do Not Resuscitate', these three letters are designed to prevent unnecessary suffering. For terminally ill patients, the letters DNR may be the difference between dying immediately or being kept alive through extreme, possibly painful, medical procedures for days, weeks or even months.

DNR is often seen as a form of euthanasia, the practice of assisting someone to die more quickly. Sometimes called 'mercy killing', euthanasia takes one of two forms: in passive **euthanasia**, death is hastened because of the withdrawal of care (e.g. switching off a life support machine) or non-intervention (e.g. following a DNR order); active euthanasia involves deliberately acting to end a person's life, for example by administering a fatal dose of pain medication. Euthanasia is an emotive subject and people often have firm views on whether such practice is right or wrong. Some people make a moral distinction between active and passive euthanasia, arguing that it is acceptable to withhold treatment and allow a terminally ill patient to die, but not to kill someone by a deliberate act. Others argue that this distinction is unfounded, since both letting someone die and actively killing someone constitute a deliberate act, the intended outcome of which is someone's death. Active euthanasia is illegal in most countries, including the UK; however, one study suggests that almost half of NHS doctors have been asked by a patient to take active steps to hasten death and a third of those asked had complied with the patient's request (Ward and Tate, 1994).

In the UK, the British Medical Association (BMA), the Royal College of Nursing (RCN) and the Resuscitation Council (UK) have provided guidelines on the use of DNR orders and are clear that these should only be issued after discussion with patients or their families. The most difficult cases are those involving patients who know they are terminally ill and are suffering a lot of pain, but who could live for several months. The guidelines (BMA et al., 2001) state that circumstances in which a DNR may be issued include:

- when a patient's condition is such that resuscitation is unlikely to succeed;

- when a mentally competent patient has consistently stated that he or she does not want to be resuscitated;

- if there is a **living will**, which says that the patient does not want to be resuscitated;

- if successful resuscitation would not be in the patient's best interest because it would lead to a poor quality of life (QOL).

The final point raises an important issue: at what point does life cease to have 'quality' and who decides that an individual's life is no longer worth living? Two main issues have been found to be important in determining terminal patients' QOL: their physical and mental state and the relationships and support provided by others (Shahidi et al., 2010). Normally, QOL is judged by individuals themselves, as QOL is defined by our subjective experiences, states and perceptions (Burckhardt and Anderson, 2003). However, some have questioned whether a terminally ill patient is always capable of judging the quality of his or her life, which raises a new question: if the patient is found incapable of judging their life quality, then who should? Should it be a family member, a medic or other healthcare professional? Consideration of QOL is closely linked to decisions about what is in an individual's best interests. The challenge is to define what a person's best interests are and how they can best be met. Can someone's best interests ever be met by withdrawing or administering a particular treatment? Advocates of euthanasia argue that it is not in the best interests of a terminally ill patient to suffer pain needlessly when his or her life is close to the end. The failure to end that suffering, even if the only way of doing so is to intentionally end the patient's life, is seen as going against the duty of the health professional to do what is best for the patient's well-being.

A final farewell

We have now reached the end of the lifespan and the end of this book. Throughout the text, the aim has been to generate critical evaluation of topics as well to provide up-to-date resources and information about human development. As you will realise by now, developmental psychology is a budding area to which new knowledge and understanding are continually being added. You have been introduced to debates new and old within the field, including:

- the relative roles of biology and environment in human development;

- continuity and discontinuity in the development of skills and abilities;

- the importance of critical or sensitive periods for the development of some functions;

- stability and change in traits and skills across the lifespan;

- the role of the individual in his or her own development.

It is our hope that the ins and outs of human development have captivated your interest in such a way that you can think of a number of examples to illustrate the above issues. It is anticipated that you have also engaged fully with the issues raised, evaluated the materials presented and reached your own evidence-based conclusions about the intricacies of human development.

Critical thinking activity

Changing trends in life expectancy

Critical thinking focus: analysis and evaluation of data

Key question: *What trends can you see in the following data sets?*

Figure 8.2 shows mortality rates for the UK in 2006. What do these data tell you about:

differences in male and female death rates in 2006;

age-related trends in mortality rates in 2006; and

at what ages male and female mortality rates are similar? Why do you think we see this pattern?

Figure 8.2:
Mortality rates per 1,000 in the UK 2006 (ONS, www.statistics. gov.uk, ONS licensed under the open government licence v 1.0)

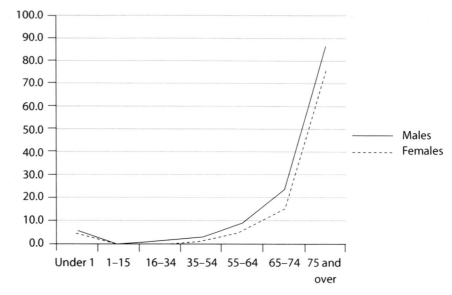

Figures 8.3 and 8.4 show the mortality rates for males and females over 30 years. Compare these graphs in order to answer the following questions.

– What differences can you see in the changes in male and female mortality rates from 1971 to 2001? Why do such differences exist?

– When was the biggest change in infant mortality rates for both males and females? What factor is most associated with high infant mortality?

Figure 8.3:
Male mortality rates per 1,000 in the UK from 1971 to 2001 (ONS, www.statistics.gov.uk, ONS licensed under the open government licence v 1.0)

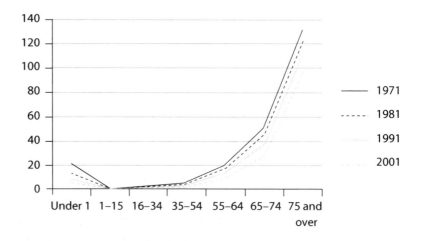

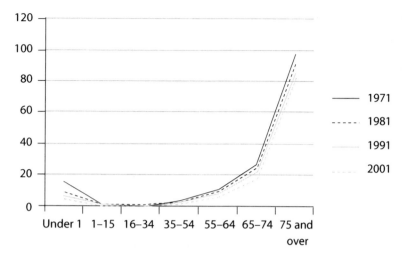

Figure 8.4: *Female mortality rates per 1,000 in the UK from 1971 to 2001 (ONS, www.statistics.gov.uk, ONS licensed under the open government licence v 1.0)*

— 1971
----- 1981
1991
2001

Critical thinking review

The patterns shown in Figure 8.2 reflect those described at the start of this chapter: females show lower mortality rates throughout most of the lifespan when compared to males; mortality rates drop after infancy, then do not start to increase until middle adulthood (35–54); and the highest increase in mortality is seen in old age. Despite improvements in infant mortality rates, the first year of life is the most dangerous one in childhood. Many infants still die during the first few weeks of life, with approximately 40 per cent of infant deaths occurring on the day of birth. Male and female mortality rates are most similar during childhood and early adolescence. Most children are at their healthiest during this period and positive parental influences are thought to contribute to this favourable statistic. Mortality statistics begin to increase in late adolescence and an individual aged 20 may be four times more likely to die than at age ten. The statistics are even more interesting when males are compared to females – there is an increased risk of death for males during these years, and in some cases a 23-year-old male may have the same risk of imminent death as a 35 year old. The reasons for this include deaths due to motor accidents, misadventure due to risk-taking, and suicide.

The data spanning 1971–2001 demonstrate another issue raised at the start of the chapter – the reduction in the gap between male and female mortality rates. While life expectancy continues to increase for both males and females, a greater increase is seen in that for males. This is thought to relate to improvements in the prevention and treatment of life-limiting disease experienced mainly by males, such as heart disease. Infant mortality rates appear to have reduced the most between 1971 and 1981, although a gradual decline is still seen from 1981 to 2001. A range of social and biological factors are associated with high infant mortality, including low birth weight, multiple births, marital status, age of the mother, country of birth of mother, and father's social class. Social class differences in infant mortality rates are wider in the post-neonatal period (deaths between 28 days and one year) than in the neonatal period (deaths under 28 days). According to Norman et al. (2008), health inequalities in infant mortality remain between different social groups. The initial rapid decline seen in this data set is therefore thought to be related to a general reduction in health inequalities in the early 1970s and 1980s (Norman et al., 2008). Further reduction in 1981–91 is thought to be related to the 'Back to Sleep' campaign, which encouraged parents to put their babies to sleep on their backs, thus reducing the number of SIDS deaths.

Skill builder activity

Quality of life and the right to die

Transferable skill focus: decision making

Key question: read the following case study, which concerns an individual approaching the end of life, and then consider the following questions.

Should Rachel be allowed to decide that she no longer wants any treatment?

Based on your knowledge of cognitive development, at what age should someone be deemed able to make their own decisions?

Is Rachel's mother right to support this decision or should she force her child to be treated?

Case study: Rachel was diagnosed with a brain tumour at the age of eight years. Now aged 12, she has spent the past four years in and out of hospital undergoing a range of treatments, including chemotherapy and radiation, but the tumour shows no signs of going away. The location of the tumour makes it inoperable and the family had all but given up hope of a cure. However, a new chemotherapy treatment has recently become available in England and is being trialled at the children's hospital where Rachel is treated and her consultant has asked if she would like to be included in the trial. Rachel and her family have been told that the treatment has a 50 per cent chance of success, but that this is the only treatment left open to her. Rachel has refused this treatment. She explained to the consultant that she has had enough of hospitals, needles and being poked and prodded. She does not want to be a guinea pig for some new treatment that might not even work. All she wants is to be able to spend time at home with her family. She accepts that refusing this treatment means that she will probably die within a few months, but thinks that the chances of success are not good enough reason for spending more time in hospital undergoing painful treatment. She has stated that if she is going to die anyway she would rather do so at home. Her mother is upset by this turn of events but says she understands Rachel's reasoning and will support her decision.

Skill builder review

The right to die is always an emotive topic and this case is made more difficult by Rachel's age. While the Mental Capacity Act 2005 provides guidelines for determining whether or not an adult is capable of making treatment decisions, there is currently no statutory legislation governing consent in children under the age of 16. However, there is a legal precedent created by the Gillick case (*Gillick* v *West Norfolk and Wisbech AHA* [1986] AC 112). The ruling of this case states that, if a minor has sufficient intelligence and understanding to enable him or her to understand the treatment and implications of treatment, then he or she is 'Gillick competent' and can consent to treatment. However, a refusal of treatment is treated differently and may be overridden by a parent or the court where such a refusal would be likely to result in the death or permanent disability of the child. The argument is that the wishes of the child can be overridden to preserve his or her long-term interests. It is an interesting differentiation that a child can be deemed capable of consent to treatment, but not of its refusal. Does this require a fundamentally different set of cognitive skills, do you think? At the age of 12, Rachel is entering Piaget's formal operational stage, suggesting that she may well be capable of the abstract and hypothetical thinking needed to make such a decision.

However, the other factor to consider is her emotional development. Some psychologists would argue that the trauma of medical treatment for life-threatening illness changes children's emotional development, including feelings of safety and security, bodily integrity and their ability to trust, all of which might compromise the child's ability to make his or her own decision. Does this mean that Rachel's mother should step in and override her daughter's choice? Is not to do so tantamount to neglectful parenting? Or perhaps we should stop and consider the pain and upset that this would put Rachel through. Would forcing treatment on her compromise her quality of life? It is important to remember that everyone has a different perspective in a situation like this: the medical team, who have been given another chance at increasing Rachel's life expectancy; her mother, who undoubtedly does not want her child to suffer, but clearly does not want to lose her either; and Rachel herself, who has experienced the illness and the treatments first hand. Whose choice should it be?

Assignments

1. How might the Kubler-Ross (1969) model of dying be applied in a hospice with terminally ill adults?

2. Evaluate the impact of social and cultural influences on our beliefs about death, dying and bereavement.

3. What is the relationship between cognitive development and children's response to loss?

Summary: what you have learned

Now you have finished studying this chapter you should:

- understand the way in which the age of the individual may impact on feelings of loss and how this is manifest in cases of bereavement or the loss of one's own life;

- be able to evaluate the impact of social and cultural factors on grief and loss, and recognise the importance of grief work;

- be able to discuss critically the role of that the community and family can play in providing end-of-life care;

- recognise the role of specialist services provided by hospices for palliative care;

- critically understand ethical issues concerning quality of life and the right to die, including the arguments for and against passive and active euthanasia;

- have developed your skills relating to the analysis and evaluation of data by considering UK mortality statistics;

- have developed your decision making related to the end-of-life choice made by a 12-year-old cancer sufferer.

Further reading

Academy of Medical Royal Colleges (2008) *A Code of Practice for the Diagnosis and Confirmation of Death*. London: AOMRC. Available online at www.aomrc.org.uk/publications/reports-guidance.html.

Guidelines for a medical definition of death: this is the code of practice followed by UK medics.

Dowdney, L (2000) Childhood bereavement following parental death. *Journal of Child Psychology and Psychiatry and Allied Disciplines*, 41(7): 819–30. Available online at www.psybc.com/pdfs/Children_and_Grief.pdf.

Considers issues surrounding bereavement for children.

Doyal L (1999) When doctors might kill their patients: the moral character of clinicians or the best interests of patients? *British Medical Journal*, 318: 1432–3. Available online at www.bmj.com/content/318/7196/1432.full?ijkey=639d06ce3dc9823e257c59796b7d02357add946c&keytype2=tf_ipsecsha.

A discussion of euthanasia.

Kellehear, A and O'Connor, D (2008) Health-promoting palliative care: a practice example. *Critical Public Health*, 18(1): 111–15.

Discusses the public health approach to care for the dying.

Glossary

accommodation — according to Piaget, this is one of the processes through which the construction of knowledge takes place. In accommodation, children modify/adapt their existing schemas to fit new information, for example separating cars from other vehicles.

adolescent egocentrism — the heightened self-consciousness of adolescence. Teenagers believe that other people are highly attentive to their appearance and behaviour, so they believe that 'all eyes are on them'.

Aids (Acquired immune deficiency syndrome) — a condition that causes the body to lose immunity to infection.

analgesics/ analgesia — group of drugs used as painkillers.

animism — a term used in developmental psychology to explain young children's patterns of thought and speech in which feelings, beliefs and desires are invested in the non-human or non-living object.

anoxia — a decreased supply of oxygen to the body tissues.

anthropology — the discipline that studies humankind.

Applied Behavioural Analysis (ABA) — a behaviourist intervention based on the principles of Dr Lovaas, in which rewards/tokens are used to manipulate children's behaviour. ABA is used with children with learning difficulties, such as autistic spectrum disorder (ASD).

artificially induce — to dilate the cervix artificially (e.g. with drugs) in order to start labour.

assimilation — according to Piaget, this is one of the processes through which the construction of knowledge takes place. In assimilation, children evaluate and try to understand new information based on their existing schemas, for example all four-wheeled vehicles are cars.

attention deficit hyperactivity disorder (ADHD) — a hyperactivity disorder characterised by an inability to focus on one task at a time and a pervasive impulsivity, often resulting in behavioural or developmental delay problems.

atypical development — refers to any development that deviates from the expected course in terms of achievement of skills and abilities.

autonomous morality	also known as moral independence. According to the Piagetian theory of moral development, this stage is characterised by a child's own determination of what is right, adapted to fit within a given circumstance.
axon	the tail-like part of a neuron, which transmits an impulse from the cell body.
behavioural	the term used to characterise the theoretical or empirical analysis of an objective behaviour.
bereavement	an emotional reaction felt after the death of a loved one.
between-group design	in this experimental design each participant group only experiences one condition of the independent variable.
blastocyst	the inner layer of cells that develops during the germinal period. These cells later develop into the embryo.
breech birth	when a baby is not in the usual position of head first at delivery. Instead, the buttock, knees or feet may come first and the head last. A breech birth increases the time of delivery, as the buttock, knees or feet do not dilate the cervix as well as the head and, due to this, mortality is as high as 10 to 20 per cent in breech births.
Caesarean delivery	also sometimes called a C-section, Caesarean section, Caesar, etc., this is a surgical procedure used to deliver a baby. This involves one or more incisions being made through the mother's abdomen and uterus.
canalised	where the development of an organism takes place along relatively predictable pathways. This suggests that environment has little effect on development.
case study	an in-depth study of an individual person or group. It often uses a combination of qualitative and quantative data to collect detailed information on one person or group.
causal relationship	the suggestion that one condition/event causes another condition/event.
centration	the centring of one's attention on an aspect of a situation to the exclusion of others. This concept is very important in Piagetian theory of cognitive development.
cerebral palsy	an umbrella term that encompasses non-progressive motor conditions, which cause physical difficulties. Cerebral refers to the cerebrum, which is the part of the brain affected, and palsy refers to difficulties with motor abilities.

chicken pox   a contagious disease that causes a rash of red spots on the body.

cliques and crowds   gatherings of people with a common interest or focus, such as music or fashion.

cognitively ready   a term used by Piaget in relation to children's development. This describes his belief that child development was a staged process, meaning that each child had to have developed certain mental abilities before they could go on to the next stage of development and learn new concepts.

cohort   a group of people who share a particular experience in a given time span, for example people born in the UK or USA between 1946 and 1964: this cohort is often referred to as the 'baby boomers'. Another example might be smokers aged between 30 and 40. Cohorts may be tracked over extended periods of time in a cohort study.

co-morbidity   the presence of either one or more disorders (or diseases) in addition to an individual's primary disease or disorder, or the effect of additional disorders or diseases on the individual.

compassionate community   a public health end-of-life care model pioneered by Allan Kellehear. In this model the community has a primary role in supporting the health and social well-being of people as they approach the end of their lives.

concept map   a visual diagram to depict the relationships between different concepts.

confounding variable   a variable that the researcher cannot systematically control and that may affect the outcomes of the research.

conservation   a Piagetian term to explain when a child (or adult) understands that a quantitative aspect of a set of materials/stimulus displayed does not change or become affected by the transformation of the display. This can be tested by the task in which water in a jar is poured into differently shaped containers and children have to state whether there is a change in the amount of water.

correlational study   the study of the extent to which one variable is related to another variable. In a positive correlation, the relationship is such that, as one variable increases, so does the other; in a negative correlation, the opposite relationship occurs and, as one variable increases, so the other variable decreases.

counterbalancing   a method used to reduce possible order effects by splitting participants into two groups, with one group completing the condition in a particular order and the other group completing the condition in the opposite order.

cranium	the part of the skull that encloses the brain.
cross-sectional research	a research method predominantly used in developmental, clinical and social psychology, in which a large group of participants from different backgrounds and ages are studied at one time point.
crystallised abilities	the information, knowledge and skills that are acquired through experience in a cultural environment.
dementia	a serious loss of cognitive ability in a previously unimpaired person, beyond what might be expected from normal ageing. It may be static, the result of a unique global brain injury, or progressive, resulting in long-term decline due to damage or disease in the body. Although dementia is far more common in the geriatric population, it may occur at any stage of adulthood.
DES	stands for diethylstilbestrol, a synthetic form of oestrogen – a female hormone. It was prescribed between 1938 and 1971 to help women with certain complications of pregnancy. Use of DES declined following studies in the 1950s that showed it was not effective in preventing pregnancy complications. However, when given during the first five months of a pregnancy, DES can interfere with the development of the reproductive system in a foetus. For this reason, although DES and other oestrogens may be prescribed for some medical problems, they are no longer used during pregnancy.
developmental niche	a theoretical framework developed by Super and Harkness to analyse and understand how social context and culture shape a child's development.
diathesis-stress model	a model that hypothesises that abnormal behaviour patterns are due to a combination of genetic susceptibility and a stressful environment.
discovery learning	an education method based on Piagetian theory. In discovery learning, active participation by the student takes place through problem-solving situations, where the learner draws on his or her own past experience and existing knowledge to discover facts and relationships and new truths to be learned. Students interact with the world by exploring and manipulating objects, wrestling with questions and controversies, or performing experiments. It is believed that, as a result, students may be more likely to remember concepts and knowledge discovered on their own because they are better able to make sense of them.
domain theory	the theory that knowledge is structured in domains.
Down's syndrome (DS)	a condition present at birth that is due to a chromosomal abnormality caused by faulty cell division soon after fertilisation. DS occurs approximately

16/17 times in every 10,000 births, and the occurrence increases as mothers become older.

ecological validity   the extent to which research findings can be generalised outside the research context. Do they reflect real life?

ectoderm   the outer layer of the embryonic cellular structure, which develops into the outer skin, nervous system, pineal gland and a part of the pituitary.

egocentric   in Piagetian theory, egocentric behaviour is displayed by young children who are unable to distinguish between their own perception of the world and that of others.

Electra complex   a psychoanalytic term used to describe a girl's romantic feelings towards her father and anger towards her mother. It is comparable to the Oedipus complex said to be experienced by boys.

embryo   an organism in the early stages of prenatal development, where there are no physical similarities to its mature form.

empiricist   empiricism is a tradition developed by John Locke and proposes that children are blank slates on which experiences are imprinted. It is only later on in life, through a long learning process, that children's perceptual and other abilities develop.

endoderm   the inner layer of the embryonic cellular structure, which develops into the digestive tract and viscera.

epidural   a form of regional anaesthesia that blocks the transmission of signals through nerves in or near the spinal cord and that can cause a loss of sensation and so relieve pain in the lower body. It is therefore sometimes offered as pain relief during childbirth. The disadvantage of an epidural is that, because it blocks all sensation, it can make the birthing process more difficult.

episiotomy   a surgical procedure in which a small incision is used to enlarge the vaginal opening in order to assist in childbirth.

ethnocentric   the perspective in which one's own ethnic group and social practices are used as the basis to evaluate the practices of other ethnic groups, with the implication that one's own ethnic group is superior.

euthanasia   a means of producing an easy and painless death, advocated by patients who are suffering from intractable pain that accompanies the terminal stages of incurable diseases.

experimental	a research design where the independent variable is manipulated.
fear of strangers	an emotive situation when a child feels apprehensive towards someone they do not know.
feral children	children who have been reared in social isolation by either animals or with no direct contact with humans.
fluid abilities	fluid intelligence or fluid reasoning is the ability to think logically and solve problems in novel situations, independent of acquired knowledge. It is the ability to analyse novel problems, identify patterns and relationships that underpin these problems and so find a solution using logic. It is necessary for all logical problem solving, especially that which is scientific, mathematical and technical.
foetal distress	this refers to signs in a pregnant women, either before or during childbirth, that may suggest that the foetus is not well.
foetus	a term used from the third month of pregnancy to describe an organism in the late stages of prenatal development.
folic acid	a vitamin given to pregnant women to aid the development of a healthy foetus, as it can reduce the risk of neural tube defects (NTDs), such as spina bifida. It is also known as vitamin B9.
forceps	a medical instrument used to grasp and hold something firmly. Forceps resemble a pair of tongs and are sometimes used in cases where the baby is not delivering. The forceps are placed around the baby's head in order to assist the delivery. Forceps are used as an alternative to the ventouse method.
Fragile X	a genetic disorder identified by a weak arm on the X chromosome.
gender identity	a child's awareness of their gender, that is, whether they are a boy or girl. It usually develops by the age of three years.
gender role	the public expression of behaviours and attitudes that indicates to others the affiliation to maleness or femaleness.
gender schema	a cognitive structure used by children to organise their gender knowledge into a set of expectations for their gender and what is appropriate to imitate.
gene mutation	a permanent change in the DNA sequence that makes up a gene, which can range from a single DNA building block to a large part of a chromosome.
genetic epistemology	the approach that focuses on the development of knowledge. This approach is underpinned by the ideas that (1) knowledge develops through organising

and adapting to one's surroundings, (2) knowledge is not based on innate ideas but on active construction by individuals and (3) this construction of knowledge occurs through the need to update knowledge through contradictions in a changing environment.

genotype the set of genes that carries hereditary factors that influence the development of an individual.

grasp reflex a neonatal reflex that occurs when something touches the palm of an infant. The infant responds by grasping tightly.

grief the intense emotional feeling associated with the loss of someone with whom a deep emotional bond existed. The emotions experienced include numbness, disbelief, separation anxiety, despair, sadness and loneliness.

gross and fine motor skills a motor skill is an action that involves the movement of muscles in the body. Gross motor skills are larger movements involving the arms, legs or the entire body – for example, crawling, running and jumping. Fine motor skills are smaller manipulative actions, such as picking things up between the thumb and finger.

habituation techniques habituation is a decrease in response to a stimulus after repeated presentations. Psychologists often use the fact that infants habituate to visual and auditory stimuli in order to assess perceptual abilities at a young age.

Heschl's gyrus a convolution of the temporal lobe that is the cortical centre for hearing and runs obliquely outward and forward from the posterior part of the lateral sulcus.

heteronomous morality also known as moral realism. According to the Piagetian theory of moral development, this is the first stage of moral development. This stage is characterised by a child accepting what is right by the rules of authority. This is also the name given to Kohlberg's first stage of moral reasoning, in which moral thinking is tied to punishment.

holophrase the utterance of a single word that forms part of a whole phrase or perhaps a sentence.

hospice a nursing home specialising in caring for terminally ill patients, so that they can live out their final days in dignity. The hospice movement is committed to making the end of life as free from pain, anxiety and depression as possible. The goals of a hospice contrast with those of a hospital, which are to cure disease and prolong life.

hypothalamus	a small (peanut-sized) but complex structure located at the base of the cerebrum that monitors basic functions such as eating, drinking and sex.
hypothetical-deductive reasoning	style of thinking that typifies Piaget's formal operational concept. It is the ability to develop hypotheses, or best guesses, about ways to solve problems. This form of reasoning is systematic and methodical.
hypothetico-deductive	refers to a method that records observations in order to develop explanatory theories, and then evaluates those theories by generating and testing hypotheses.
id	a Freudian term to explain the instinctive innate pre-birth nature of a person's personality. The id is the pre-socialised infantile part of a person's personality.
innate	refers to characteristics believed to exist at birth due to genetic factors; something that is instinctive, not learned.
insecure-avoidant	a type of attachment behaviour, in which a child treats their parent and the stranger in a similar way, and appears to show little distress when left with the stranger.
insecure-disorganised	a type of attachment behaviour, in which a child's responses to a parent/caregiver are either confused or apprehensive, showing avoidance or resistance. In other words, the child shows a lack of attachment behaviour.
insecure-resistant	a type of attachment behaviour, in which a child becomes very distressed upon separation from a parent, but because of over-activation with the parent, with little interest in the environment, then finds it difficult to be comforted by the parent upon reunion.
interconnectivity	early brain growth includes the development of neural pathways and synaptic connections. This interconnectivity between neurons is important for healthy brain functioning and is thought to be strengthened by repeated use of pathways.
internal working model (IWM)	a model that suggests that children have an internal representation of their relationship with their mother, or other attachment figure. It is suggested that these cognitive structures embody the child's memories of the day-to-day interactions with the attachment figure, and these schemas/structures are then used as a guide to the child's actions with the attachment figure.
interviews	a qualitative approach where data is collected in a conversation-like style with participants. Interviews can be structured, with pre-questions for each participant, or unstructured, where there is no set list of questions.

joint-action formats	a term coined by Jerome Bruner to refer to the joint attention episodes that characterise parent–child interactions. According to Bruner, these episodes are essential for learning new skills, including language.
joint attention	the process by which one person alerts another to a stimulus via non-verbal means, such as gazing or pointing. For example, the infant may look first at an object, then the mother quickly follows, to focus also on the object. This joint attention provides opportunities to learn and is important for relationship formation.
language acquisition device (LAD)	an innate mechanism hypothesised by Noam Chomsky, in which children are pre-programmed with the underlying rules of universal grammar and, based on the language the child is exposed to, the child will select the appropriate rules for the language spoken.
language acquisition support system (LASS)	Bruner's term to describe the range of interactive precursors, such as joint picture book reading, that help support language development in children. These social interactions provide a scaffolding environment to structure the child's early language utterances.
larynx	the top part of the windpipe, containing the vocal cords.
latching on	when a breastfeeding baby correctly positions its mouth around the nipple in order to feed.
leukaemia	a life-threatening disease characterised by abnormally low levels of white blood cells in the blood and body tissue.
libido	a Freudian psychoanalytical term to explain mental or physical sexual desire or pleasure.
lifespan approach	the understanding of a person's development through life from birth to death.
living will	a form of advanced medical directive that defines treatment preference at the end of life, if the patient cannot make medical decisions on their own behalf.
locomotor functions	functions related to movement from place to place, such as crawling, walking and running.
longitudinal study	a study of an individual or group of individuals over a long time period.
matched design	where participants in each condition/group of a research design are paired on a specific variable or set of variables.
maternal responsiveness	a key aspect of mothering described by John Bowlby, in which the mother is sensitive to the child's needs, meaning that her response to the child is contingent on the child's needs.

maturation	the biological process that underpins growth and development; the genetic instructions facilitating the development of instinctive behavioural patterns when a certain growth point or time period has been reached.
menopause	the gradual but permanent cessation of a woman's menstrual activity.
mental operations	the set of mental abilities and skills that allow a child to process and manipulate information so as to solve problems.
meshing	describes the way in which a mother and child will interact closely, and in perfect harmony, especially during breastfeeding.
mesoderm	the middle layer of the embryonic cellular structure, which develops into the muscles and bones.
meta-analysis	the statistical procedure that combines the findings from a number of studies to determine whether there is a significant trend.
microencephaly	a neurodevelopmental disorder in which the circumference of the head is smaller than that of another person of the same sex and age.
mitosis	a cell division process in which somatic cells divide into daughter cells with a completely complementary set of chromosomes.
model	an informal theory that illustrates relationships observed in data or nature.
motherese	sometimes also called parentese or baby talk, this refers to the way in which carers alter their speech patterns to fit the developmental level of the child. Characteristics of motherese include short sentences, a high pitch and sing-song intonation. Babies appear to prefer to listen to motherese and this is thought to focus their attention and so aid language learning.
mourning	the actions or expressions of a person who is bereaved.
multidimensional variables	factors that are represented across more than one dimension. In relation to human development, this infers that development consists of multiple interrelated changes, such as biological, social, emotional and cognitive changes.
multidirectional	in relation to human development, this means that, as some capacities/behaviours decrease, others will expand.
multidisciplinary	as a person's development is multidimensional and multidirectional, it should therefore be seen that different professionals such as psychologists, sociologists, neuroscientists and medical researchers all have different but complementary perspectives on age-related changes.

myelination	this is the process in which myelin (the fatty sheath that covers the axon of a neuron) is formed around the neurons. Myelination occurs in the sixth month of a foetus's life and continues through childhood. Myelin increases the speed at which chemical messages can be passed from cell to cell in the nervous system.
nativist	nativism is a contrasting approach to empiricism. Nativists suggest that children's skills and abilities are present at birth, and that newborns are therefore not blank slates.
neonate	a newborn child.
neo-Piagetians	developmental theorists who have elaborated Piaget's theory, giving more emphasis to information processing, strategies and precise cognitive steps.
neural tube	a hollow structure that features in the development of the central nervous system, formed through the fusion of the neural folds.
neuro-imaging studies	studies that use techniques such as CT and MRI scans to produce detailed images of brain structures. Other brain imaging techniques such as functional MRI scans (fMRI) can help build up a picture of the relationship between brain structure, neurological processes and behaviours. For example, fMRI scanners allow study participants to be presented with a range of stimuli, including visual images, sounds and touch stimuli, or to perform different actions such as pressing a button or moving a joystick. Consequently, fMRI can be used to reveal the brain structures and processes associated with perception, thought and action.
neuron	a nerve cell that handles information processing at the cellular level.
non-nutritive sucking preference procedure	a procedure to assess an infant's attention and perceptual processes by recording the rate of the infant's sucking on a pacifier nipple or dummy. Sucking on the nipple produces stimuli, such as a voice recording or a set of images, rather than nutrients/food. If an infant sucks more at a specific set of stimuli or sucks in order to produce that stimulus, it is inferred that they are showing a preference for that stimulus.
norm	a value that is used in statistical analyses to compare individual/group conditions; it is usually used to refer to a typical or usual value or behaviour.
object permanence	a child's ability to understand that an object exists even if the object is no longer visible to the eye.
observation	a qualitative research method that watches and records participants' behaviour.

Oedipal complex	in Freudian terms, this is a subconscious sexual desire in a male child for the parent of the opposite sex, usually accompanied by hostility to the parent of the same sex.
oestrodiol	the predominant sex hormone in females. This hormone is the one responsible for the growth of the female uterus, Fallopian tubes and vagina. It promotes breast development and the growth of the outer genitals. It also plays a role in the distribution of body fat in women and stops the process of growing taller.
ontogeny	the development of an individual organism.
operant conditioning	the association made between a behaviour and the consequence of the behaviour, controlled by a discriminative stimulus. This consequence can either reinforce behaviour or, if aversive, the behaviour is discouraged from reoccurring.
overextension	young children's extension of a word to cover events/objects beyond that which the word is normally used for, such as calling all animals 'doggie'.
palliative care	the active holistic care of patients with advanced progressive illness. It includes the management of pain and other symptoms. The aim of palliative care is to enable an individual to live as well as possible with the effects of the disease.
palmar grasp	stroking an infant's palm causes the fingers to close around the object used. This grip is strong but unpredictable; it may be sufficient to support the child's weight, yet the child may also release their grip suddenly and without warning. This reflex is seen at birth but disappears at around five or six months of age. It is thought to be the precursor of the purposive grasp, which develops at around four months.
perinatal	refers to the period immediately before and after birth.
pharynx	the part of the throat situated immediately behind the mouth and nasal cavity. The pharynx is part of the digestive system and also the respiratory system; it is also important in vocalisation.
phenotype	the observable, physical structure and function of an organism.
phoneme	the smallest unit of speech that constitutes a change in meaning, such as 'rate' and 'late'; the two words mean something completely different but only differ by one phoneme.
phylogeny	the evolution of behaviour.

pincer grasp	the grasping of an object between the thumb and forefinger. The ability to perform this task is a milestone of fine motor development in infants, usually occurring from nine to 12 months of age.
pituitary gland	the 'master gland' of the endocrine system, as it regulates the actions of the other endocrine glands.
placenta	the 'life support system' for a foetus. It is an organ consisting of embryonic and maternal tissue, to which the foetus is attached via the umbilical cord.
plasticity	(1) refers to the extent to which the direction of development is guided by environmental factors as well as initiated by genetic factors. According to this idea, all organisms, including humans with the same genotype, vary in developmental pattern, in phenotype or in behaviour according to varying environmental conditions. (2) This term is also sometimes used to refer specifically to the flexibility of the brain tissue to assume the functions normally carried out by other tissue.
positivist approach	an approach that suggests that human experiences and social behaviours can be reduced to observable, measurable and categorised facts.
prenatal	prior to birth.
proto-dialogue	early interaction between mother and child that exhibits the characteristics of conversation (dialogue), such as turn-taking, mutuality and synchronicity These proto-dialogues develop out of pseudo-dialogues.
proximity seeking behaviours	in attachment theory, this describes the child's efforts to gain (or regain) contact with the mother or other carer. These behaviours include clambering on to the adult, creeping, crawling or walking and actually making contact, through the child's own efforts.
pseudo-dialogue	synchronised interaction between adult and infant in which the adult structures the interaction so that the infant appears to be an active participant in the 'dialogue'.
puberty	the part of an individual's development where the sex organs become reproductively functional.
qualitative	a research method that emphasises collecting data on the meaning of the behaviour or experiences for the individual/group concerned. Data are collected through various approaches, such as interviews or participant observations, and are then normally transcribed and analysed using theoretical approaches such as grounded theory and discourse analysis.

quantitative	a research method that reduces all data to numbers. Data are collected through experiments and statistical tests and are then used to analyse the data to find out relationships or correlations in data sets.
quasi-experimental	a study where the researcher does not have control over all variables. Often used to refer to the use of naturally occurring phenomena that cannot be manipulated by the researcher for ethical reasons. For example, if testing the contribution of fathers to child development, it would not be ethical to assign some children to families with fathers and others to fatherless families. Instead, comparisons are made between families where fathers are or aren't present by choice.
questionnaire survey	a study where a pre-set list of questions is sent out to a large number of people to complete individually.
random sampling	a sampling method in which every member of the population has an equal chance of being selected.
reinforcement	the strengthening of learning through a bond between a response and a tangible reward.
relativistic thinking	the assumption that knowledge is constructed by each individual through a unique personal framework.
resilience	the ability of people to cope with stress and adversity.
reversibility	in a series of operations, if reversing their order will restore the original state. In part of Piaget's conservation theory, understanding that this is possible results in the ability to conserve.
rouge test	a test used to measure young children's self-concepts. In the test, a dot of red lipstick/face paint is put on the child's face before he or she is put in front of a mirror, to see whether the child touches the red dot. If so, it is then determined that the child has acquired a self-concept or recognition of self.
rubella	also known as German measles. It is a mild disease but can have serious complications for women who are in the early stages pregnancy, as the foetus could potentially develop cognitive problems, heart disease or deafness.
scaffolding	an interactive process in which an adult/older peer behaviourally structures a task for the child to respond to. As the child's ability to complete the task increase, the peer or adult decreases/ modifies the structural support until the child can learn independently.

schizophrenia	an umbrella term for a number of psychotic disorders with various cognitive, emotional and behavioural manifestations.
secure base	a concept related to attachment theory, which states that the carer provides a secure and dependable base for the child to explore the world.
self-concept	a domain-specific evaluation of the self.
self-esteem	the degree to which an individual values his or her own self, skills and abilities. An individual with high self-esteem places a high value on him- or herself.
separation anxiety	a psychoanalytical term that hypothesises the anxiety a child would experience though the loss of a mother.
sexual dimorphism	an individual has two distinct forms, which are differentiated on the basis of sex characteristics.
social learning	a process based on the works of Bandura and Walters, which suggests that someone will imitate observed behaviour in another person if it appears that the behaviour will have reinforcing consequences, and will inhibit the behaviour if the observed consequence is punishment.
socio-cultural context	an approach that attempts to understand the impact of an individual's environment on their development.
specific learning difficulties	a condition/disorder that significantly affects a child's learning in comparison to the majority of children of their age.
spina bifida	a developmental birth defect caused by the incomplete closure of the embryonic neural tube.
standardised test	a measure that has been through empirical analysis to ensure reliability and validity.
Strange Situation	an experimental method developed by Mary Ainsworth, in which a young child is placed in increasingly strange situations to observe their emotional reactions.
sub-clinical disease	the period prior to the appearance of the symptoms of a disease. The disease is developing but no signs have yet been noticed by the individual or others around them.
sudden infant death syndrome (SIDS)	a term used to explain the sudden or inexplicable death of an infant or very young child. Sometimes referred to as 'cot death'.

symbolic interactionist theory	an important perspective in the social sciences that places emphasis on micro-scale social interaction. This approach is derived from American pragmatism, especially the work of George Herbert Mead and Charles Cooley. According to Mead, people interact with each other by interpreting or defining each other's actions instead of merely reacting to each other's actions.
symbolic play	imaginative play, where a child may pretend to be other people or act out 'real-life situations', such as playing nurses and doctors, or pretending that an object is another object, such as using a banana as a telephone.
syphilis	an infectious venereal disease that enters the nervous system through a break in the skin or a mucous membrane, most commonly during sexual inter-course.
tabula rasa	from the Latin meaning 'blank slate'. This is the phrase that John Locke used to refer to a child's mind at birth, which he believed was unformed and featureless.
telegraphic speech	a term developed by Roger Brown to explain a characteristic of children's early stages of language, where a highly reduced form of speech, in which unessential words are left out, just as in a telegram.
teratogen	a Greek word meaning 'creating a monster'– a reference to an environmental hazard/abnormality that can occur in prenatal development, through, for example, drugs or harmful substances.
testosterone	the primary testicular hormone in men, which stimulates the maturation of the male genitals, the development of hair growth, the production of sperm and voice changes.
thalidomide	a drug that was given to pregnant women in the 1950s to prevent morning sickness, which led to babies being born with severe limb deformities if taken during the first two months of pregnancy.
theory	an interconnecting set of statements that structure how we observe and categorise facts about the world.
theory of mind	the understanding that other people have different emotions, thoughts and feelings from oneself.
transactional model	describes the way in which innate skills and abilities interact with the environment. In this model, the child's behaviour can change the social context of development by influencing the response of others to them. In the same way,

the pre-existing beliefs etc. of the individuals in the child's environment will influence how they respond to the child. In this way the child and context shape each other.

trophoblast
a cell that develops at the first stage of pregnancy on the outer layer of a blastocyst and provides nutrients to the embryo and develops into a large part of the placenta.

ulnar grasp
an early manipulatory skill used by infants in which objects are grasped by pressing the fingers against the palm.

umbilical cord
the vascular tube that connects the foetus with the placenta and passes oxygen and nutrients.

underextension
the limiting of a word meaning to too few instances by a young child, for example when a child restricts the word 'dog' to situations in which the child is playing with a toy, but then fails to refer to the animal at the park as a 'dog'.

ventouse
a vacuum device used to assist with labour if it has not progressed adequately. It is attached to the baby's head.

visual cortex
the part of the brain specialised in processing information and in pattern recognition.

within-group design
all participants experience all levels of the independent variable.

zone of proximal development (ZPD)
the conceptual zone/space between a child completing a task on his or her own and completing the task with assistance from an adult or older peer.

References

Abrams, D, Eilola, T and Swift, H. (2009) *Attitudes to Age in Britain 2004–2008*. Research report no. 599. London: Department for Work and Pensions. Available online at http://research.dwp.gov.uk/asd/asd5/rports2009-2010/rrep599.pdf (accessed 10 March 2011).

Academy of Medical Royal Colleges (AOMRC) (2008) *A Code of Practice for the Diagnosis and Confirmation of Death*. London: AOMRC. Available online at www.aomrc.org.uk/publications/reports-guidance.html.

Adams, MJ (1990) *Beginning to Read: Thinking and learning about print*. Cambridge, MA: MIT Press.

Adolph, KE (2002) Learning to keep balance, in Kali, R (ed.) *Advances in Child Development and Behaviour*. San Diego, CA: Academic Press.

Aguiar, A and Baillargeon, R (2002) Developments in young infants' reasoning about occluded objects. *Cognitive Psychology*, 39: 116–57.

Ainsworth, M and Bell, S (1970) Attachment, exploration and separation: illustrated by the behaviour of 1 year olds in a Strange Situation. *Child Development*, 41: 49–65.

Alberts, A, Elkind, D and Ginsberg, S (2007) The personal fable and risk-taking in early adolescence. *Journal of Youth and Adolescence*, 36: 71–6.

Alder, EM and Ross, LA (2000) Menopausal symptoms and the domino effect. *Journal of Reproductive and Infant Psychology*, 18: 75–8.

Alexander, G, Wilcox, T and Woods, R (2008) Sex differences in infants' visual interest in toys. *Archives of Sexual Behavior*, 38(3): 427–33.

Amara, CE, Rice, CL, Koval, JJ, Paterson, DH, Winter, EM and Cunningham, DA (2003) Allometric scaling of strength in an independently living population age 55–86 years. *American Journal of Human Biology*, 15: 48–60.

Archer, J (1999) *The Nature of Grief: The evolution and psychology of reactions to loss*. New York: Routledge.

Aries, P (1981) *The Hour of our Death*. New York: Oxford University Press.

Arnett, JJ (1992) Reckless behaviour in adolescence: a developmental perspective. *Developmental Review*, 12: 339–73.

Arnett, JJ (1999) Adolescent storm and stress reconsidered. *American Psychologist*, 54: 317–26.

Arnett, JJ (2000) Emerging adulthood: a theory of development from the late teens through the twenties. *American Psychologist*, 55: 469–80.

Arnett, JJ (2004) *Emerging Adulthood: The winding road from the late teens through the twenties*. New York: Oxford University Press.

Arnett, JJ (2006) Emerging adulthood in Europe: a response to Bynner. *Journal of Youth Studies*, 9: 111–23.

Atchley, RC (1976)*The Sociology of Retirement*. New York: Shenkman.

Azmitia, M, Kamprath, N and Linnet, J (1998) Intimacy and conflict: on the dynamics of boys' and girls' friendships during middle childhood and adolescence, in Meyer, L, Grenot-Scheyer, M, Harry, B, Park, H and Schwartz, I (eds) *Understanding the Social Lives of Children and Youth*. Baltimore, MD: PH Brookes.

Baillargeon, E, Baillargeon, R, Spelke, E and Wasserman, S (1985) Object permanence in five-month-old infants. *Cognition*, 20: 191–208.

Baillargeon, R (2002) The acquisition of physical knowledge in infancy: a summary in eight lessons, in Goswami, U (ed.) *Handbook of Child Cognitive Development*. Oxford: Blackwell.

Baltes, PB (2003) On the incomplete architecture of human ontogeny: selection, optimization and compensation as foundation for developmental theory, in Staudinger, UM and Lindenberger, U (eds) *Understanding Human Development*. Boston: Kluwer.

Bandura, A (1963) The role of imitation in personality development. *Journal of Nursery Education*, 18: 207–15.

Bandura, A (1986) *Social Foundations of Thought and Action: A social cognitive theory*. Englewood Cliffs, NJ: Prentice Hall.

Bannister, D and Agnew, J (1977) The child's construing of self, in Cole, JK (ed.) *Nebraska Symposium on Motivation 1976*. Lincoln, NE: University of Nebraska.

Baron-Cohen, S, Leslie, AM and Frith, U (1985) Does the autistic child have a theory of mind. *Cognition*, 21: 37–46.

Basseches, M (1984) *Dialectical Thinking and Adult Development*. Norwood, NJ: Ablex.

Bates, JE (2003) Temperamental unadaptability and later internalising problems as moderated by mothers' restrictive control. Paper presented at the meeting for the Society for Research in Child Development, Tampa, FL.

Baumeister, RF, Campbell, JD, Krueger, JI and Vohs, KE (2003) Does high self esteem cause better performance, interpersonal success happiness or healthier lifestyles? *Psychological Science in the Public Interest*, 4(1): 1–44.

Bayley, N (1993) *Bayley Scales of Infant Development* (2nd edn). San Antonio, TX: Psychological Corporation.

Bem, SL (1989) Genital knowledge and gender constancy in preschool children. *Child Development*, 60: 649–62.

Bergen, D (1988) Stages of play development, in Bergen, D (ed.) *Play as a Medium for Learning and Development*. Portsmouth: Heinemann.

Bering, JM and Bjorklund, DF (2004) The natural emergence of afterlife reasoning as a developmental regularity. *Developmental Psychology*, 40: 217–33.

Berko Gleason, J (1973) Code switching in children's language, in Moore, TE (ed.) *Cognitive Development and the Acquisition of Language*. New York: Academic Press.

Bielak, AM (2010) How can we not 'lose it' if we still don't understand how to 'use it'? Unanswered questions about the influence of activity participation on cognitive performance in older age: a mini-review. *Gerontology*, 56: 507–19.

Bigelow, BJ (1977) Children's friendship expectations: a cognitive-developmental study. *Child Development*, 48: 246–53.

Birren, JE, Butler, RN and Greenhouse, SW et al. (eds) (1963) *Human Aging: A biological and behavioral study*. Washington, DC: US Government Printing Office.

Blackburn, JA and Papalia, DE (1992) The study of adult cognition from a Piagetian perspective, in Sternberg, RJ and Berg, CA (eds) *Intellectual Development*. New York: Cambridge University Press.

Blakemore, SJ and Choudhury, S (2006) Development of the adolescent brain: implications for executive function and social cognition. *Journal of Child Psychology and Psychiatry*, 47: 296–312.

Blaskewicz Boron, J, Turiano, NA, Willis, SL and Schaie, KW (2007) Effects of cognitive training on change in accuracy in inductive reasoning ability. *Journal of Gerontology*, 62(3): 179–86.

Blatchford, P (1998) *Social Life in School*. London: Falmer.

Blatchford, P, Creeser, R and Mooney, A (1990) Playground games and play time: the children's view. *Educational Research*, 32: 163–74.

Blatchford, P, Pellegrini, T, Baines, E and Kentaro, K (2002) *Playground Games: Their social context in elementary/junior school*. Final report to the Spencer Foundation. Available online at www.break time.org.uk/SpencerFinalReport02.pdf (accessed 10 March 2011).

Bloom L, Lifter, K and Broughton, J (1985) The convergence of early cognition and language in the second year of life: problems in conceptualisation and measurement, in Barrett, M (ed.) *Children's Single-word Speech*. London: Wiley-Blackwell.

Bloom, L (1998) *Language Acquisition in its Developmental Context*. Oxford: Oxford University Press.

Bluebond-Langner, M (1977) Meanings of death to children, in Feifel, H (ed.) *New Meanings of Death.* New York: McGraw-Hill.

Blumenthal JA, Babyak MA, Moore KA, Craighead, WE, Herman, S, Khatri, P, Waugh, R, Napolitano, MA, Forman, LM, Appelbaum, M, Doraiswamy, PM and Krishnan, KR (1999) Effects of exercise training on older patients with major depression, *Archives of Internal Medicine*, 159: 2349–56.

Blumstein Posner, R (2006) Early menarche: a review of research on trends in timing, racial differences, etiology and psychosocial consequences. *Sex Roles*, 54(5–6): 315–22.

Bombar, ML and Littig, LW (1996) Babytalk as a communication of intimate attachment: an initial study in adult romances and friendships. *Personal Relationships*, 3(2): 137–58.

Bower, B (1985) The left hand of math and verbal talent. *Science News*, 127(17): 263.

Bowlby, J (1951) *Maternal Care and Mental Health.* Geneva: World Health Organization.

Bowlby, J (1969) *Attachment and Loss: Vol. 1: Attachment.* New York: Basic Books.

Boyatzis, CJ and Watson, MW (1993) Preschool children's symbolic representation of objects through gestures. *Child Development*, 67(3): 729–35.

Boysson-Bardies, B (1999) *How Language Comes to Children: From birth to two years* (trans. M DeBevoise). Cambridge, MA: MIT Press.

Bretherton, I and Mulholland, KA (1999) Internal working models in attachment relations: a construct revisited, in Cassidy, J and Shaver, PR (eds) *Handbook of Attachment: Theory, research and clinical applications* (pp89–111). New York: Guilford.

Bril, B (1999) Dires sur les enfants selon les cultures, in Bril, B, Dansen, PR, Sabatier, C and Krewer, B (eds) *Propos sur l'enfant et l'adolescent. Quel enfans pour quelles cultures?* Paris: L'Harmattan.

Brim, OG, Ryff, CD and Kessler, RC (2004) *How Healthy are We? A national study of of well-being at midlife*, London: University of Chicago Press.

Bronfenbrenner, U (1977) Toward an experimental ecology of human development. *American Psychologist*, 32: 513–31.

Brown, R (1973) *A First Language: The early stages.* Cambridge, MA: Harvard University Press.

Brown, R and Hanlon, C (1970) Derivational complexity and order of acquisition in child speech, in Hayes, J (ed.) *Cognition and the Development of Language.* New York: Wiley.

Bruner, JS (1975) The ontogenesis of speech acts. *Journal of Child Language*, 2: 1–19.

Bruner, JS (1983) *Child's Talk: Learning to use language.* New York: Norton.

Bruner, JS (1985) *Actual Minds, Possible Worlds.* Cambridge, MA: Harvard University Press.

Bruner, JS (1993) Explaining and interpreting: two ways of using mind, in Harman, G (ed.) *Conceptions of the Human Mind: Essays in honor of George A Miller.* Hillsdale, NJ: Lawrence Erlbaum.

Bruton, C (2007) Do we send our children to school too young? *The Times,* 6 September. Available online at http://women.timesonline.co.uk/tol/life_and_style/women/families/article2392738.ece. (accessed 12 March 2011).

Buhrmester, D (1990) Intimacy of friendship, interpersonal competence, and adjustment during preadolescence and adolescence. *Child Development,* 61: 1101–11.

Buhrmester, D (1996) Need fulfillment, interpersonal competence, and the developmental contexts of early adolescent friendship, in Bukowski, W, Newcomb, A and Hartup, W (eds) *The Company They Keep.* New York: Cambridge University Press.

Burckhardt, CS and Anderson, KL (2003) The quality of life scale (QOLS): reliability, validity, and utilization. *Health and Quality of Life Outcomes,* 1: 60.

Burke, DM and Shafto, MA (2004) Aging and language production. *Current Directions in Psychological Science,* 13: 21–4.

Burke, DM and Shafto, MA (2008) Language and aging, in Craik, FIM and Salthouse, TA (eds) *The Handbook of Aging and Cognition.* New York: Psychology Press.

Bushnell, IWR (2003) Newborn face recognition, in Pascalis, O and Slater, A (eds) *The Development of Face Processing in Infancy and Early Childhood: Current perspectives.* New York: Nova Science.

Byrnes, BM and Gavin, DAW (1996) The Shavelson model revisited: testing for structure of academic self-concept across pre-early, and late adolescence. *Journal of Educational Psychology,* 88: 215–28.

Caley, L, Syms, C, Robinson, L, Cederbaum, J, Henry, M and Shipkey, N (2008) What human service professionals know and want to know about fetal alcohol syndrome. *Canadian Journal of Clinical Pharmacology,* 15: e177–e123.

Carneiro, P, Heckman, JJ and Vytlacil, E (2001) *Estimating the Return to Education when it Varies among Individuals.* Available online at www.iza.org/en/papers/Vytlacil131101.pdf (accessed 12 March 2011).

Carstensten, LL (1992). Motivation for social contact across the lifespan: a theory of socio-emotional selectivity, in Jacobs, Janis E (ed.) *Nebraska Symposium on Motivation: Developmental perspectives on motivation* (Current theory and research in motivation). Nebraska, NE: University of Nebraska Press.

Carter-Saltzman, L (1980) Biological and sociocultural effects on handedness: comparison between biological and adoptive families. *Science,* 209 (4462): 1263–5.

Case, R (1999) Neopiagetian theories of cognitive development Neo-Piagetian theories of cognitive development, in Beilin, H and Pufall, P (eds), *Piaget's Theory: Prospects and possibilities* (pp61–104). Hillsdale, NJ: Erlbaum.

Casey, BJ, Giedd, JN and Thomas, KM (2000) Structural and functional brain development and its relation to cognitive development. *Biological Psychology*, 54(1–3): 241–57.

Chachkes, E and Jennings, R (1994) Latino communities: coping with death, in Dane, B and Levine, C (eds) *AIDS and the New Orphans: Coping with death*. Westport, CT: The Greenwood Press.

Charles, ST and Mavandadi, SK (2004) Social support and physical health across the life span: socioemotional influences, in Lang, FR and Fingerman, KL (eds) *Growing Together: Personal relationships across the life span*. New York: Cambridge University Press.

Chomsky, N (1979) Human language and other semiotic systems. *Semiotica*, 25: 31–44.

Cintas HM (1989) Cross-cultural variation in infant motor development. *Physical and Occupational Therapy in Pediatrics*, 8: 1–20.

Clark, R, Hyde, JS, Essex, MJ and Klein, MH (2006) Length of maternity leave and quality of mother–infant interactions. *Child Development*, 68, 2: 364–83.

Clark, DC, Pynoos, MD and Goebel, AE (1994) Mechanisms and processes of adolescent bereavement, in Haggerty, RJ, Sherrod, LR, Garmezy, N and Rutter, M (eds) *Stress, Risk and Resilience in Children and Adolescence*. Cambridge: Cambridge University Press.

Cohen, LB and Cashon, CH (2003) Infant perception and cognition, in Lerner, R, Easterbrooks, A and Mistry, J (eds) *Comprehensive Handbook of Psychology: Vol. 6, Developmental psychology. Part Two: Infancy* (pp65–89). New York: Wiley and Sons.

Cole, M (1990) Cognitive development and formal schooling: the evidence from cross-cultural research, in Moll, LC (ed.) *Vygotsky and Education*. New York: Cambridge University Press.

Cole, PM and Tan, PZ (2007) Emotion socialization from a cultural perspective, in Grusec, JE and Hastings, PD (eds) *Handbook of Socialization*. New York: Guilford.

Coleman, JC (1978) Current contradictions in adolescent theory. *Journal of Youth and Adolescence*, 7: 1–11.

Colonnesi, C, Stamms, GJ and Koster, I (2010) The relationship between pointing and language development, *Developmental Review*, in press.

Commons, ML, Richards, FA and Armon, C (1984) *Beyond Formal Operations: Late adolescent and adult cognitive development*. New York: Praeger.

Cook, AS and Dworkin, DS (1992) *Helping the Bereaved: Therapeutic interventions for children, adolescents and adults*. New York: Basic Books.

Cooley, CH (1902) *Human Nature and the Social Order*, New York: Charles Scribner's Sons.

Cordier, S (2008) Evidence for a role of paternal exposures in developmental toxicity. *Basic and Clinical Pharmacology and Toxicology*, 102: 176–81.

Croghan, R, Griffin, C, Hunter J and Phoenix, A (2006) Style failure: consumption, identity and social exclusion. *Journal of Youth Studies*, 9(4): 463–78.

Csikszentmihalyi, M and Larson, R (1984) *Being Adolescent: Conflict and growth in the teenage years*. New York: Basic Books.

Cuddy-Casey, M and Orvaschel, H (1997) Children's understanding of death in relation to child suicidality and homicidality. *Clinical Psychology Review*, 17: 33–45.

Damon, W and Hart, D (1988) *Self-understanding in Childhood and Adolescence*. New York: Cambridge University Press.

Darwin, C (1859) *On the Origin of Species*, London: John Murray.

Davies, BE, Moon, RM, Sachs, MC and Ottolini, CY (1998) Effects of sleep position on infant motor development. *Pediatrics*, 102: 1135–40.

Davies-Floyd, RE and Sargeant, CF (1997) *Childbirth and Authoritative Knowledge: Cross-cultural perspectives*, Berkeley, CA: University of California Press.

DeCasper, AJ and Spence, MJ (1986) Prenatal maternal speech influences newborns' perception of speech sounds. *Infant Behavior and Development*, 9: 133–50.

Demetriou, A, Christou, C, Spanoudis, G and Platsidou, M (2002) The development of mental processing: efficiency, working memory, and thinking. *Monographs of the Society for Research in Child Development*, 67(1): serial no. 268.

Department for Education and Skills (DfES) (2007) *Raising Expectations: Staying in education and training post–16*. Green Paper, March. www.dfes.gov.uk/publications/raisingexpectations/

Department of Health (DoH) (2004) *National Service Framework for Children, Young People and Maternity Services*, September. www.dh.gov.uk/PolicyAndGuidance/HealthAndSocialCareTopics/ChildrenServices/ChildrenServicesInformation/fs/en

Department of Health (DoH) (2008) *End of Life Care Strategy: Promoting high quality care for all adults at the end of life*, July. www.dh.gov.uk/en/Publicationsandstatistics/Publications/PublicationsPolicyAndGuidance/DH_086277

Derbyshire, E (2007) The importance of adequate fluid and fibre intake during pregnancy. *Nursing Standard*, 21(24): 40–3.

Diamond, AD (1985) Development of the ability to use recall to guide action as indicated by infants' performance on AB. *Child Development*, 56: 868–83.

Diamond, LM (2000) Sexual identity, attractions, and behavior among young sexual-minority women over a two-year period. *Developmental Psychology*, 36: 241–50.

Donaldson, M (1978) *Children's Minds*. London: Croom Helm.

Dontigny, L, Arsenault, M-Y and Martel, M-J et al. (2008) Rubella in pregnancy. *Journal of Obstetrics and Gynaecology Canada*, 30(2): 152–68.

Dorn, LD, Dahl, RE, Woodward, HR and Biro, F (2006) Defining the boundaries of early adolescence: a user's guide to assessing pubertal status and pubertal timing in research with adolescents. *Applied Developmental Science*, 10: 30–56.

Doyle, AM, Lechiler, RI and Turka, LA (2004) Organ transplantation: halfway through the first century. *Journal of the American Society of Nephrology*, 15: 2965–71.

Dunn, J (1988) *The Beginnings of Social Understanding*. Oxford: Blackwell.

Durston, S, Davidson, MC, Tottenham, N, Galvan, A, Spicer, J, Fossella, JA and Casey, BJ (2006) A shift from diffuse to focal cortical activity with development. *Developmental Science*, 9(1): 1–8.

Duschl, R, Schweingruber, H and Shouse, A (eds) (2007) *Taking Science to School: Learning and teaching science in grades K–8*. Washington, DC: National Academies Press.

Earles, JL and Salthouse, TA (1995) Interrelations of age, health, and speed. *Journal of Gerontology*, 50(1): 33–41.

Edwards SL and Sarwark, JF (2005) Infant and child motor development. *Clinical Orthopaedics*, 434: 33–9.

Eisenberg, N and Fabes, RA (1998) Prosocial development, in Eisenberg, N (ed.) *Handbook of Child Psychology, Vol. 3: Social, emotional, and personality development*. New York: Wiley.

Ekerdt, DJ, Bossé, R and Levkoff, S (1985) An empirical test for phases of retirement: findings from the Normative Aging Study. *Journal of Gerontology*, 40: 95–101.

Ekerdt, DJ, Kosloski, K and Deviney, S (2000) The normative anticipation of retirement by older workers. *Research on Aging*, 22: 3–22.

Elkind, D (1978) Understanding the young adolescent. *Adolescence,* 13(49): 127–34.

Enzinger, C, Fazekas F, Matthews, PM and Ropele S et al. (2005) Risk factors for progression of brain atrophy in aging: six-year follow-up of normal subjects. *Neurology*, 64(10): 1704–11.

Epstein, JL (1986) Friendship selection: developmental and environmental influences, in Meuller, E and Cooper, C (eds) *Process and Outcome in Peer Relationship*. New York: Academic Press.

Erikson, EH (1950) *Childhood and Society,* New York: WW Norton.

Erikson, EH (1963) *Childhood and Society* (2nd edn). New York: Norton.

Evans, JL (2006) The emergence of language: a dynamical systems account, in Hoff, E and Shatz, M (eds) *Blackwell Handbook of Language Development*. Wiley Online Library.

Fan, Y, Batmanghelich, N, Clark, CM, Davatzikos, C and Alzheimer's Disease Neuroimaging Initiative (2008) Spatial patterns of brain atrophy in MCI patients, identified via high-dimensional pattern classification, predict subsequent cognitive decline. *Neuroimage*, 39: 1731–43.

Faulkner, KW (1997) Talking about death with a dying child. *American Journal of Nursing*, 97: 65–9.

Fein, GG (1986) Pretend play, in Gorlitz, D and Wohlwill, JF (eds) *Curiosity, Imagination and Play*. Hillsdale, NJ: Lawrence Erlbaum.

Fenner, F, Henderson, DA, Arita, I, Jezek, Z and Ladnyi, ID (1988) *Smallpox and Its Eradication*. Geneva: World Health Organization.

Fenson, L, Dale, PS, Reznick, JS, Bates, E, Thal, DJ and Pethick, SJ (1994) Variability in early communicative development. *Monographs of the Society of Research in Child Development*, 59: serial no. 242.

Fentress, JC and Mcleaod, PJ (1986) Motor patterns in development, in Blass, EM (ed.) *Handbook of Behavioural Neurobiology, Vol. 8: Developmental psychology and developmental neurobiology*. New York: Plenum.

Fernald, A (1985) Four-month-old infants prefer to listen to motherese. *Infant Behaviour and Development*, 8: 181–95.

Fiedler, DC (1997) Authoritative knowledge and birth territories in contemporary Japan, in Davis-Floyd, R and Sargent, C (eds) *Childbirth and Authoritative Knowledge: Cross-cultural perspectives*. Berkeley, CA: University of California Press.

Field, D (1981) Can preschool children really learn to conserve? *Child Development*, 52: 326–34.

Fischer, JL, Sollie, DL, Sorell, GT, Green, SK (1989) Marital status and career stage influences on social networks of young adults. *Journal of Marriage and the Family*, 51: 521–34.

Flavell, JH and Miller, PH (1998) Social cognition, in Kuhn, D and Siegler, RS (eds) *Handbook of Child Psychology, Vol. 2: Cognition, perception, and language*. New York: Wiley.

Flavell, JH, Miller, PH and Miller, SA (1993) *Cognitive Development* (3rd edn). Englewood Cliffs, NJ: Prentice Hall.

Flint, M (1982) Male and female menopause: a cultural put on, in Voda, AM, Dinnerstein, M and O'Donnell, SR (eds) *Changing Perspectives on Menopause*. Austin, TX: University of Texas Press.

Fotenos, AF, Mintun, MA, Synder, AZ, Morris, JC and Buckner, RL (2008) Brain volume decline in aging: evidence for a relation between socioeconomic status, preclinical Alzheimer disease, and reserve. *Neurology*, 65(1): 113–20.

Fraser, AM, Brockert, JE and Ward RH (1995) Association of young maternal age with adverse reproductive outcomes. *New England Journal of Medicine*, 332: 1113–17.

Freud, A (1958) Adolescence, in *The Writings of Anna Freud, Vol. 5: Research at the Hampstead Child-Therapy Clinic and other papers 1956–1965*, New York: Indiana University of Pennsylvania.

Freud, S (1905) Three essays on the theory of sexuality, in Strachey, J (ed. and trans.) (1953) *The Standard Edition of the Complete Psychological Works of Sigmund Freud, Vol. 7*. London: Hogarth Press.

Freud, S (1917) *A General Introduction to Psychoanalysis*. New York: Washington Square Press.

Friedberg, L (2003) The impact of technological change on older workers: evidence from data on computers. *Industrial and Labor Relations Review*, 56: 511–29.

Frisen, A and Holmqvist, K (2010) Physical, sociocultural, and behavioral factors associated with body-esteem in 16-year-old Swedish boys and girls. *Sex Roles*, 63: 373–85.

Galloway, JC and Thelen, E (2004) Feet first: object exploration in young infants. *Infant Behavior and Development*, 27: 107–12.

Gershkoff-Stowe, L and Thelen, E (2004) U-shaped changes in behaviour: a dynamic systems perspective. *Journal of Cognition and Development*, 5: 11–36.

Ghayas, S and Adil, A (2007) Effect of handedness on intelligence level of students. *Journal of the Indian Academy of Applied Psychology*, 33(1): 85–91.

Gilligan, C (1982) *In a Different Voice: Psychological theory and women's development*. Cambridge, MA: Harvard University Press.

Gilligan, C (1996) The centrality of relationships in psychological development: a puzzle, some evidence and a theory, in Noam, GG and Fischer, KW (eds) *Development and Vulnerability in Close Relationships*. Hillsdale, NJ: Lawrence Erlbaum.

Gold, EB, Sternfeld, B, Kelsey, JL, Brown, C and Mouton C et al. (2000) The relation of demographic and lifestyle factors to symptoms in a multi-ethnic population of 40–55-year-old women. *American Journal of Epidemiology*, 152: 463–73.

Gopnik, A (1993) How we know our minds: the illusion of first-person knowledge of intentionality. *Behavioral and Brain Sciences*, 16: 1–14.

Gordon-Salant, S, Yeni-Konshian, G, Fitzgibbons, PJ and Barrett, J (2006) Age-related differences in identification and discrimination of temporal cues in speech segments. *Journal of the Acoustical Society of America*, 119(4): 2455–66.

Graber, JA and Brooks-Gunn, J (2001) Body image, in Lerner, RM and Learner, JV (eds) *Adolescence in America*. Santa Barbara, CA: ABC-CLIO.

Grady, CL, Springer, MV, Hongwanishkul, D, McIntosh, AR and Winocur, G (2006) Age-related changes in brain activity across the adult lifespan. *Journal of Cognitive Neuroscience*, 18: 227–41.

Graham, P and Rutter, M (1985) Adolescent disorders, in Rutter, M and Hersov, L (eds) *Child and Adolescent Psychiatry: Modern approaches* (4th edn). Oxford: Blackwell Scientific.

Grieg, A and Taylor, J (1999) *Doing Research with Children*. London: Sage.

Grossbart, TA and Sarwer, DB (2003) Psychosocial issues and their relevance to the cosmetic surgery patient. *Seminars in Cutaneous Medical Surgery*, 22(2): 136–47.

Guisinger, SJ and Blatt, S (1994) Individuality and relatedness: evolution of a fundamental dialectic. *American Psychologist*, 49: 104–11.

Gunnar, MR and Quevedo, K (2007) The neurobiology of stress and development. *Annual Review of Psychology*, 58: 145–73.

Hall, GS (1891) The contents of children's minds on entering school. *Pedagogical Seminary*, 1: 139–73.

Hall, GS (1904) *Adolescence: Its psychology and its relations to physiology, anthropology, sociology, sex, crime, religion and education*. New York: Appleton.

Hall, GS (1912) *Founders of Modern Psychology*. New York and London: Appleton.

Hall, GS (1922) *Senescence*. London and New York: Appleton.

Hannan, TE (1992) An examination of spontaneous pointing in 20- to 50-month-old children. *Perceptual and Motor Skills*, 74: 651–8.

Hansson, RO, DeKoekkoek, PD, Neece, WM and Patterson, DW (1997) Successful aging at work: annual review, 1992–1996: the older worker and transitions to retirement. *Journal of Vocational Behavior*, 51: 202–33.

Hanushek, EA (2003) *The Economics of Schooling and School Quality*. London: Edward Elgar.

Hardy, I, Jonen, A, Möller, K and Stern, E (2006) Effects of instructional support within constructivist learning environments for elementary school students' understanding of 'floating and sinking'. *Journal of Educational Psychology*, 98: 307–26.

Harkness, S and Super, CM (1995) Culture and parenting, in Bornstein, MH (ed.) *Handbook of Parenting, Vol. 3*. Hillsdale, NJ: Lawrence Erlbaum.

Harris, M (1992) *Language Experience and Early Language Development: From input to uptake*. Hove: Lawrence Erlbaum.

Harris, M, Barlow-Brown, F and Chasin, J (1995a) The emergence of referential understanding: pointing and the comprehension of object names. *First Language*, 15: 19–34.

Harris, M, Yeeles, C, Chasin, J and Oakley, Y (1995b) Symmetries and asymmetries in early lexical comprehension and production, *Journal of Child Language*, 22: 1–18.

Harris, PL (1989) Object permanence in infancy, in Slater, A and Bremner, JG (eds) *Infant Development: Recent advances*. Hove: Lawrence Erlbaum.

Harris, PL (2006) Social cognition, in Kuhn, D and Siegler, R (eds) *Handbook of Child Psychology, Vol. 2: Cognition, perception, and language* (6th edn). New York: Wiley.

Hartup, WW (1996) The company they keep: friendships and their developmental significance. *Child Development*, 67: 1–13.

Hayden, KM, Zandi, PP, Lyketsos, CG, Khachaturian, AS and Bastian, LA et al. (2006) Vascular risk factors for incident Alzheimer disease and vascular dementia: the Cache County study. *Alzheimer Disease and Associated Disorders*, 20(2): 93–100.

Hayslip, B and Hansson, RO (2003) Death awareness and adjustment across the life span, in Bryant, CD (ed.) *Handbook of Death and Dying*. Thousand Oaks, CA: Sage.

Heath, S (2008) *Housing Choices and Issues for Young People in the UK*. York: Joseph Rowntree Foundation. Available at www.ecotec.com/pdfs/2325-young-people-housing.pdf

Hedlund, B and Ebersole, P (1983) A test of Levinson's mid-life re-evaluation. *Journal of Genetic Psychology*, 143: 189–92.

Hepper, PG, *Shahidullah, S and White, R (1991) Handedness in the human fetus. Neuropsychologia*, 29: 1107–11.

Herkert, B (2000) Communicating grief. *Omega: Journal of Death and Dying*, 41: 93–116.

Hermans, H and Oles, P (1999) Midlife crisis in men: affective organization of personal meanings. Human Relations, 52: 1403–26.

Hertz-Piciotto, I, Park, HY and Dostal, M (2008) Prenatal exposure to persistent and non-persistent organic compounds and effects on immune system development. *Basic and Clinical Pharmacology and Toxicology*, 102: 146–54.

Hiley, CM and Morley, C (1995) What do mothers remember about the 'back to sleep' campaign? *Archives of Diseases in Childhood,* December, 73(6): 496–7.

Hines, M and Brooks, G (2005) *Sheffield Babies Love Books: An evaluation of the Sheffield Bookstart project*. Sheffield: City of Sheffield.

Hochschild, A and Machong, A (1989) *The Second Shift: Working parents and the revolution at home.* New York: Viking Penguin.

Hoffman, ML (2000) *Empathy and Moral Development: Implications for caring and justice.* Cambridge: Cambridge University Press.

Holtzen, DW (2000) Handedness and professional tennis. *International Journal of Neuroscience.* 105: 109–19.

Hopkins, B (1991) Facilitating early motor development: an intracultural study of West Indian mothers and their infants living in Britain, in Nugent, JK, Lester, BM and Brazelton, TB (eds) *The Cultural Context of Infancy, Vol. 2.* Norwood, NJ: Ablex.

Hughes, M (1975) Egocentrism in preschool children. Unpublished PhD thesis. University of Edinburgh.

Hunt, CE and Hauck, FR (2006) Sudden infant death syndrome. *Canadian Medical Association Journal,* 174(13): 1861–9.

Huttenlocher, PR and Kubicek, L (1983) The source of relatedness effects on naming latency. *Journal of Experimental Psychology: Learning, Memory and Cognition,* 9(3): 486–96.

Inhelder, B and Piaget, J (1964) *The Early Growth of Logic in the Child* (trans. 1969). New York: Norton.

Inoff-Germain, G, Chrousos, G, Arnold, G, Nottelmann, E, and Cutler, G (1988). Relations between hormone levels and observational measures of aggressive behavior of young adolescents in family interactions. *Developmental Psychology,* 24: 129–39.

Iverson, P, Kuhl, PK, Akahane-Yamada, R, Diesch, E and Tohkura, Y et al. (2003) A perceptual interference account of acquisition difficulties in non-native phonemes. *Cognition,* 87: B47–57.

Jacobsson, KC and Rowe, DC (1999) Genetic and environmental influences on the relationship between family connectedness, and adolescent depressed mood. *Developmental Psychology,* 35: 926–39.

Jaffee, S and Hyde, JS (2000) Gender differences in moral orientation: a meta-analysis. *Psychological Bulletin,* 126: 703–26.

James, W (1890) *The Principles of Psychology.* New York: Dover.

Jenkins, SR (1989) Longitudinal prediction of women's careers: psychological, behavioral, and social-structural influences. *Journal of Vocational Behavior,* 34: 204–35.

Johnson-Laird, PN (1993) How the mind thinks, in Harman, G (ed.) *Conceptions of the Mind: Essays in honor of George A. Miller.* Hillsdale, NJ: Lawrence Erlbaum.

Kagan, J (2003) Biology, context and developmental enquiry. *Annual Review of Psychology*, 54: 1–23.

Kagan, J, Articus, D and Snidman, N et al. (1994) Reactivity in infants: a cross-national comparison. *Developmental Psychology*, 30: 342–5.

Kalish, RA (1987) Death and dying, in Silverman, P (ed.) *The Elderly as Modern Pioneers*. Bloomington, IN: Indiana University Press.

Kalish, RA and Reynolds, DK (1976) *Death and Ethnicity: A psycho-cultural study*. Los Angeles, CA: University of Southern California Press.

Kamptner, LN (1988) Identity development in early adolescence: causal modeling of social and familial influences. *Journal of Youth and Adolescence*, 17: 493–513.

Kastenbaum, R (2000) *The Psychology of Death*. New York: Springer Link.

Kaye, K and Brazelton, TB (1971) Mother–infant interaction in the organization of sucking. Paper presented to the Society for Research in Child Development, Minneapolis, MN, March.

Kaye, K and Fogel, A (1980) The temporal structure of face-to-face communication between mothers and infants. *Developmental Psychology*, 16: 454–64.

Kefalas, M, Furstenberg, F and Napolitano, L (2005) *Marriage is More than Being Together: The meaning of marriage among young adults in the United States*. Available online at www.transad. pop.upenn.edu/downloads/kefalasmarriagenorms.pdf (accessed 12 March 2011).

Kellehear, A. (2005) *Compassionate Cities: Public health and end of life care*. Milton Park: Routledge.

Kellehear, A and O'Connor, D (2008) Health-promoting palliative care: a practice example. *Critical Public Health*, 18(1): 111–15.

Kelly, E (1994) Racism and sexism in the playground, in Blatchford, P and Sharp, S (eds) *Breaktime and the School: Understanding and changing playground behaviour*. London: Routledge.

Killen, M (2007) Children's social and moral reasoning about exclusion. *Current Directions in Psychological Science*, 16: 32–6.

Killen, M and Stangor, C (2001) Children's social reasoning about inclusion and exclusion in gender and race peer group contexts. *Child Development*, 72: 174–86.

Kim, U and Berry, JW (1993) *Indigenous Psychologies: Research and experience in cultural context*. Newbury Park, CA: Sage.

Kivipelto, M, Ngandu, T and Fratiglioni, L et al. (2005) Obesity and vascular risk factors at midlife and the risk of dementia and Alzheimer disease. *Archives of Neurology*, 62: 1556–60.

Kivipelto, M, Ngandu, T and Laatikainen T et al. (2006) Risk score for the prediction of dementia risk in 20 years among middle aged people: a longitudinal, population-based study. *Lancet Neurology*, 5: 735–41.

Kinzie, MB and Joseph, DR (2008) Gender differences in game activity preferences of middle school children: implications for educational game design. *Educational Technology Research and Development*, 56: 643–63.

Kirchmeyer, C (2006) The difference effects of family on objective career success across gender: a test of alternative explanations. *Journal of Vocational Behavior*, 68: 323–46.

Knecht, S, Dräger, B, Deppe, M, Bobe, L and Lohmann, H (2000) Handedness and hemispheric language dominance in healthy humans. *Brain*, 123(12): 2512–18.

Koenig, JI, Kirkpatrick, B and Lee, P (2002) Glucocorticoid hormones and early brain development in schizophrenia. *Neuropsychopharmacology*, 27: 309–18.

Kohlberg, L (1958) The development of modes of moral thinking and choice in the years 10 to 16. Unpublished doctoral thesis, University of Chicago.

Kohn, A (1993) Preschoolers' reasoning about density: will it float? *Child Development*, 64: 1637–50.

Krueger, C, Holditch-Davis, D, Quint, S and DeCasper, A (2004) Recurring auditory experience in the 28- to 34-week-old fetus. *Infant Behavior and Development*, 27: 537–43.

Kubler-Ross, E (1969) *On Death and Dying*. New York: Macmillan.

Kuhl, P (2000) A new view of language acquisition. *Proceedings of the National Academy of Science*, 97(22): 11850–7.

Kuhl, P, Stevens, E, Hayashi, A, Deguhi, T, Kirlani, S and Iverson, P (2006) Infants show a facilitation for native language phonetic perception between 6 to 12 months. *Developmental Science*, 9: F13–21.

Kurinczuk, JJ, Hollowell, J, Brocklehurst, P and Gray, G (2009) *Inequalities in Infant Mortality Project Briefing Paper 1: Infant mortality: overview and context*. Oxford: National Perinatal Epidemiology Unit.

Lamb, T and Yang, JF (2000) Could different directions of infant stepping be controlled by the same locomotor central pattern generator? *Journal of Neurophysiology*, 83: 2814–24.

Leaper, C (2002) Parenting girls and boys, in Bornstein, MH (ed.) *Handbook of Parenting, Vol. 1: Children and parenting*. Mahwah, NJ: Lawrence Erlbaum.

Leavitt, LA and Hall, D (2004) *Social and Moral Development: Emerging evidence on the toddler years*. Princeton, NJ: Johnson and Johnson Pediatric Institute.

Leslie, AM and Thaiss, L (1992) Domain specificity in conceptual development: neuropsychological evidence from autism. *Cognition*, 43: 225–51.

Lester, BM, Boukydis, CFZ and Twomey, JE (2000) Maternal substance abuse and child outcome, in Zeanah, CH Jr (ed.) *Handbook of Infant Mental Health*. New York: Guilford.

Levinson, DJ (1986) *The Seasons of a Man's Life*. New York: Alfred Knopf.

Levinson, DJ (1996) *The Seasons of a Woman's Life*. New York: Alfred Knopf.

Lewis, K and Brooks-Gunn, J (1979) *Social Cognition and the Acquisition of the Self*. New York: Plenum.

Lewis, M (1990) Social knowledge and social development. *Merrill-Palmer Quarterly*, 36: 93–116.

Liddle, B and Nettle, D (2006) Higher-order theory of mind and social competence in school-age children. *Journal of Cultural and Evolutionary Psychology*, 4: 231–46.

Liebal, K, Behne, T, Carpenter, M and Tomasello, M (2009) Infants use shared experience to interpret pointing gestures. *Developmental Science*, 12(2): 264–71. Available online at http://email.eva.mpg.de/~tomas/pdf/LiebalEtal_SharedExperience_2009.pdf (accessed 12 March 2011).

Lieven, EVM (1994) Crosslinguistic and crosscultural aspects of language addressed to children, in Gallaway, C and Richards, BJ (eds) *Input and Interaction in Language Acquisition*. Cambridge: Cambridge University Press.

Lynn, J (2001) Serving patients who may die soon and their families: the role of hospice and other services. *Journal of the American Medical Association*, 285(7): 925–32.

Maccoby, EE (2002) Gender and group processes. *Current Directions in Psychological Science*, 11: 54–8.

Maccoby, EE (2003) Parenting effects, in Borkowski, JG, Ramey, SL and Bristol-Power, M (eds) *Parenting and the Child's World*. Mahwah, NJ: Lawrence Erlbaum.

Maclean, M, Bryant, P, and Bradley, L (1987) Rhymes, nursery rhymes, and reading in early childhood. *Merrill-Palmer Quarterly*, 33: 255–81.

Main, M and Solomon, J (1986) Discovery of an insecure-disorganized/disoriented attachment pattern, in Brazelton, TB and Yogman, MW (eds) *Affective Development in Infancy*. Norwood, NJ: Ablex.

Main, M and Solomon, J (1990) Procedures for identifying infants as disorganized/disoriented during the Ainsworth Strange Situation, in Greenberg, MT, Cicchetti, D and Cummings, EM (eds) *Attachment in the Preschool Years: Theory, research and intervention*. Chicago, IL: University of Chicago Press.

Marcia, JE (1987) The identity status approach to the study of ego identity development, in Honess, T and Yardley, K (eds) *Self and Identity: Perspectives across the lifespan*. London: Routledge and Kegan Paul.

Marcia, JE (1993) The status of the statuses: research review, in Marcia, JE Waterman, AS Matteson, DR Archer, SL and Orlofsky, JL (eds) *Identity: A handbook for psychosocial research* (pp22–41). New York: Springer-Verlag.

Marcia, JE (2002) Identity and psychosocial development in adulthood. *Identity*, 2: 7–28.

Marmot, M, Shipley, M, Brunner, E and Hemingway, H (2001) Relative contribution of early life and adult socioeconomic factors to adult morbidity in the Whitehall II Study. *Journal of Epidemiology and Community Health*, 55: 301–7.

Martin, M and Willis, SL (2005) *Middle Adulthood: A lifespan perspective*. Thousand Oaks, CA: Sage.

Mastropieri, D and Turkewitz, G (1999) Prenatal experience and neonatal responsiveness to vocal expressions of emotion. *Developmental Psychobiology*, 35(3): 204–14.

Metcalf, P and Huntington, R (1991) *Celebrations of Death: The anthropology of mortuary ritual*. Cambridge, Cambridge University Press.

Matthews, TJ, Menacker, F and MacDorman, MF (2003) Infant mortality statistics from the 2002 period: linked birth/infant death data set. *National Vital Statistics Reports*, 52(2): 1–28. Hyattsville, MD: National Center for Health Statistics.

Matychuk, P (2005) The role of child-directed speech in language acquisition: a case study. *Language Sciences*, 27: 301–79.

McCabe, MP, Ricciardelli, LA and Finemore, J (2002) The role of puberty, media, and popularity with peers as strategies to increase weight, decrease weight and increase muscle tone among adolescent boys and girls. *Journal of Psychosomatic Research*, 52: 145–53.

McGuffin, P, Plomin, R, DeFries, JC and McClearn, GE (2001) *Behavioral Genetics*. (4th edn). New York: Worth Publishers.

McMaster, J, Pitts, M and Poyah, G (1997) The menopausal experiences of women in a developing country: 'there is a time for everything: to be a teenager, a mother and a granny'. *Women's Health*, 26(4): 1–13.

Mead, GH (1934) *Mind, Self and Society from the Standpoint of a Social Behaviourist*. Chicago, IL: University of Chicago Press.

Meier, BP and Hinsz, VB (2004) A comparison of human aggression committed by groups and individuals: an interindividual-intergroup discontinuity. *Journal of Experimental Social Psychology*, 40: 551–59.

Menary, R (2007) *Cognitive Integration: Mind and cognition unbounded*. Basingstoke: Palgrave Macmillan.

Metz, D and Underwood, M (2005) *Older, Richer, Fitter: Identifying the customer needs of Britain's ageing population*. London: Age Concern Books.

Miles, S (2000) *Youth Lifestyles in a Changing World*, Buckingham: Open University Press.

Miles, S, Cliff, D and Burr, V (1998) 'Fitting in and sticking out': consumption, consumer meanings and the construction of young people's identities, *Journal of Youth Studies*, 1: 81–91.

Miller, JG and Bersoff, DM (1992) Culture and moral judgment: how are conflicts between justice and interpersonal responsibilities resolved? *Journal of Personality and Social Psychology*, 62(4): 541–54.

Miller, PH (2002) *Theories of Developmental Psychology* (4th edn). New York: Worth Publishers.

Milner, M (2004) *Freaks, Geeks, and Cool Kids: American teenagers, schools, and the culture of consumption*. New York: Routledge.

Mitchell, G (2008) *Palliative Care: A patient-centred approach*. Oxford: Radcliffe Publishing.

Moon, C and Fifer, WP (2000) Evidence of transnatal auditory learning. *Journal of Perinatology*, 20: S37–S44.

Moor, H, Jones, M, Johnson, F, Martin, K, Cowell, E and Bojke, C (2006) *Mathematics and Science in Secondary Schools:the Deployment of Teachers and Support Staff to Deliver the Curriculum* (DfES Research Report 708). London: DfES. Available at www.dfes.gov.uk/research/data/uploadfiles/ RR708.pdf

Munakata, Y (1998) Infant perseveration and implications for object permanence theories: a PDP model of the AB task. *Developmental Science*, 1(2): 161–84.

National Cancer Institute, US National Institutes of Health (2010) *Grief, Bereavement, and Coping with Loss*. Bethesda, MD: NCI. Available online at www.cancer.gov/cancertopics/pdq/supportive care/bereavement/Patient/allpages (accessed 12 March 2011).

National Research Council (NRC) (1996) *Mathematics and Science Education Around the World: What can we learn from the Survey of Mathematics and Science Opportunities (SMSO) and the Third International Mathematics and Science Study (TIMSS)?* Washington, DC: National Academy Press.

Nebot, M, Borrell. C and Villalb. JR (1997) Adolescent motherhood and socioeconomic factors: an ecological approach. *European Journal of Public Health*, 7 (2): 144–8.

Nelson, K (1996) *Language in Cognitive Development: The emergence of the mediated mind*. New York: Cambridge University Press.

Nelson, CA, Thomas, KM and de Hann, M (2006) in Nelson, CA, Thomas, KM and de Haan, M (2007) *Neural Bases of Cognitive Development: Handbook of child psychology*.

Newcomb, AF, Bukowski, WM and Pattee, L (1993) Children's peer relations: a meta-analytic review of popular, rejected, neglected, controversial, and average sociometric status. *Psychological Bulletin*, 113: 99–128.

Newell, KM, Vaillancourt, DE and Sosnoff, JJ (2006) Aging complexity and motor performance, in Birren, JE and Schaie, KW (eds) *Handbook of the Psychology of Aging* (6th edn). San Diego, CA: Academic Press.

Nicolson, RI, Fawcett, AJ and Dean, P (2001) Developmental dyslexia: the cerebellar deficit hypothesis. *Trends in Neurosciences*, 24(9): 508–11.

Norgate, SH (1997) Research methods for studying the language of blind children, in Hornberger, NH and Corson, D (eds) *The Encyclopedia of Language and Education, Vol. 8: Research methods in language and education*. The Netherlands: Kluwer Academic Publishers.

Norman, P, Gregory, I, Dorling, D and Baker, A (2008) Geographical trends in infant mortality: England and Wales 1970–2006. *Health Statistics Quarterley*, 40, 18–29.

Nottelmann, ED, Susman, EJ, Blue, JH, Inoff-Germain, G and Dorn, LD (1987) Gonadal and adrenal hormone correlates of adjustment in early adolescence, in Lerner, RM and Foch, TT (eds) *Biological-psychosocial Interactions in Early Adolescence*. Hillsdale, NJ: Lawrence Erlbaum.

Nunes, T, Schliemann, AD and Carraher, DW (1993) *Street Mathematics and School Mathematics*, New York: Cambridge University Press.

Obler, LK (2005) Nancy Dorian, in Brown, K (ed.) *Encyclopedia of Language and Linguistics* (2nd edn), Oxford: Elsevier.

Office for National Statistics (2010) *Population Trends*, Winter. Available at www.statistics.gov.uk/populationtrends/downloads/poptrends142web.pdf

Ojeman, GA (1984) Common cortical and thalamic mechanisms for language and motor functions. *American Journal of Physiology*, 246: 901–3.

Ozer, DJ and Benet-Martinez, V (2006) Personality and the prediction of consequential outcome. *Psychology*, 57: 402–21.

Parker, J and Gottman, J (1989) Social and emotional development in a relational context, in Bernat, T and Ladd, G (eds) *Peer Relationships in Child Development*. New York: Wiley and Sons.

Parker, JG and Seal, J (1996) Forming, losing, renewing and replacing friendships: applying temporal parameters to the assessment of children's friendship experiences. *Child Development*, 67 (5): 2248–68.

Parkes, CM (1972) *Bereavement: Studies of grief in adult life*. Harmondsworth: Penguin.

Parkes, CM (1986) *Bereavement: Studies of grief life* (2nd edn). London: Tavistock.

Parten, MB (1932) Social participation among pre-school children. *Journal of Abnormal and Social Psychology*, 27: 243–69.

Patiniotis, J and Holdsworth, C (2005) 'Seize that chance!': Leaving home and transitions to higher Education'. *Journal of Youth Studies*, 8(1): 81–95.

Perry, WG (1970) *Forms of Intellectual and Ethical Development in the College Years*. New York: Holt, Rhinehart.

Philips, SD (1982) Career exploration in adulthood. *Journal of Vocational Behaviour*, 20: 129–40.

Phoenix, A (2005) Young people and consumption: communalities and differences in the construction of identities, in Tufte, B, Rasmussen, J and Christensen LB (eds) *Frontrunners or Copycats?* Copenhagen: Copenhagen Business School Press.

Piaget, J (1923) *Language and Thought of the Child*. London: Routledge.

Piaget, J (1952) *The Origins of Intelligence in Children*. New York: International Universities Press.

Piaget, J (1962) *Play, Dreams and Imitation in Childhood*. New York: Norton.

Piaget, J (1983) Piaget's theory, in Mussen, P (ed). *Handbook of Child Psychology*, Vol. 1 (4th edn). New York: Wiley.

Piaget, J and Inhelder, B (1969) *The Psychology of the Child*. London: Routledge and Kegan Paul.

Pine, KJ, Messer, DJ and St John, K (2001) Children's misconceptions in primary science: a survey of teachers' views. *Research in Science and Technology Education*, 19(1): 79–96.

Pinker, S (2003) Language as an adaptation to the cognitive niche, in Christiansen, M and Kirby, S (eds) *Language Evolution: States of the art*. New York: Oxford University Press.

Pinker, S (2007) The evolutionary social psychology of off-record indirect speech acts. *Intercultural Pragmatics*, 4(4): 437–61.

Pinquart, M and Sorensen, S (2000) Influences of socioeconomic status, social network, and competence on subjective well-being in later life: a meta-analysis. *Psychology and Aging*, 15: 187–224.

Proffitt, JB, Coley, JD, and Medun, DL (2000) Expertise and category based induction. *Journal of Experimental Psychology: Learning, Memory, and Cognition*, 26: 811–28.

Pujol,J, López-Sala, A, Sebastián-Gallés, N, Deus, J, Cardoner, N, Soriano-Mas, C, Moreno, A and Sans, A (2004) Delayed myelination in children with developmental delay detected by volumetric MRI. *NeuroImage*, 22 (2): 897–903.

Pujol, J, Soriano-Mas, C, Ortiz, H, Sebastián-Gallés, N, Losilla, JM and Deus, J (2006) Myelination of language-related areas in the developing brain. *Neurology*, 66(3): 339–43.

Ragow-O'Brien, D, Hayslip, B and Guarnaccia, CA (2000) The impact of hospice on attitudes toward funerals and subsequent bereavement adjustment. *Journal of Death and Dying*, 41(4): 291–305.

Rapkin A, Tsao, JC, Turk, N Anderson, M and Zelter, LK (2006) Relationships among self-rated tanner staging, hormones, and psychosocial factors in healthy female adolescents. *Journal of Pediatric Adolescent Gynecology*, 19: 181–7.

Reiner, WG and Gearhart, JP (2004) discordant sexual identity in some genetic males with cloacal exstrophy assigned to female sex at birth. *New England Journal of Medicine*, 350: 333–41.

Reis, H T, Lin, Y, Bennett, ME, and Nezlek, JB (1993) Change and consistency in social participation during early adulthood. *Developmental Psychology*, 29: 633–45.

Rhodes, SR (1983) Age-related differences in work attitudes and behaviour: a review and conceptual analysis. *Psychological Bulletin*, 93: 328–67.

Richards, M, Hardy, R andWadsworth, ME (2003) Does active leisure protect cognition? Evidence from a national birth cohort. *Social Science and Medicine*, 56: 785–92.

Robins, RW, Trzesniewski, KH, Tracey, JL, Gosling, SD and Potter, J (2002) Global self-esteem across the life span. *Psychology and Aging,* 17: 423–34.

Rohrich, RJ (2000) The millennium cosmetic surgery: Who are we? Where are we going? *Plastic Reconstruction Surgery*, 105(1): 225.

Rosenberg, M (1979) *Conceiving the Self*. New York: Basic Books.

Rosenblatt, PC (1993) The social context of private feelings, in Stroebe, MS Stroebe W and Hansson RO (eds) *Handbook of Bereavement: Theory, research and intervention*. New York: Cambridge University Press.

Rosenbloom, C and Bahns, M (2006) What can we learn about diet and physical activity from master athletes? *Holistic Nursing Practice*, 20(4): 161–6.

Rothbaum, F, Weisz, J, Pott, M, Miyake, K and Morelli, G (2000) Attachment and culture: security in the United States and Japan. *American Psychologist*, 55: 1093–1104.

Rowe, R, Maughan, B, Worthman, C, Costello, E and Angold, A (2004) Testosterone, antisocial behaviour, and social dominance in boys: pubertal development and biosocial interaction. *Biological Psychiatry*, 55: 546–52.

Royal College of Obstetricians and Gynaecologists (RCOG) (2004) *Management of HIV in Pregnancy. Guideline No. 39*, 1–12.

Rubia, K, Overmever, S, Taylor, E, Brammer, M, Williams, SC R, Simmons, A, Andrew, C and Bullmore, ET (2000) Functional frontalisation with age: mapping neurodevelopmental trajectories with fMRI. *Neuroscience and Biobehavioral Reviews*, 24 (1): 13–19.

Rubin, KH, Bukowski, W and Parker, JG (1998) Peer interactions, relationships, and groups, in Eisenberg, N (ed.) *Handbook of Child Psychology, Vol. 3: Social, emotional, and personality development* (6th edn). New York: Wiley.

Ruble, DN and Martin, CL (1998) Gender development, in Eisenberg, N (eds) *Handbook of Child Psychology, Vol. 3: Social, emotional, and personality development* (6th edn). New York: Wiley.

Rymer, R (1993) *Genie: Escape from a silent childhood.* Harmondsworth: Penguin Books.

Salthouse, TA (2009) When does age-related cognitive decline begin? *Neurobiology of Aging*, 30: 507–14.

Sameroff, AJ (1991) The social context of development, in Woodhead, M, Carr, R and Light, P (eds) *Becoming a Person*, London: The Open University Press/Routledge.

Sameroff, AJ and Chandler, MJ (1975) Reproductive risk and the continuum of caretaker casualty, in Horowitz, FD (ed.) *Review of Child Development Research, Vol. 4.* Chicago, IL: University of Chicago Press.

Sammons, P, Elliot, K, Sylva, K, Melhuish, M, Siraj-Blatchford and Taggart, B (2004). The impact of pre-school on young children's cognitive attainments at entry to reception. *British Education Research Journal*, 30 (5): 691–712.

Samson, MM, Meeuwsen, IB, Crowe, A, Dessens, JA, Duursma, SA and Verhaar, HJ (2000) Relationships between physical performance measures, age, height and body weight in healthy adults. *Age and Ageing*, 29: 235–42.

Sarigiani, AC and Petersen, PA (2000) Adolescence: puberty and biological maturation, in Kazdin, A (ed.) *Encyclopedia of Psychology*. Washington, DC, and New York: American Psychological Association/Oxford University Press.

Sassler, S, Ciambrone, D and Benway, G (2008) Are they really mama's boys/daddy's girls? The negotiation of adulthood upon returning to the parental home. *Sociological Forum*, 23 (4): 670–98.

Saunders, C and Clark, D (ed.) (2002) *Cicely Saunders: Founder of the hospice movement: Selected letters 1959–1999.* Oxford: Oxford University Press.

Schachter, SC and Ransil, BJ (1996) Handedness distributions in nine professional groups. *Perceptual and Motor Skills*, 82: 51–63.

Schaie, KW (2006) Intelligence, in Schultz, R (ed.) *Encyclopedia of Aging* (4th edn). New York: Springer.

Schulenberg, JE and Zarrett, NR (2006) Mental health during emerging adulthood: continuity and discontinuity in courses, causes, and functions, in Arnett, JJ and Tanner, JL (eds) *Emerging Adults in America: Coming of age in the 21st century*. Washington, DC: American Psychological Association.

Seale, C (1991) *Caring for People who Die*. Paper presented at British Sociological Association Conference on Health and Society, University of Manchester.

Selman, RL (1980) *The Growth of Interpersonal Understanding*. New York: Academic Press.

Shahidi, J, Bernier, N and Cohen, SR (2010) Quality of life in terminally ill cancer patients: contributors and content validity of instruments. *Journal of Palliative Care*, 26(2): 88–93.

Shan, Z, Liu, JZ, Sahgal, V, Wang, B, and Yue, GH (2005) Selective atrophy of left hemisphere and frontal lobe of the brain in old men. *Journal of Gerontology:* Series A, biological sciences and medical sciences, 60 (2): 165–74.

Shatz, M and Gelman, R (1973) The development of communication skills. *Monographs of the Society for Research in Child Development*, 38: serial no. 152.

Shea, AK and Streiner, M (2008) Cigarette smoking during pregnancy. *Nicotine and Tobacco Research*, 10 (2), 267–78.

Shirley, MM (1933) *The First Two Years: A study of 25 babies, Vol. 1: Post natal and locomotor development*. Minneapolis, MN: University of Minnesota Press.

Short, G (1999) Children's grasp of controversial issues, in Woodhead, M, Faulkner, D and Littleton, K (eds) *Making Sense of Social Development*, London: Routledge.

Shulman, S and Ben-Artzi, E (2003) Age-related differences in the transition from adolescence to adulthood and links with family relationships. *Journal of Adult Development*, 10(4): 217–26.

Shweder, RA and Levine, RA (eds) (1994) *Culture Theory: Essays on mind, self and emotion*. Cambridge: Cambridge University Press.

Siegal, M and Beattie, K (1991) Where to look first for children's knowledge of false beliefs. *Cognition*, 38: 1–12.

Siegal, M and Peterson, CC (1994) Children's theory of mind and the conversational territory of cognitive development, in Lewis, C and Mitchell, P (eds) *Origins of an Understanding of Mind*. Hove: England: Erlbaum.

Siegler, RS (1986) *Children's Thinking*. Englewood Cliffs, NJ: Prentice-Hall.

Simmons, RG and Blyth, DA (1987) *Moving into Adolescence: The impact of pubertal change and school context*. New York: Aldine De Gruyter.

Simonton, DK (1990). Creativity in the later years: optimistic prospects for achievement. *Gerontologist, 30,* 626–31.

Sinnott JD (1994) *Interdisciplinary Handbook of Life Span Learning*. Westport, CT: Greenwood.

Singh, L, Morgan, JL and Best, CT (2002) Infants' listening preferences: Babytalk or happy talk?, *Infancy*, 3: 365–94.

Sinnott, JD (1996). The developmental approach: postformal thought as adaptive intelligence, in Blanchard-Fields, F and Hess, TM (eds) *Perspectives on Cognitive Change in Adulthood and Aging* (pp358–83). New York: McGraw-Hill.

Skinner, BF (1936) *The Behavior of Organisms: An experimental analysis*. New York: Appleton-Century-Crofts.

Slobin, DI (1972) Children and language: they learn the same way all around the world. *Psychology Today*, 6(2): 71–4.

Smith, LB, Thelen, E, Titzer, R and McLin, D (1999) Knowing in the context of acting: the task dynamics of the A-not-B error. *Psychological Review*, 106(2): 235–60. Available online at www.indiana.edu/~cogdev/labwork/SmithThelen1999.pdf (accessed 12 March 2011).

Snarey, JR, Reimer, J and Kohlberg, L (1985) The development of social-moral reasoning among kibbutz adolescents: a longitudinal cross-cultural study. *Developmental Psychology*, 20: 3–17.

Snow, CE (1972) Mother's speech to children learning language. *Child Development*, 43 (2): 549–65.

Snowdon (2002) *Aging with Grace: What the nun study teaches us about leading longer, healthier, and more meaningful lives*. New York: Bantam.

Springer, SP and Deutsch, G (1985) *Left Brain, Right Brain*. New York: WH Freeman.

Stattin, H and Magnusson, D (1990) *Paths Through Life, Vol. 2: Pubertal Maturation in Female Development*. Hillsdale NJ: Lawrence Erlsbaum.

Stevens, MM and Dunsmore, JC (1996) Adolescents who are living with a life-threatening illness, in Corr, CA and Balk, DE (Eds) *Handbook of Adolescent Death and Bereavement*, New York: Springer.

Stipek, DJ (2003) School entry age, in Tremblay, RE, Peters, RDeV, Boivin, M and Barr, RG (eds) *Encyclopedia on Early Childhood Development*. Montreal: Centre of Excellence for Early Childhood Development. Available online at www.child-encyclopedia.com/documents/StipekANGxp.pdf (accessed 12 March 2011).

Stroebe, MS (1998) New directions in bereavement research: exploration of gender differences. *Palliative Medicine*, 12(1): 5–12.

Super, C (1976) Environmental effects on motor developments: the case of 'African infant precocity'. *Developmental Medicine and Child Neurology*, 18: 561–7.

Super, D, Savickas, M, and Super, C (1996). The life-span, life-space approach to careers, in D. Brown, L Brooks, and Associates (Eds.), *Career Choice and Development* (3rd ed., 121–78). San Francisco: Jossey-Bass.

Susman, EJ (2006) Puberty revisited: models, mechanisms and the future. Paper presented at the Society for Research on Adolescence, San Francisco.

Swain, J, Tasgin, E, Mayes, L, Feldman, R, Constable, R and Leckman, J (2008) Maternal brain response to own baby cry is affected by caesarean section delivery. *Child Psychology and Psychiatry*, 49(10): 1042–52.

Talge, N M, Neal, C and Glover, V (2007) Antenatal maternal stress and long-term effects on child neurodevelopment: how and why? *Journal of Child Psychology and Psychiatry*, 48 (3–4): 245–61.

Thelen, E (1995) Motor development: a new synthesis. *American Psychologist*, 50: 79–95.

Thiessen, ED, Hill, EA and Saffran, JR (2005) Infant-directed speech facilitates word segmentation. *Infancy*, 1: 53–71.

Thompson, RA (2006) The development of the person, in Eisenberg, N (ed.) *Handbook of Child Psychology, Vol. 3: Social, emotional, and personality development* (6th edn). New York: Wiley.

Thompson, PM, Giedd, JN, Woods, RP, MacDonald, D, Evans, AC and Toga, AW (2000) Growth patterns in the developing brain detected by using continuum mechanical tensor maps. *Nature*, 404, 190–3.

Thornton, R and Light, LL (2006) Language comprehension and production in normal aging, in Birren, JE and Schaie, KW (eds) *Handbook of the Psychology of Aging* (6th edn). San Diego, CA: Elsevier.

Thorpe, G (1993) Enabling more dying people to remain at home. *British Medical Journal*, 307 (6909): 915–18.

Tomasello, M (2006) Acquiring linguistic constructions, In Kuhn, D and Siegler, R (eds) *Handbook of Child Psychology, Vol. 2: Cognition, perception, and language* (6th edn). New York: Wiley.

Turiel, E (1983) *The Development of Social Knowledge: Morality and convention*. Cambridge: Cambridge University Press.

Uchino, B, Cacioppo, JT and Kiecolt-Glaser, JK (1996) The relationship between social support and physiological processes: a review with emphasis on underlying mechanisms and implications for health. *Psychological Bulletin*, 119: 488–531.

Upton, P and Eiser, C (2006) School experiences after treatment for a brain tumour. *Child: Care, Health and Development*, 32(1): 9–17.

Urberg, KA and Kaplan, MG (1989) An observational study of race-, age-, and sex-heterogeneous interaction in preschoolers. *Journal of Applied Developmental Psychology*, 10: 299–311.

Vacca, JL, Vacca, RT, Gove, MK, Burkey, RC and Lenhart, LA (2006) *Reading and Learning to Read* (6th edn). Boston, MA: Allyn and Bacon.

Valenzuela, M, Breakspear, M and Sachdev, P (2007) Complex mental activity and the aging brain: molecular, cellular and cortical network mechanisms. *Brain Research Reviews*, 56: 198–213.

van Ijzendoorn, M and Kroonenberg, P (1988) Cross cultural patterns of attachment: a meta analysis of the Strange Situation. *Child Development*, 59: 147–56.

van Solinge, H and Henkens, K (2005) Couples' adjustment to retirement: a multi-actor panel study. *Journal of Gerontology: Psychological Sciences*, 60(1): S11–S20.

Viholainen, H, Ahonen, T, Cantell, M, Lyytinen, P and Lyytinen, H (2002) Development of early motor skills and language in children at risk for familial dyslexia. *Developmental Medicine and Child Neurology*, 44: 761–9.

von Hofsten, C, Kochukhova, O and Rosander, K (2007) Predictive tracking over occlusions by 4-month-old infants. Developmental Science, 10(5): 625–40.

Vurpillot, E (1968) The development of scanning strategies and their relation to visual differentiation. *Journal of Experimental Child Psychology*, 6: 632–50.

Vygotsky, LS (1930/1978) *Mind in Society: The development of higher psychological processes.* Cambridge, MA: Harvard University Press.

Vygotsky, LS (1962) *Thought and Language.* New York: Wiley.

Vygotsky, LS (1986) The genetic roots of thought and speech, in Kozulin, A. (ed. and trans.) *Thought and Language.* Cambridge, MA: MIT Press.

Wade, B and Moore, M (1993) *Experiencing special education: what young people with special educational needs can tell us.* Buckingham: Open University Press.

Wade, B and Moore, M (1998) An early start with books: literacy and mathematical evidence from a longitudinal study. *Educational Review*, 50: 135–45.

Walker, LJ (1989) A longitudinal study of moral reasoning. *Child Development*, 60: 157–66.

Ward, BJ and Tate, PA (1994) Attitudes among NHS doctors to requests for euthanasia. *British Medical Journal*, 308: 1332.

Wargo Aitkins, J, Bierman, K and Parker, JG (2005) Navigating the transition to junior high school: the influence of pre-transition friendship and self-system characteristics. *Social Development*, 14: 42–60.

Waterman, AS (1992) Identity as an aspect of optimal psychological functioning, in Adams, GR Gullotta, TP and Montemayor, R (eds) *Adolescent Identity Formation* (50–72). Newbury Park, CA: Sage.

Waters, G and Caplan, D (2005) The relationship between age, processing speed, working memory capacity, and language comprehension. *Memory*, 13(3–4): 403–13.

Watson, JB (1913) Psychology as the behaviorist views it. *Psychological Review*, 20: 158–77.

Watson, JB (1924) *Behaviourism*, New York: Norton.

Watson, JB (1928) *Psychological Care of the Infant and Child*. New York: Norton.

Wegman, ME (2001) Infant mortality in the 20th century: dramatic but uneven progress. *Journal of Nutrition*, 131: 401S–408S.

Wellman, HM and Gelman, SA (1998) Knowledge acquisition in foundational domains, in Kuhn, D and Siegler, RS (eds) *Handbook of Child Psychology, Vol. 2: Cognition, perception, and language* (5th edn). New York: Wiley.

Wendell, C, Zonderman, A, Metter, J, Najjar, SS and Waldstein, SR (2009) Carotid intimal medial thickness predicts cognitive decline among adults without clinical vascular disease. *Stroke*, 40: 3–180.

Wheldhall, K and Poborca, B (1980) Conservation without conversation? An alternative non-verbal paradigm for assessing conservation of liquid quantity. *British Journal of Psychology*, 71: 117–34.

Whitbourne, SK (2005) *Adult Development and Aging: Biopsychological perspectives* (2nd edn). New York: Wiley.

White, J, Moffit, T, Earls, F, Robins, L and Silva, P (1990) How early can we tell? Predictors of childhood conduct disorder and adolescent delinquency. *Criminology*, 28: 507–27.

Whitney, I and Smith, PK (1993) A survey of the nature and extent of bullying in junior/middle and secondary schools. *Educational Research*, 35(1): 3–25.

Wiesner, M and Ittel, A (2002) Relations of pubertal timing and depressive symptoms to substance use in early adolescence. *Journal of Early Adolescence*, 22: 5–23.

Willis, SL and Schaie, KW (2006) Cognitive functioning among the baby boomers: longitudinal and cohort effects, in Whitbourne, SK and Willis, SL (eds) *The Baby Boomers*. New York: Lawrence Erlbaum.

Wimmer, H and Perner, J (1983) Beliefs about beliefs: representation and constraining function of wrong beliefs in young children's understanding of deception. *Cognition*, 13: 103–28.

Wold, G (2004) *Basic Geriatric Nursing*. St Louis, MO: Mosby.

Wood, DJ, Bruner, JS and Ross, G (1976) The role of tutoring in problem-solving. *Journal of Child Psychology and Psychiatry*, 17(2): 89–100.

Woodward, AL and Markman, EM (1998) Early word learning, in Kuhn, D and Siegler. RS (eds), Damon, W (series ed.) *Handboook of Child Psychology, Vol. 2: Cognition, perception, and language* (5th edn) pp371–420). New York: Wiley.

Woolley, JD (1997) Thinking about fantasy: are children fundamentally different thinkers and believers than adults? *Child Development*, 68: 991–1011.

World Health Organization (WHO) (1990) *Technical Report Series 804: Cancer pain and palliative care.* Geneva: WHO.

Yan, B and Arlin PK (1995) Nonabsolute/relativistic thinking: a common factor underlying models of postformal reasoning? *Journal of Adult Development*, 2: 223–40.

Yang, Q, Wen, SW, Leader, A, Chen, X, Lipson, J and Walker, M (2007) Paternal age and birth defects: how strong is the association? *Human Reproduction*, 22: 696–701.

Yung, LM, Laher, I, Yao, X, Chen, ZY, Huang, Y and Leung, FP (2009) Exercise, vascular wall and cardiovascular diseases: an update (part 2). *Sports Science*, 39(1): 45–63.

Zarbatany, L, McDougall, P and Hymel, S (2000) Gender-differentiated experience in the peer culture: links to intimacy in preadolescence. *Social Development*, 9(1): 62–79.

Zhang, LF (2002) Thinking styles and cognitive development. *Journal of Genetic Psychology*, 163: 179–95.

Index

Page references in *italic* type indicate relevant figures and tables.